Memories, Memorials, and Monuments

Hodgin Hall – Exterior – with "U" Sign, circa 1926 (Center for Southwest Research, UNM Libraries).

Memories, Memorials, and Monuments

A Companion to Only in New Mexico:
An Architectural History of the
University of New Mexico:
The First Century 1889–1989

Van Dorn Hooker, FAIA, and Ann Hooker Clarke

Foreword by V.B. Price

Park Place Publications • Pacific Grove, California

Cover image: UNM Meditation Chapel's stained class doors, "Tree of Life," designed and fabricated by Denise Taylor. Photograph by Suzanne Mortier.

Memories, Memorials, And Monuments
A Companion to Only in New Mexico:
An Architectural History of the University of New Mexico:
The First Century, 1889–1989
Van Dorn Hooker, FAIA, and Ann Hooker Clarke
Foreword By V.B. Price

© 2019 Ann Hooker Clarke
All rights reserved.
FIRST EDITION
ISBN 978-1-943887-63-7
Library of Congress Control Number: 2019936998

Text and Cover Design by Patricia Hamilton
Published by Park Place Publications
Pacific Grove, California

Only in New Mexico: An Architectural History of the
University of New Mexico: The First Century, 1889–1989
    Library of Congress Cataloging-in-Publication Data:
    Hooker, Van Dorn, 1921–2015
    Only in New Mexico: an architectural history of the University of New Mexico: the first century, 1889–1989 / Van Dorn Hooker with Melissa Howard and V.B. Price—1st ed.
        p.   cm.
    Includes bibliographical references.
    ISBN 0-8263-2135-6 (cloth: alk. paper)
    1. University of New Mexico—Buildings—History.
    I. Howard, Melissa.
    II. Price, V.B. (Vincent Barrett)
    III. Title
    LD3781.N534 H66 2000
    $727^1.3^1 0978961$—dc21
    99-006976

Contents

List of Figures xiv
Acknowledgements xviii
Dedication xix
Preface xxi
Foreword xxiii
Introduction xxv
Note xxvii

SECTION ONE – CENTRAL / MAIN CAMPUS

THE ALUMNI MEMORIAL CHAPEL 5
    War Dead Commemorated 7
ROBERT O. ANDERSON SCHOOL OF MANAGEMENT 10
    Jackson Student Center 11
    The Roger H. Jehenson Tree 11
    Parish Memorial Library 12
    Eric Pillmore Room for Ethics 12
    The H. Raymond Radosevich Room 12
    McKinnon Center for Management 13
THE ANTHROPOLOGY BUILDING 13
    The Clark Field Library and Archive 14
    The "Nibs" Hill Student Lounge 14
    The Maxwell Museum 14
    The Alfonso Ortiz Center for Intercultural Studies 15
    Rodey Hall 15
    The Hibben Center for Archaeologial Research 16
    The Seaweed Totem Pole (Smith Family Totem Pole) 16
THE SCHOOL OF ARCHITECTURE AND PLANNING 17
    George Pearl Hall 17
    The Rainosek Gallery 17
BANDELIER EAST (ORTEGA HALL I) 18
BANDELIER WEST 19
    The Van Dorn Hooker III Rose Garden 19
CARLISLE GYMNASIUM 19
    Elizabeth Waters Center for Dance at Carlisle Gym 20
    The Korber Radio Station 21

Contents continued ...

CASTETTER HALL (BIOLOGY) 21
    The Castetter Garden 21
    Loren Potter Wing 22
CENTENNIAL ENGINEERING CENTER 22
    The Robert J. Stamm Commons 23
CLARK HALL (CHEMISTRY) 23
    The Jesse E. Riebsomer Wing 24
CIVIL ENGINEERING - WAGNER HALL 24
COMMUNICATION AND JOURNALISM 25
    The Will Harrison Grove 25
    The Tony Hillerman Memorial Plaque 26
    The Keen Rafferty Reading Room 27
COUNSELING, ASSISTANCE, AND REFERRAL SERVICE (CARS) 28
    Maria Palacios Memorial Tree 28
DORMITORIES AND DINING HALLS 28
    Coronado Hall 28
    DeVargas Hall and Laguna Hall 29
    La Posada Dining Hall and Howard Mathany Room 29
    Mathias Lambert Custers Cottage ("Ladies Cottage") 30
    Hokona Hall I 30
    Hokona Hall II 30
    Lena C. Clauve Lounge 31
    The Conrado Gutierrez, Patrick McNamara, and Joyce Rogers Room 31
    Joyce Rogers Memorial Religious Studies Library 32
    Kwataka Hall 33
    Alvarado Hall 33
    Santa Ana and Santa Clara Dormitories 33
    Oñate Hall 34
    Solon Rose Cottage 34
    Yatoka Hall 34
EARL'S GROTTO 35
BRATTON HALL I (ECONOMICS) 35

COLLEGE OF EDUCATION COMPLEX   36
    Frank Angel Latin American Program in Education (LAPE) Conference Room   36
    The Richard E. Lawrence Courtyard   37
    Manzanita Center   37
    Masley Hall and Gallery   38
    Simpson Hall (Home Economics)   38
    Travelstead Hall   39
    Tireman Learning Materials Center   40
    The Simon P. Nanninga Conference Room   40
    The Anita Osuna Carr Library   41

THE ESTUFA   41

FARRIS ENGINEERING CENTER   42

THE FINE ARTS CENTER   42
    UNM Art Museum   42
    Clinton Adams Gallery   43
    Beaumont Newhall Study Room   43
    Enyeart/Malone Library and Archive   44
    Bunting Visual Resources Library   44
    Lannan Reading Room   44
    Van Deren Coke Photography Gallery and Van Deren and Joan Coke Library   45
    The Kurt Frederick Rehearsal Hall   45
    Keller Recital Hall   46
    Mattox Sculpture Center   46
    Popejoy Hall   47
    The Popejoy Trees   48
    Robb Archive of Southwestern Folk Music   48
    Rodey Hall and Rodey Theater   49
    The John Sommers Gallery   50
    Tamarind Institute   50
    Hartung Hall   50

FORD UTILITIES CENTER   51

CAMP FUNSTON   52

HADLEY HALL I   52

HADLEY HALL II   53

Contents continued ...

HODGIN HALL ("MAIN BUILDING")   53
- The Charles Hodgin Elm and Hodgin Grove   54
- Parsons Grove   54
- The Irma Bobo Room   55
- The Glenn Emmons Room   55
- The Gazebo   56
- The Dorothy and Ray Hickman Parlor   56
- The Huggett-Heald Tree and Plaque   56
- The Lettermen's Wing and John C. "Luke" Luksich Foyer   57
- The Horace F. McKay Lobby   57
- The Faulhaber Stained Glass Window   58
- John D. Robb Bust and Rodey Awards   58
- Wall Plaques   58
- The Memorial Concrete Benches and Kiwanis Fountain   58
- Dr. Karen Abraham Courtyard   58
- Tight Grove   59
- Lobo Sculpture   60
- Lobo Head   60

HUMANITIES BUILDING AND SMITH PLAZA   61
- Sherman E. Smith Plaza   61
- The Franklin Dickey Memorial Theater   62
- The Leon Howard Library and Conference Room   62

JOHNSON CENTER AND GYM[253] AND JOHNSON FIELD   63
- Lobo Statue   64
- "Spirit Of The Lobos"   65
- Vivian H. Heyward Exercise Physiology Teaching Laboratory   66
- Seidler Natatorium   66

JONSON GALLERY   67
- The Robert Wood Johnson Foundation   67

LOGAN HALL   68

MARRON HALL   68

MESA VISTA HALL I   69
- Mesa Vista Hall   69
- The John W. "Wolfie" Smeltzer Garden   69

MITCHELL HALL (CLASSROOM BUILDING)   71

NAVAL SCIENCES BUILDING   72
- The Hank Willis Library   72

NORTHROP HALL (GEOLOGY)   73
    The Silver Family Geology Museum   73

ORTEGA HALL II   74
    The Robert Manly Duncan Reading Room   75

PARSONS HALL AND PARSONS GROVE   76

THE JOHN AND JUNE PEROVICH BUSINESS CENTER   77

SARA RAYNOLDS HALL   78

REGENER HALL   78

SCHOLES HALL   79
    Thomas Reaser Roberts Room   80

DANE SMITH HALL   81
    The Student Grove   81

STUDENT HEALTH CENTER AND UNDERGRADUATE STUDIES   82
    Student Health Center   82
    Dudley Wynn Honors Center   82
    Lawrence R. Klausen Memorial Park   83

STUDENT SERVICES CENTER BUILDING —UNIVERSITY ADVISEMENT AND ENRICHMENT CENTER)   84
    The Karen Glaser Conference Room   84

THE NEW MEXICO STUDENT UNION BUILDING   84
    Esther Thompson Gallery   85

TAPY HALL   85

WOODWARD HALL   86

ZIMMERMAN LIBRARY   87
    Zimmerman Field   88
    The Raul D. Dominguez Memorial Garden/Smith Patio   89
    Clinton P. Anderson Room   89
    The Anderson Spruce   90
    The Thomas Bell Room   90
    The Alice S. Clark Room   91
    The Ford Room   91
    The Sigmund and Estelle Herzstein Room   91
    The John Gaw Meem Archive of Southwestern Architecture   92
    The Frank Waters Room   93
    The Willard Reading Room   93

Endnotes: Section One   94

Contents continued ...

SECTION TWO—NORTH CAMPUS

THE LAW SCHOOL
- Bratton Hall II (Bratton Hall)   113
- Judge Sam Gilbert Bratton Plaque   113
- William E. Bondurant Lecture Hall   114
- Bruce King Reading Room and Archive   114
- The Edward, Beatrice and John Rickert Memorial Garden   114
- Utton Transboundary Resources Center   115
- Henry P. Weihofen Faculty Library   116
- The Frederick Hart Wing   117
- The John Morgan-Johnson Tsosie Patio   117
- Robert Desiderio Seminar Room   118
- The James Quinn Memorial Tree   118
- The Mary Coon Walters Classroom   118
- Other Donor Named Rooms in UNM School of Law   118

THE NEW MEXICO LAW CENTER   119
- The Pamela B. Minzer Law Center   119

THE MEDICAL SCHOOL   120
- Reginald Heber Fitz Hall (Basic Medical Sciences Building)   120
- Frederick Harvey, MD, Library Room   120
- The Sidney Soloman Conference Room   121
- Interior Garden Memorial to Joseph P. Leonard   121

UNM CANCER CENTER AND CANCER RESEARCH AND TREATMENT CENTER   122
- Carl Anderson and Marie Jo Anderson Charitable Foundation Healing Garden and Pool   122
- The Philip and Olga Eaton Sculpture Garden of Healing   123
- UNM Helix Garden Memorial   124
- Billy McKibben Recognition Plaque   124
- Steve Schiff Center for Skin Cancer Research   125

CARRIE TINGLEY HOSPITAL   126

CASA ESPERANZA (HOUSE OF HOPE)   127

DOMENICI CENTER FOR HEALTH SCIENCES EDUCATION   127
- The Fred H. Hanold, MD, Memorial Student Study Room   128
- The Leonard M. Napolitano, PhD, Anatomical Education Center   128

PETE AND NANCY DOMENICI HALL (THE MIND INSTITUTE) 129
    The Ronald McDonald House 130
MEDICAL SCHOOL MEMORIAL TREES 130
    The Fred A. Collatz III, MD, Memorial Tree 130
    The Jeanne Smith Jordan Memorial Tree 131
    Michael J. McCaughey Memorial Tree 131
NOVITSKI HALL 131
THE COLLEGE OF NURSING 132
    The Diane Lynn Adamo Tree 132
THE UNIVERSITY OF NEW MEXICO HOSPITAL (UNMH) 133
    The Jonathan Abrams, MD, Art Gallery 133
    Barbara and Bill Richardson Pavilion 134
    Adult Emergency Department Exam Room 1 – Will Ferguson and Associates 135
    Geoffrey S.M. Hedrick Imaging Suite 135
    First Floor Main Lobby – Gerald and Barbara Landgraf 136
    Newborn Intensive Care Unit – The Thomas Silva Family Lounge 136
    Dr. Edward "Ed" William Sengel, III, Consulting Room, Pediatric Special Services 137
    Carrie Tingley Rehabilitation Unit 137
    Pediatric Intensive Care Unit – Patient Rooms – Lyle and Gale McDaniels 137
    Pediatric Surgery Center – Staff Lounge – Charles Kassell 137
    Jeff Apodaca Multi-Media Center 137
    Pete's Playground 138
    The Tree of Life Project – The Meditation Room 139
    The A. Earl and Agnes Walker Library 139
    Additional Contributions to The Richardson Pavilion 140
    Lions Club Eye Clinic 140

Endnotes: Section Two 141

Contents continued ...

SECTION THREE—SOUTH CAMPUS

    AMBROSE ALDAY BATTING COMPLEX   149

    "THE PIT" (DREAMSTYLE BASKETBALL ARENA)   149
        Larry Chavez and Joyce Hitchner Sports Bar   150
        Bob King Court   150
        Pete McDavid Room   150

    JOHN BAKER MEMORIAL WARMUP LOUNGE   151

    THE UNM CHAMPIONSHIP GOLF COURSE   152
        The Patty Howard Golf Complex   152

    RUDY DAVALOS BASKETBALL CENTER   153

    THE L.F. "TOW" DIEHM ATHLETIC FACILITY   154

    BRIAN URLACHER INDOOR PRACTICE FACILITY   155

    THE LINDA ESTES TENNIS COMPLEX   156
        Randy Briggs Tennis Domes   156
        Ted Russell Tennis Arena   157

    COLLEEN MALOOF ATHLETIC ADMINISTRATION BUILDING   158

    JAMES CRAIG ROBERTSON SOCCER FIELD   158

    UNIVERSITY SCIENCE AND TECHNOLOGY PARK   159
        Dikewood Building   159
        Research Park Streets   160
            Basehart Street   160
            Bradbury Drive   160
            Avenida César Cháves   160
            Goddard Street   161
            Langham Street   161
            Shields Street   162
            Springer Street   162

    UNIVERSITY STADIUM ("DREAMSTYLE STADIUM")   163
        Branch Field   163
        Franco-Scott Memorial Patio   164

Endnotes: Section Three   166

SECTION FOUR—OTHER PLACES

ALUMNI MEMORIAL CLOCK   171
THE CARMEN L. ALVAREZ ELM TREE   171
BLAIR'S GARDEN   171
THE TEJAY R. COLLINS PLAQUE   172
MARY A. BURROWS   172
CORNELL MALL   172
   The Belén Marbles Fountain   173
THE DUCK POND   174
   The Enarson Bench   175
THE FRANK B. FEATHER TREE   176
THE F. CHRIS GARCIA TREE   176
THE LARRY GALLEGOS TREE   177
THE LINDA HUTCHINS MEMORIAL   177
THE CHARLOTTE AND WILLIAM KRAFT MEMORIAL ROSE GARDEN   178
THE MACKEL FAMILY TREES   178
THE JENNIE P. MORROS TREE   178
TRIBUTE TO MOTHER EARTH   179
DEBORAH K. LAPOINTE MEMORIAL TREE   180
DAVID KENT MARQUESS MEMORIAL   180
100 TREES FOR 100 YEARS   181
JOHN K. PRENTICE TREE   181
THE CYNTHIA AND DAVID EDWARD STUART MARKER   182
THE JACKIE LAWTON WELLS TREE   182
THE FRANK RUMINSKI TREE   183
THE HECTOR A. TORRES TREE   183
STREET NAMES   184
   Tucker Road   184
THE STOUT MEDAL MEMORIAL GARDEN   185
MELISSA ANN STERLING TREE   185
THE USS NEW MEXICO QUEEN OF THE PACIFIC FLEET BELL TOWER   185
YALE PARK   186
THE LONG'S 100 POPLAR TREES   187
MICHAEL LEYBA MEMORIAL   187
THE HODGIN HALL ILLUMINATED "U" SIGN   187
ZIMMERMAN CHAPEL   188
Endnotes: Section Four   189
   Author References   191
   About the Authors   192

LIST OF FIGURES

SECTION ONE – CENTRAL / MAIN CAMPUS

Fig. 1. Alumni Memorial Chapel – Exterior – Spring Blossoms	5
Fig. 2. Alumni Memorial Chapel – Interior – Reredos	6
Fig. 3. Alumni Memorial Chapel – Interior – Names of War Dead	7
Fig. 4. Anderson School of Management – Sign on Building	10
Fig. 5. Bust of Robert O. Anderson, 1917-2007	10
Fig. 6. Jackson Student Center	11
Fig. 7. The Roger H. Jehenson Tree	11
Fig. 8. Jehenson Plaque	11
Fig. 9. Parish Memorial Library	12
Fig. 10. The First Student Union Building	13
Fig. 11. Anthropology – Maxwell Museum – Interior – Rug	14
Fig. 12. Anthropology – Exterior – Maxwell Museum Entrance	14
Fig. 13. Hodgin Hall – Exterior – Rear of Building with "U" Sign and Rodey Hall, circa 1920s	15
Fig. 14. Hibben Center for Archeology Research – Exterior – Dedication Plaque	16
Fig. 15. Hibben Center	16
Fig. 16. The Seaweed Totem Pole	16
Fig. 17. Bandelier Hall East – Exterior – Two Young Trees, circa 1920s	18
Fig. 18. Bandelier Hall West – Snowfall	19
Fig. 19. Bandelier Hall East – Van Dorn Hooker III Memorial Garden	19
Fig. 20. Van Dorn Hooker III Marker	19
Fig. 21. Carlisle Gymnasium – Exterior – Looking Southwest, circa 1920s	19
Fig. 22. Carlisle Gymnasium – Exterior – Electric Tower, 1928	21
Fig. 23. Castetter Hall – Looking Northwest, circa 1950s	21
Fig. 24. Library – Zimmerman – Exterior – Cactus Garden in Snow (Castetter Garden)	21
Fig. 25. Castetter Hall – Potter Wing, 1967	22
Fig. 26. Engineering – Centennial Under Construction; Mechanical Also Shown, 2008	22
Fig. 27. Centennial Engineering, 2013	22
Fig. 28. Clark Hall – Chemistry Building	23
Fig. 29. Engineering – Wagner Hall – Exterior – Civil Engineering, circa 1950s	24
Fig. 30. Communication and Journalism Building – View from Central Avenue, 1963	25
Fig. 31. Hillerman Plaque	26
Fig. 32. Maria Palacios Tree	28
Fig. 33. Dormitory – Coronado Hall – Looking East Across Dirt Lot, 1964	28
Fig. 34. Dormitory – DeVargas Hall – Upper Story Windows, 1970	29
Fig. 35. Dining Hall – La Posada – Exterior – Building Sign, circa 1970s	29
Fig. 36. Dormitory – Hokona I – View Across Lawn, circa 1910s	30
Fig. 37. Hokona I	30
Fig. 38. Dormitory – Hokona II – South Entrance, 1997-98	30
Fig. 39. Dormitory – Hokona II – Aerial View Looking Northeast, 1964	30
Fig. 40. Faculty Housing – 1925 Las Lomas Road – Lena Clauve's House, 1995	31
Fig. 41. Dormitory – Kwataka Hall – Exterior, circa 1920s	33
Fig. 42. Dormitory – Santa Ana Hall – Looking Northwest, circa 1960s	33
Fig. 43. Dormitory – Santa Clara Hall – Looking North Over Hill, 1979	33
Fig. 44. Dormitory – Oñate Hall – White Metal Fence, circa 1970s	34
Fig. 45. Dormitory – Yatoka Hall – Cars Parked in Front, circa 1920s	34
Fig. 46. Bratton Hall I – Economics, 1967	35

Fig. 47. College of Education – Manzanita Center – Children with Wooden Toys, circa 1960s — 37
Fig. 48. College of Education – Simpson Hall – Blue Tarp on Building Sign (Mrs. Simpson), 1989 — 38
Fig. 49. College of Education – Travelstead Hall – John Tatschl and Stained Glass Window — 39
Fig. 50. Travelstead Hall — 39
Fig. 51. The Estufa – Looking Northeast at Door on Side, 1932 — 41
Fig. 52. Engineering – Farris – Looking West from Regener Hall Plaza, circa 1970s — 42
Fig. 53. Fine Arts Center – Exterior –North Doors, circa 1970s — 42
Fig. 54. John Donald Robb with Kurt Frederick (right) — 45
Fig. 55. Fine Arts Center – Keller Hall – Set for "The Magic Flute," 1964 — 46
Fig. 56. Maddox Sculpture Center — 46
Fig. 57. Fine Arts Center – Popejoy Hall – Interior – Orchestra on Stage, 1973 — 47
Fig. 58. The Popejoy Trees — 48
Fig. 59. Hodgin Hall – Exterior – Rear of Building with "U" Sign and Rodey Hall, circa 1920s — 49
Fig. 60. Tamarind Institute, circa 1970 — 50
Fig. 61. Tamarind Institute, 2013 — 50
Fig. 62. Ford Utilities Center – Snow on Ground, circa 1950s — 51
Fig. 63. Ford Utilities Center, 2013 — 51
Fig. 64. Hadley Hall I – Front Entrance and Young Trees, circa 1890s — 52
Fig. 65. Hadley Hall I – Building in Ruins after Fire, circa 1910 — 52
Fig. 66. Engineering – Hadley Hall II – Car Parked in Front, 1920 — 53
Fig. 67. Left, University of New Mexico Building: Hodgin Hall under construction, 1892 — 53
Fig. 68. Center, Hodgin Hall – Exterior – View from Redondo Road, 1980 (during restoration) — 53
Fig. 69. Right, Hodgin Hall, 2013 — 53
Fig. 70. Irma Bobo Room, Hodgin Hall — 55
Fig. 71. Hodgin Hall – Gazebo Construction with Snow, 1991 — 56
Fig. 72. Horace F. McKay Lobby — 57
Fig. 73. Class of 1921 Bench — 58
Fig. 74. Hodgin Hall – Exterior – winter in Tight Grove, circa 1909 — 59
Fig. 75. Tight Grove Plaque — 59
Fig. 76. Lobo sculpture by Michelle Middleton located in Tight Grove — 60
Fig. 77. Hodgin Hall – Tatschl Lobo Head and Logan Hall, 1991 — 60
Fig. 78. Humanities Building – Looking Southeast across Smith Plaza, circa 1970s — 61
Fig. 79. Homecoming – Vendors on Smith Plaza, 1972 — 61
Fig. 80. Left, Commencement – Ceremony in Johnson Gym, circa 1961 — 63
Fig. 81. Right, Aerial Photo – Looking West across Johnson Field,1971 — 63
Fig. 82. Left, Johnson Field — 63
Fig. 83. Right, Johnson Center – Exterior – West Entrance, 1974 — 63
Fig. 84. Landscaping – Sculpture – Lobo Statue by John Tatschl, 1965 — 64
Fig. 85. Landscaping – Sculptures – Lobo Statue at Stanford Entrance, circa 1950s — 64
Fig. 86. Johnson Center – Interior – Seidler Natatorium, circa 2000 — 66
Fig. 87. Jonson Gallery – Looking Southeast, circa 1970s — 67
Fig. 88. Logan Hall – Psychology – Looking Southwest, 1972 — 68
Fig. 89. Marron Hall – Looking across Redondo Road, 1998 — 68
Fig. 90. Mesa Vista Hall – Exterior – Looking East from Cornell Mall, circa 1990s — 69
Fig. 91. The John W. Smeltzer Garden — 69
Fig. 92. Mitchell Hall – Exterior – Snowfall, 1997 — 71
Fig. 93. Naval Sciences Building – Looking Southeast across Dirt Lot, 1941 — 72
Fig. 94. Hank Willis Plaque — 72
Fig. 95. Geology – Northrup Hall – Looking across Yale Boulevard, 1953 — 73
Fig. 96. Ortega Hall and the Center of the Universe, 1998 — 74
Fig. 97. Parsons Hall, 1928 — 76
Fig. 98. John and June Perovich Business Center — 77

List of Figures continued ...

Fig. 99. Sara Raynolds Hall – Exterior – Looking North, 1921	78
Fig. 100. Physics Lab and Lecture Hall – Regener Hall – Exterior, 1972	78
Fig. 101. Scholes Hall, 1939	79
Fig. 102. Thomas Reaser Roberts Plaque	80
Fig. 103. Dane Smith Hall – Exterior – Cyclist on Path, 2001	81
Fig. 104. Student Health Center	82
Fig. 105. Lawrence R. Klausen Memorial Park	83
Fig. 106. Lawrence R. Klausen Memorial Plaque	83
Fig. 107. Student Services Center – Exterior – Looking North across Courtyard, 1984	84
Fig. 108. Engineering – Civil – Tapy Hall – Front Lawn, circa 1950s	85
Fig. 109. Woodward Hall – Exterior – Walkway, circa 1970s	86
Fig. 110. Library – Zimmerman – Exterior – East Side Prior to Additions, circa 1938	87
Fig. 111. Zimmerman Stadium and Zimmerman Library, circa 1960s	88
Fig. 112. Library – Zimmerman – Exterior – Raul D. Dominguez Memorial Garden	89
Fig. 113. Library – Interior – Zimmerman – Clinton P. Anderson Reading Room, 1985	89
Fig. 114. Anderson Spruce	90
Fig. 115. Library – Zimmerman – Interior – Outside View of Willard Reading Room, 1940	93

SECTION TWO – NORTH CAMPUS

Fig. 1. Bratton Hall II – Law School – Exterior Entry Doors, Trees, and Bicycle Racks, circa 1970s	113
Fig. 2. Bratton Hall II – Law School – Exterior Close-up on Doors, 1998	113
Fig. 3. Bratton Hall I – Plaque	113
Fig. 4. Fred Hart Wing	117
Fig. 5. John Morgan and Johnson Tsosie Patio	117
Fig. 6. John Morgan and Johnson Tsosie Marker	117
Fig. 7. Pamela B. Minzer Law Center, Court of Appeals (Albuquerque)	119
Fig. 8. Basic Medical Sciences – Horizontal View, 1998	120
Fig. 9. Reginald Heber Fitz Hall, 2014	120
Fig. 10. Cancer Research and Treatment Center – Front Entrance, 1998	122
Fig. 11. Cancer Research Center, 1974	122
Fig. 12. Healing Garden Rendering	122
Fig. 13. Philip and Olga Eaton Sculpture Garden of Healing	123
Fig. 14. Carrie Tingley Hospital	126
Fig. 15. Casa Esperanza	127
Fig. 16. Domenici Center for Health Sciences Education	127
Fig. 17. Leonard M. Napolitano, Ph.D., Anatomical Education Foundation Center	128
Fig. 18. Pete and Nancy Domenici Hall and MIND Institute	129
Fig. 19. Ronald McDonald House	130
Fig. 20. Fred A. Collatz III, MD Memorial Elm Tree	130
Fig. 21. Jeanne Smith Jordan Plaque	131
Fig. 22. Novitski Hall – Dental Hygiene School, 1978	131
Fig. 23. The Adamo Tree	132
Fig. 24. UNM Hospital – Aerial View, 1966	133
Fig. 25. University of New Mexico Hospital today	133
Fig. 26. Abrams Gallery	133
Fig. 27. Barbara and Bill Richardson Pavilion	134
Fig. 28. Pete's Playground	138
Fig. 29. Tree of Life Door by Denise Taylor, University Hospital	139

SECTION THREE – SOUTH CAMPUS

Fig. 1. University Arena – The Pit – Exterior – Northeast Corner, North Side, 1998 — 149
Fig. 2. "The Pit" Basketball Arena, 2013 — 149
Fig. 3. Left, Track at UNM South Campus — 151
Fig. 4. Center, John Baker Memorial Warm Up Lounge — 151
Fig. 5. Right, John Baker Plaque — 151
Fig. 6. UNM Championship Golf Course — 152
Fig. 7. Patty Howard Golf Complex — 152
Fig. 8. Rudy Davalos Basketball Center — 153
Fig. 9. L.F. "Tow" Diehm Athletic Facility – Close-up of Front Doors, 1998 — 154
Fig. 10. Brian Urlacher Indoor Practice Facility — 155
Fig. 11. Linda Estes Tennis Complex — 156
Fig. 12. Randy Briggs Tennis Domes interior — 156
Fig. 13. Randy Briggs Tennis Domes — 156
Fig. 14. Ted Russell Tennis Arena — 157
Fig. 15. Colleen Maloof Athletic Administration Building — 158
Fig. 16. South Campus Running Track and Soccer Field, 1998 — 158
Fig. 17. Dikewood Building, University Science and Technology Park — 159
Fig. 18. Left, University Stadium – Stadium Seating and Press Boxes, 1998 — 163
Fig. 19. Center, University Stadium Press Box — 163
Fig. 20. Right, UNM Stadium — 163

SECTION FOUR – OTHER PLACES

Fig. 1. Alumni Clock, circa 1990s — 171
Fig. 2. Alumni Memorial Clock – Two Faces — 171
Fig. 3. Cornell Mall – Woman with Books, circa 1960s — 172
Fig. 4. Cornell Mall, 2013 — 172
Fig. 5. Fine Arts Center – Exterior – Fountain — 173
Fig. 6. The Duck Pond – After Completion of Construction, 1975 — 174
Fig. 7. The Duck Pond – Looking North from South of Bridge, 1995 — 174
Fig. 8. The Enarson Bench — 175
Fig. 9. Marker – Audrey Pitt and Harold Enarson — 175
Fig. 10. Jennie P. Morros Tree — 178
Fig. 11. Jennie P. Morros Marker — 178
Fig. 12. Landscaping – Fountain – Tribute to Mother Earth, 1997 — 179
Fig. 13. Tribute to Mother Earth Plaque — 179
Fig. 14. John K. Prentice Tree — 181
Fig. 15. John K. Prentice Plaque — 181
Fig. 16. Frank Ruminski Tree — 183
Fig. 17. Student Publications – Navy ROTC – Bell Tower, 1967 — 185
Fig. 18. Bell Tower, 2013 — 185
Fig. 20. Yale Park Sculpture – "Spirit Mother" During Snowfall, 1997 — 187
Fig. 21. Yale Park Sculpture – "Cultural Crossroads" Snow-covered Ground, 1997 — 187
Fig. 22. Hodgin Hall – Exterior – with "U" Sign, circa 1926 — 187
Fig. 23. Hodgin Hall "U" Today — 187
Fig. 24. Edward A. Zimmerman Plaque — 188
Fig. 25. Zimmerman Chapel Interior — 188

Acknowledgements

My thanks to the many University people, friends and relatives of people noted in the book, who have helped me find information. I am sure I have omitted some, so please forgive me. I thank you too.

Van Dorn Hooker, FAIA, and University Architect Emeritus, 2014

Karen Abraham	*Lindsay R. Gilbert, Jr.*	*Robert Meyer*
Rudolfo Anaya	*Jennifer George*	*John Perovich*
Jan Bandrofchak	*Marcia Glenn*	*Price V.B.*
Nancy J. Bell	*Carolyn Gonzales*	*Roberta Ricci*
Audra Bellmore	*Terry Gugliotta*	*Nancy Rice*
Breda Bova	*Laura J. Hall*	*Edmund P. "Ned" Ross*
Anne J. Brown	*Helen Harris*	*Richard Ruminski*
Andrew John Burgess	*Fred Hart*	*Lawrence Schuster*
Patricia "Pat" Cain	*Nancy Herbet*	*David S. Stuart*
John Martin "Jack" Campbell	*John H. Hooker*	*Michelle Tatlock*
Shannan Carter	*Melissa Howard*	*Kenneth Thompson*
Tim Cass	*Pam Hurd-Knief*	*Hazel Tull-Leach*
Mary Conrad	*Peter B. Ives*	*Jill Trujillo*
David Darling	*Mary Kinney*	*Portia Vescio*
William E. "Bud" Davis	*Kathy Kolankiewicz*	*Mary Vosovich*
Chris Deal	*Robert "Bob" Lalicker*	*Robert Ware*
Rose Diaz	*Kay Marr*	*Chuck Wellborn*
Philip Eaton	*Nancy Brown-Martinez*	*Ellen P. Wenzel*
Henry Ellis	*Anne M. Massmann*	*Maria Wolfe*
Kara Evans	*Peggy McBride*	*Roger Wrolstad*
Christina Fenton	*Laura McNamara*	*Acela "Lucy" Yebra*
Craig Fertig	*Cindy Morris*	
Kathleen Ferris	*Suzanne Mortier*	

Special thanks are extended to the following for assistance with photographs: UNM Archivist *Portia Vescio* and her predecessor *Terry Gugliotta* for researching and providing historic photographs from the digital archives maintained at the UNM Center for Southwest Research; *Suzanne Mortier*, former University Landscape Architect; *Michelle Tatlock*, Department of Spiritual Care and Education, UNM Hospital, and unknown sources.

Ann Hooker Clarke, 2019

Dedication

Memories, Memorials, and Monuments,
my late father Van Dorn Hooker's last manuscript,
is a tribute to his love of the University, the State of New Mexico,
its people, history, art, and architecture.

Memories, Memorials and Monuments: A Companion to Only in New Mexico: An Architectural History of the University of New Mexico is therefore dedicated to Van Dorn Hooker, University Architect Emeritus; the many people who shared his commitment to the University by assisting him in his research; and the students, staff, professors, and others who are remembered in the named places and objects found at the University. He was compelled to his last breath to complete this manuscript, ever worried that many of the memories, memorials, and monuments, from what in time will be seen as the early years of the University, would eventually be lost or forgotten in a changing campus environment.

ANN HOOKER CLARKE, MAY 2010

John K. Prentice Tree (Photograph by Suzanne Mortier, UNM Landscape Architect, 2013).

Preface

Walter Lippman, a writer of the last century, wrote the following:

When shall we recognize the truth of our situation? Only when we see ourselves and the events of our day as one act in a drama that began long before we were born and will not be played out until long after we are dead. We shall never manage the present, or make any sense of it, unless we have explained our past well enough to imagine our future. Coping adequately with the present requires an understanding of the historic continuum. The present constitutes but a fleeting point in time emerging from the long and direction-pointing past into the ever arriving future.

COURTESY OF JOHN DURRIE
UNIVERSITY SECRETARY EMERITUS

The memory of a university is short. Students attend for a few years, usually one to six or seven. Professors stay for a time until they move on up the academic ladder at some other university or retire from academia. For the staff, thirty years is a long time, twenty or less is more the norm. Often someone leaves such a mark on the institution that his or her contemporaries want to create a memorial to commemorate their service to the University.

Then the next generation comes along and wonders who that person was and what they did. Often the meaning of a memorial and the life and times of the person being commemorated is lost in the passing of time. Perhaps this book will answer some of these questions in the far distant future, providing stories of the history of the University of New Mexico and the people who gave so much of their lives or money to the University that parts of it still carry their names.

VAN DORN HOOKER, FAIA

Zimmerman Library – east side prior to additions, circa 1938 (Center for Southwest Research, UNM Libraries)

Foreword

Ever wonder who Keen Rafferty, Tom Popejoy, Dane Smith, Lena Clauve, John D. Robb, France Scholes, Frances Marron, or Sherman Smith were? They all have plaques, statues, buildings, reading rooms or some outdoor spaces named after them at the University of New Mexico, along with a couple of hundred other teachers, administrators, benefactors, and students who have honored the University with their service and talent from 1889 to 2012.

If you have always felt the nagging prod of curiosity when you see such names on campus, this fascinating book by Van Dorn Hooker, FAIA, will satisfy your hunger and delight your sense of history.

Hooker was the award-winning mastermind of UNM's unique architectural heritage when he was the University Architect and Associate Professor of Architecture from 1963 to 1987. He spent many years of retirement researching and writing about UNM. His Only in New Mexico, an architectural history of the school, is a classic. In this book, Hooker reveals some of the inner history of the university. He is a graceful and ardent storyteller with a gift of getting charmingly straight to the point.

He compiles here a vast array of personal stories, legends, amazing achievements, and little known facts about the people the University has chosen to honor by naming a physical space after them. It is, in a sense, a people's history of the school.

A university is its people, and its values are displayed by whom it chooses to thank. Hooker's research makes it clear that UNM has named buildings, monuments, and memorials not only for people who donated large sums of money to the school, but also for those who brought honor to it, who cared for it, who nurtured its sense of excellence, and who guarded its New Mexico spirit.

Such notables as Tony Hillerman, Mathias Lambert Custers, Patrick McNamara, Caswell Silver, Joaquin Ortega, Frank Waters, Larry Willard, Pamela B. Minzer, A.C. "Scotty" Scott and Henry C. Franco, Josephine Parsons, student Hugh Carlisle, Norris Bradbury, and John Perovich all have some part of UNM's physical environment named after them. You can learn about them by reading this warm and engaging labor of love that Van Dorn Hooker has created with such admirable attention to detail and to the significance of the lives UNM has chosen to praise.

People who love UNM will love this book, especially those of us who walk on campus all the time and wonder to ourselves with increasing intensity as we pass the names on auspicious buildings and quiet plaques, "Who was that?"

V.B. Price, Albuquerque, NM, 2014

Raul Dominguez Memorial Garden (Photograph by Richard Reck, Center for Southwest Research, UNM Libraries).

Introduction

This book is intended to give the reader some information about the people for whom places and objects, such as buildings, rooms, streets, plazas, and trees, on the University of New Mexico, Albuquerque Central, North, and South Campuses have been named. I have also included people for whom such places and objects, long torn down or forgotten, were named. Also included is information about the names of some places and objects not named for people, like The Estufa and University Stadium.

I especially want to acknowledge Terry Gugliotta, University Archivist, and her staff, the staff at the UNM Center for Southwest Research, Suzanne Mortier, University Landscape Architect, and Jennifer George, UNM Department of Anthropology, for their extraordinary dedication and skill in assisting me, not just throughout the research, but particularly in the final stages of preparing the manuscript. Without their efforts, this compilation of memories might have itself been forgotten.

The University of New Mexico will continue to grow as long as there is demand for it to grow, and buildings will be torn down to make way for larger buildings. This book provides a glimpse of what happened between 1889 and 2012 – not even a blink of the eye in the long light of history, but 120 years in the life of the University of New Mexico.

Finding biographical information about people for whom buildings and other places and objects were named proved to be very interesting, though difficult. Obituaries helped a bit, but many of these were merely announcements of funerals or memorial services. Conversations with surviving friends and family members, when they could be found, were also helpful. Many university people had newspaper articles written about themselves, but that required long searches. The staff in the Center for Southwest Research and Terry Gugliotta, the University Archivist, and her staff were most helpful. Others to whom I am indebted appear in the Acknowledgments.

The location of named places and objects goes all the way from Popejoy Hall, named for past UNM President Tom Popejoy and where thousands of people attend performances each month, to an obscure little garden plot that few people ever see in the courtyard of Mesa Vista Hall named for an outstanding student, John "Wolfie" Smeltzer. Some are named for people who did notable things for the University, and some for people whose friends or relatives wanted to commemorate them more personally and bought space. Thus, items are named for professors, Doctors of Medicine, athletes, groundskeepers, administrators, students, alumni and kinfolk. This book is a compilation of what I could find on the University campuses in Albuquerque that bear people's names. I'm sure I have missed some, please forgive me.

A naming committee must approve naming of places and objects before the requests go to the Board of Regents for final consideration, though not everything goes to the committee.[1] In some instances, naming is informal, such as planting and naming a tree. Most of the names of buildings and outdoor spaces are, or were, approved by the Board of Regents, but some names have come about by common usage, like Johnson Field.

In the early days of the University, most of the appellations were made for people who had made significant contributions in teaching, research, sports and other ways to the University. The Board of Regents recently promulgated Regents Policy 1020, Naming UNM Facilities, Spaces, Endowments and Programs followed by a UNM Policy with the same title, revised September 6, 2005.[2] These documents spell out in detail procedures for getting places and objects named, including how much money a person, friends, or a corporation must contribute to get his, her or its name on something.

Many named places and objects have been lost as buildings have been remodeled or torn down. Plaques and memorial markers have been removed for various reasons and could not be found. In some cases names have been carried over to new structures, as with Bratton Halls I and II.

Researching the book has been an enjoyable experience for me over some five years of off and on digging. I have found many interesting items about many people, many of whom were my friends who did great things for the University. In the future, I hope a way will be found to honor people who will have made significant contributions at UNM, but whose families and friends do not have the funds to buy the space for a memorial. I also hope hear that this book becomes the first in a series as I am confident that future generations at UNM would want the reasons for the memorials, not just at the Albuquerque campuses, but also elsewhere at UNM, to not be forgotten. As the University evolves, each has a story to tell.

This book is divided into four sections: Central/Main Campus, North Campus, South Campus, and Other Spaces. Included in the latter are pedestrian malls, plazas, streets, groves of trees, and other non-building memorials not otherwise included in the main sections.

For more information about people who have memorials named for them, the University Archives at Zimmerman Library would be a good starting point.

Van Dorn Hooker, FAIA
UNM University Architect Emeritus
UNM Associate Professor of Architecture Emeritus
May 2010

---

1   See https://www.unmfund.org/memorials-tributes/ (last accessed Feb. 2, 2019).
2   UNM Policy Office, "Regents' Policy Manual – Section 2.11: Naming University Facilities, Spaces, Endowments, and Programs," https://policy.unm.edu/regents-policies/section-2/2-11.html (last accessed Feb. 2, 2019).

Note

> [I]t would be helpful for the General Library to have among its archives a roster of memorials of buildings and other facilities, giving brief biographical information about persons memorialized. It being noted that considerable information of this sort is presently in hand, it was agreed that the Campus Planning Committee would consider the matter further, and particularly the desirability of making such information readily accessible to the public.[1]

My father, Van Dorn Hooker, passed away in 2015 at age 93 in Albuquerque. He came to UNM as University Architect in the early 1960s from private practice in Santa Fe and retired as University Architect Emeritus in 1984. His vision was to make the world a better place, and to that end, his legacy can be found throughout the UNM campus, his several books and articles, and in his efforts to create the University Archives.

Van Dorn Hooker was also deeply interested in history, architectural history, art, and people. He spent the last several years of his life researching the history of the people for which places and things at UNM have been named or for which memorials were placed. He was grateful for the assistance he received from many people, including those listed in the Acknowledgements, and especially the staff of the University Archives and the University Planning, Design & Construction Office, which houses the current University Architect..

The compendium at hand, which is admittedly incomplete and limited to the Albuquerque campus, may be read as a companion to Van Dorn Hooker's books *Only in New Mexico: An Architectural History of the University of New Mexico, the First Century 1889-1989*, and the large format picture book *The University of New Mexico* (with V.B. Price and photographer Richard Reck). This compendium also augments the related book *Miracle on the Mesa: A History of the University of New Mexico, 1889-2003* by former UNM President William "Bud" E. Davis.

As an aid to readers, archivists, historians, and the families of those memorialized, I have corrected a few dates and filled in some gaps based on obituaries and other readily available biographical information from digital sources.[2] I have included historical photographs where available from such sources as the UNM Center for Southwest Research through the New Mexico Digital Collections website. I am especially grateful to Portia Vescio, University Archivist, and Suzanne Mortier, former University Landscape Architect for their assistance. Special thanks also to Denise Taylor of Taylor Made Glass, LLC, for information about the Tree of Life stained glass featured on the cover, and to Patricia Hamilton of Park Place Publications, in Pacific Grove, California, for her care and expertise in formatting the manuscript and facilitating its publication.

The campus began with a scattering of buildings on a treeless mesa at the eastern edge of Albuquerque that has since given way to a vibrant and green campus within the larger metropolitan area. Many of the earliest buildings depicted in the older black and white images may not be easily recognizable today. Nonetheless, I included these images to depict the buildings and places at or close to the time they were named.

As with any change in the built environment, some named buildings and several markers have been lost to time. Background information is scattered or missing. My hope is that this first compendium, which is not intended to be a treatise, will serve as a major starting point for interested readers. I further believe that my father and the many people who assisted him in his research would wish that this initial work will spur others, including those associated with the satellite campuses, to carry on the effort as the University continues to change and new people are memorialized.

Ann Hooker Clarke, Carmel Valley, California, 2019

---

1. http://digitalrepository.unm.edu/cgi/viewcontent.cgi?article=1325&context=bor_minutes (last accessed November 14, 2017).
2. Please note that the URL links included in the endnotes may need to be copied into one's browser. The editor acknowledges that some digital sites may become obsolete over time.

Memories, Memorials, and Monuments

Lobo in Tight Grove (Source unknown).

Section One—Central/Main Campus

Hadley Hall and Hodgin Hall 1890 (Center for Southwest Research, UNM Libraries).

THE ALUMNI MEMORIAL CHAPEL[1]

*Fig. 1. Alumni Memorial Chapel – Exterior – Spring Blossoms
(Photograph by Terry Gugliotta, Center for Southwest Research, UNM Libraries).*[2]

The concept of a memorial chapel at the University of New Mexico began to form shortly after the end of World War II and was realized in 1962. The Alumni Association raised more than $75,000 toward the construction of the chapel, now known as the Alumni Memorial Chapel, and received a loan from the University to complete the project. The design, modeled in Pueblo Mission Style, was based on a sketch by John Gaw Meem,[3] who designed some of the early buildings on campus. To date, the drawing by Meem has not been found. The project architects were the firm of Holien and Buckley. Edward O. Holien was the designer.

Today, the University Alumni Association manages the Alumni Memorial Chapel and new Chapel Garden for use by UNM alumni, personnel, and friends for weddings, memorial services, funerals, and occasional religious gatherings.[4] The Alumni Association in 2013 created a "Celebration Wall" where photo tiles (without captions) may be donated to commemorate special events held in the chapel.[5]

The brass bells over the front entrance were contributed by the Atchison, Topeka and Santa Fe Railroad. The bells were removed from retired steam locomotives and installed upon completion of the chapel. Chi Omega sorority donated the carillon in 1975.

The Christus, a forty-two-inch tall carving in cedar wood, was created by sculptor John Tatschl for the late Professor of Art, Dr. Ralph Douglass, his wife Miriam, and their daughter Marilyn. Professor Douglass was an internationally known calligrapher who taught art and calligraphy at UNM for many years. He also chaired the Art Department for ten years and retired from the University in 1961. The Douglass family donated the Christus to the University Alumni Chapel in memory of Professor Douglass's son Donald Ralph Douglass, who was killed in the Battle of the Bulge in 1945, and the other 134 alumni and students who gave their lives in World War II.

The Christus, originally installed in a niche in the lobby of the original part of the Zimmerman Library, was later moved to a more prominent location in the building. With the renovation of the Chapel in 1994, the Christus was moved once again to the Alumni Memorial Chapel for inclusion with the other war memorials. Soon after the installation, however, objections were raised regarding the religious nature of the statue, and the University placed the statue in storage.

The pipe organ in the choir loft was constructed by Dr. Wesley T. Selby. Professor Selby imported the organ parts from an Illinois factory and assembled it in the chapel loft. The nine-stop baroque organ is the only one of its kind in New Mexico and was named in memory of Walter Keller, former Chair of the Department of Music, who passed away in 1970. (See also discussion regarding Keller Hall.)

The electronic organ in the chapel was donated in memory of Willa Adela (Tucker) Zimmerman, wife of James F. Zimmerman (former UNM President), by her daughters Helen Emily Z. Brandenburg and Elizabeth "Libby" Z. Cottle. This organ was installed soon after construction on the chapel was completed.

Sculptor John Tatschl designed the altar screen, or reredos, using donated materials. Graduate students Richard Lee Masterson and Donald Duncan assisted. Bernalillo County Salvage Board and Raymond Seder, Class of 1911, funded construction of the screen. However, funding shortages required that the panels be installed initially without painted images.

Fig. 2. Alumni Memorial Chapel – Interior- Reredos (Center for Southwest Research, UNM Libraries).[6]

In late 1983, private funds permitted the employment of a Santero, John M. Gonzales, to paint retablos, or images, of saints having special meaning in New Mexico[7] on the panels in the reredo. Although the committee appointed to oversee the project was careful to exclude any image that might be offensive to any religion, the screen does contain religious imagery and is covered by a screen for some services. A plaque dedicated to Thomas Sydney Bell, New Mexico's first Rhodes Scholar, reads:

> The United States Flag and Painted Reredos Screen
> are Gifts of William B. Macey and Jean Mullins Macey
> in Memory of Thomas Sydney Bell.

WAR DEAD COMMEMORATED IN ALUMNI CHAPEL[8]

Fig. 3. Alumni Memorial Chapel – Interior – List of Names (Center for Southwest Research, UNM Libraries).[9]

At the entrance to the Alumni Memorial Chapel, a plaque reads:

> Dedicated to the Memory
> of the War Dead of the
> University of New Mexico
> by Alumni and Friends. 1960.

Inside, panels on the south wall of the nave list the names of UNM alumni killed in American wars. As of this writing, the names are listed as follows:

WORLD WAR I

Floyd Leslie Bradley	Hugh A. Carlisle	William Lampton
Harry Boyette Lee	Howard E. Morrow	

WORLD WAR II

William M. Agnew, Jr.	James P. Allen	C. Richard Arnds
Charles E. Ashton	Glenn Bailey	Napoleon R. Baldonado
Fritz G. Barnes	Robert S. Barth	A.R. Beauchamp
Robert J. Beckham	L.C. (Bill) Bennett	Glenn R. Bergquist
Kenneth E. Berryhill	Robert Bigelow	William R. Black
Robert Bledsoe	C.M. Botts, Jr.	Jack P. Bowman
Joseph W. Britian, Jr.	Wilbur P. Broemel	James W. Brown
George H. Browne	Barney T. Burns	Dan Burns
Lewis Butler	Ellis Simpson Byers	Edward N. Calame
Harry M. Calame	Llewellyn Calkins	Charles C. Clancey
Mansal R. Clark, Jr.	Charles Goggeshall	Paul D. Colvin, Jr.
Buford F. Cooksey	Maurice G. Covington	Dean H. Craft
Robert A. Craig	Wilson C. Currier, Jr.	H. Quentin Daniel
Gilbert F. Davidson	Dwayne A. Davis	James C. DeBaca
Dale E. Dellinger	Wayne B. Denton	Ralph Monyhan Dienst
James Lawrence Douglas	Donald Ralph Douglass	Francis A. Dunphy
Michael R. Duran	Jack L. Ellis	James L. Elrod
John M. Erbacher	Ernest P. Everheart	Jack Evins

WORLD WAR II *(continued)*

John W. Fleming
John W. Gentry
Harry D. Giles
Justin Gray, Jr.
John Eugene Griffith
William A. Harrington, Jr.
Clyde H. Hill
James E. Hubbell
Robert D. Jackson
George D. Johnson, Jr.
Davis Kells
Robert W. Korber
Floyd C. Leeds
Jesus Soria Llamas
Joe T. Lujan, Jr.
Robert H. McDougal
James L. McNaughton
Donald B. Martz
William H. Meyer
Edward L. Morris
William McRae Norris
Lawrence O'Neil
Duward N.B. Passmore
Jack E. Peterson
Marion Plomtequx
Charles M. Raymond
Albert E. Rey
Lester L. Roberts
Frank J. Sanchez
Charles A. Schubert
Robert Spears
Carl A. Staber
Walter J. Sullivan
Thomas C. Terry

Otto P. Fellin, Jr.
Willard G. Gieske
Ernest E. Gill
Robert H. Greenwell
Otto B. Hammersmith
Robert L. Harrison
Reese L. Hill
Andrew Jackson Hughes
Carter B. Johnson
Thomas M. Jorgensen
Dean R. Kendall, Jr.
Edwin S. Landon
Cleveland H. Letton
Hardy V. Logan, Jr.
Ross A. McCollum
John R. McFie, Jr.
Donald W. Mabry
Louis L. Medina
Guthrie McNabb Miller, Jr.
William F. Murphy
John Norton
En-Kuei Pao (Richard Baugh)
John P. Patton
Elmer M. Pettine
Eddie Pope
Claude Reece
Malcolm H. Richter
Titus Rouse
Bertram Sandoval
Caesar J. Selva
Homer Spensley
Richard M. Strong
James W. Syme
Glen T. Thompson

Frank B. Furby
Troy D. Gilbert
Cesar L. Gonzales
John J. Griffin
Crokett L. Harmon
Loys Voss Hayes
George T. Holton
Glenn E. Hunt
Donald M. Johnson
Osborn Keller
Ray Kenny
Edward Larner
Dr. Ray Lindenschmidt
Richard N. Long
Arthur W. McCormick
Paul McLaughlin
Charles L. Maggart
Lionel Melendez
Paul Moore
William Norris
Barton St. Vrain Oglesby
Ted E. Parker
Newton J. Patton
Franklin L. Pierce
Charles A. Rodoslovich
Kenneth Reid
Richard Riley
James E. Sadler
Frederick McCreary Schneider
James D. Smith
Robert B. Spruill
Philip E. Sullivan
Charles Tannehill
James F. Thompson

Dana Paul Todd
Lee C. Tucker
Charles Wallach
John Jerome Wilcoxson
Oliver B. Witten
Robert E. Young

Thomas S. Trinkle
Donald Vasquez Urquhart
William H. Watson
Thomas N. Wilkerson, Jr.
Harold A. Wood

Martin Trujillo
Charles E. Van
Robert S. Wilcox
Frederick E. Wilson, Jr.
Allen D. Young

KOREAN CONFLICT

Richard C. Clinite
Hugh Jenkins
John J. Leonard
Kay Sherrill Platt
William H. Suffern, Jr.

William A. Fairchild, Jr.
Karl George Koenig
Larry T. Mitchell
Robert Wayne Shirley
Howard M. Tohill

Francis A. Holcomb
Frederick N. Larrivee, Jr.
Marquis H. Oracion
Darrell O. Smith
Maurice Robert Tyner

VIETNAM WAR

Michael Thomas Adams
Charles Dominic Caserio
Michael Randell Earl
Gary Lee Gaziala
Stephen Kenneth Jennings
Frederic Runyon Koch
John Ault Le Compte
William Dale Marshall, Jr.
Larry Dalton Phelps
Patrick Salazar
William Weiberg

Robert C. Barnes
Kenneth Richard Clough
Martin Vincent Fanning
Lloyd Lee Gooding
Michael Thomas Jones
Kenneth B. Kozai
Conrad Lerman Gerald
Scott Winston McIntire
John David Rogers
Randall Keith Teter
Victor D. Westphall III

Edmond David Bilbrey
Donald Gene Denney
John Wesley Frink
Albert C. James
Edward Lewis Jory, Jr.
Mitchell Sim Lane
David Markland
Jesse Mitchem
Mel Ernest Salazar, Jr.
Terry Leo Trainer

AFGHANISTAN AND IRAQ WARS

Tamara Long Archuleta

Thomas J. Casey

Raymond Estelle II

ROBERT O. ANDERSON SCHOOL OF MANAGEMENT[10]

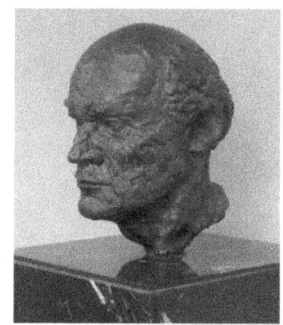

Fig. 4. Anderson School of Management – Sign on Building (Photograph by Terry Gugliotta, Center for Southwest Research, UNM Libraries).[11]

Fig. 5. Bust of Robert O. Anderson, 1917-2007 (Photograph by Suzanne Mortier, UNM Landscape Architect, 2013).

The building known as the Robert O. Anderson School of Management was constructed in 1968 for the College of Business Administration. The College of Business Administration was then located in the since demolished Yatoka Hall. The design of the new building was described as recalling some of the early Santa Fe buildings such as Sena Plaza, which is a two-story adobe with balconies, and early University buildings such as the first Hokona Hall. President Tom Popejoy once stated that the building was "not strictly traditional, but regional." John Reed was the architect for the project.

In 1985, architect James Brown, a partner with Hutchinson, Brown, and Partners, presented the final design of a building for the Anderson School of Management to the Board of Regents. Brown also presented proposals for the Parish Library[12] and the Social Sciences building[13] in this meeting. He described the design of the graduate school as being a transition between the traditional pueblo style on the Central campus and the contemporary style of the medical school buildings on the North Campus.

The Anderson School of Management was named for Robert Orville Anderson.[14] The Board of Regents held dedicatory ceremonies on May 3, 1974, "…honoring a distinguished international business management statesman."

Anderson was born in Chicago, Illinois, on April 13, 1917, and earned a Bachelor of Business from the University of Chicago. He was with the American Mineral Spirits Company from 1939 to 1941, served as President of Malco Refining Company, which he merged into the Atlantic Refining Company and later with Richfield Oil Company to form ARCO. He served for many years as Chairman of the Board and Chief Executive Officer of ARCO, which has been credited with discovering the vast Prudhoe Bay Oil Field in Alaska. Andersen led a seven-company effort to build the Alaskan pipeline in 1974. Along with his brother Donald, he later established the Hondo Oil and Gas Company.

Anderson served as trustee of the University of Chicago and the California Institute of Technology, as well as a regent at New Mexico State University in Las Cruces, New Mexico. He supported many philanthropic and environmental organizations and received many awards, including the American Petroleum Institute's Gold Medal, and several honorary degrees, including in 1966 an honorary Doctor in Literature from UNM. He died at his home in Roswell on December 2, 2007.

Jackson Student Center[15]

Fig. 6. Jackson Student Center (Photograph by UNM Newsroom).[16]

In 2006, the area under the cantilevered third story of the Anderson School of Management was enclosed with largely glass walls. The two-story space is known as the Paul R. Jackson Student Center, named by Mr. Jackson's son, Steven P. Jackson, who made a large donation for the project. Wells Fargo also contributed funds.

Paul Jackson was a local insurance businessman, former Citizens Bank board member, and influential Albuquerque business leader. The space was designed to allow informal interactions between students and faculty, serve as a gathering space for study groups, student clubs, and organizations, and as a venue for lectures, dinners, and receptions. The mezzanine, which houses the Student Financial Services Center, includes electronic screens and stock tickers, which are used as part of the Portfolio Management Practicum class.

The Roger H. Jehenson Tree

Fig. 7. The Roger H. Jehenson Tree (Photograph by Suzanne Mortier, UNM Landscape Architect, 2013).

Fig. 8. Jehenson Plaque (Photograph by Suzanne Mortier, UNM Landscape Architect, 2013).

On the south side of the Anderson School of Management, a purple leaf plum tree was planted and dedicated to Professor Roger H. Jehenson, former faculty member of the business school. Professor Jehenson was born in Brussels, Belgium, studied in Belgium and Canada, and received his doctorate from Yale. He died in an automobile accident in 1986. Jehenson was known for his commitment to interdisciplinary study. The American Sociological Association in its obituary spoke of Prof. Jehenson as a "scholar par excellence."[17] The commemorative plaque is inscribed:

> Roger H. Jehenson, November 30, 1986,
> In Loving Memory, Teacher and A Great Friend.

Parish Memorial Library

Fig. 9. Parish Memorial Library (Center for Southwest Research, UNM Libraries).

The Parish Memorial Library within the Anderson School of Management contains the business and management collections and was named for former Professor and Dean William J. Parish. Born in Franklin, Pennsylvania, Dean Parish graduated from Brown University in 1929. After contracting tuberculosis, Parish came to Albuquerque in 1939 and joined the UNM faculty in 1943 as an assistant professor. Parish received his doctorate from Harvard University in 1950 and became a full professor at UNM in 1955. Parish served as Dean of the College of Business Administration from 1959 to 1963 when he was appointed Dean of the University Graduate School. Parish gave the UNM Research Lecture in 1959. After he died in 1964, his family donated a commemorative plaque in 1968 and has continued to donate generously to Parish Library.[18]

Eric Pillmore Room for Ethics[19]

The Eric Pillmore Room for Ethics (Room 234 of the Anderson School of Management) houses the New Mexico Ethics Alliance. Eric Pillmore, a 1975 Anderson School of Management graduate, was the Senior Vice President of Corporate Governance at Tyco International Corporation until 2007. Pillmore had been hired to restore Tyco's reputation and install a working program of ethics following a company scandal involving the improprieties of a former CEO.

Before assuming his post at Tyco, Pillmore held executive positions at Multilink Technology Corporation, General Instrument Corporation, and General Electric. He later worked for Deloitte's Center for Corporate Governance[20] and established his own consulting firm. He has lectured at business schools around the country regarding ethics and governance. Pillmore has worked to establish curriculum for college accounting courses that integrate ethical concepts and principles into material used by business students nationwide. Pillmore serves on several boards of directors and the Anderson School National Advisory Board. He was honored in 2004 by being added to the Anderson School Hall of Fame,[21] and in 2006, he received the Zimmerman Award from the UNM Alumni Association.[22]

The H. Raymond Radosevich Room[23]

The H. Raymond Radosevich Room for Management of Technology and Entrepreneurship in the Anderson School of Management was dedicated in 2007. Radosevich joined the University in 1976 and served as Professor and Associate Dean until 1985, then Dean until 1989. From 1980 until he became Dean, Radosevich was President of the New Mexico Technological Program, a non-profit corporation for the development of new high-technology firms.

Radosevich held academic appointments at Carnegie Mellon University, the University of Kansas, and Vanderbilt University and earned master and doctorate degrees in industrial management from Carnegie Mellon as well as a master's degree in mechanical engineering from the University of Minnesota. Radosevich retired from UNM.

McKinnon Center for Management

In 2017, a new center for management building was constructed and named for Sonnet and Ian McKinnon, Albuquerque natives, whose donation also benefited the University's athletics program. After graduating from the Anderson School in 1993 with a B.B.A. in finance, Sonnet with her father Don Goodenough formed a manufacturing company. The company built wine and beer tanks and brewing systems for commercial beer producers worldwide. Sonnet has supported young people to be the first in their families to attend college. She served the UNM Foundation Board of Directors from 2006 to 2010. Ian, who is a managing partner at Ziff Brothers Investments in New York, received a B.A. from Occidental College and an M.B.A. from Harvard Business School. He was a finalist for both the Rhodes and Marshall Scholarships. Ian is the son of Karen McKinnon Stibolt who earned her B.A. and M.A. at UNM, and the late Daniel A. McKinnon III, a former New Mexico Supreme Court Justice who received his B.S. degree from UNM.[24]

THE ANTHROPOLOGY BUILDING

Fig. 10. *The first Student Union Building which later became home to the Department of Anthropology and the Maxwell Museum, 1937 (Center for Southwest Research, UNM Libraries).*[25]

The first Student Union building (SUB) was designed by architect John Gaw Meem and constructed in 1936-37 using Public Works Administration (PWA) funds matched with state bonds. The University dedicated the building on September 25, 1937, following a football game. Afterwards, the University held an open house and a dance. The building included a soda fountain obtained from a downtown pharmacy and installed in the basement, which became a gathering place for students. The original plan also included a patio. After a new SUB was completed in 1959, this building became home to the Department of Anthropology.

The Clark Field Library and Archive[26]

The Clark Field Library and Archive, whose name was proposed by Professor John "Jack" Martin Campbell, is a collection of anthropological books and material contributed by Mr. Clark Field, the father of Dorothy Maxwell. Mr. Field went to Oklahoma as a "Sooner" when the state opened its borders to settlers and spent the rest of his life there as a newspaperman interested in anthropology. He collected Native American art. In 1966, the Anthropology Department renamed its library in 1966 the Clark Field Library and Archive. Today, the Clark Field Library and Archive is managed jointly by the Anthropology Department and the Maxwell Museum, contains more than 10,000 books, many journal titles, all departmental Ph.D. dissertations and selected theses, and an extensive map collection.

The "Nibs" Hill Student Lounge

The "Nibs" Hill name was given informally to a student lounge and study on the second floor of the Anthropology Building. The lounge lasted a very short time before being taken over for a computer room.

Willard W. "Nibs" Hill received his B.A. from the University of California, Berkeley, and his doctorate from Yale in 1937. He joined the Department of Anthropology in 1937, "… bringing broad experience in North American ethnology and especially Navajo studies" as noted by Philip Bock in his history of the Department. Hill became Chair of the Department in 1947, a position he held for many years, before retiring from UNM in 1971.[27] His popularity with students and the friendship of President Tom Popejoy and Vice President France Scholes helped him start a doctoral program in the Anthropology Department.

The Maxwell Museum[28]

Fig. 11. Anthropology - Maxwell Museum – Interior – Rugs (Center for Southwest Research, UNM Libraries).[29]

Fig. 12. Anthropology – Exterior – Maxwell Museum Entrance (Center for Southwest Research, UNM Libraries).[30]

In 1964, Professor Willard Hill was succeeded by John Martin "Jack" Campbell. Prof. Campbell[31] during his eight years as the Chair of Anthropology also served three years as Director of the Maxwell Museum. Founded in 1932 by Edgar Lee Hewitt (who had founded the Department of Anthropology), the Anthropology Museum was moved into the new Administration Building (now Scholes Hall) in 1936 and remained there until 1963, when an addition to the Anthropology Building could accommodate it. In the late 1960's, Campbell initiated an expansive construction program in anthropology, which included a much enlarged museum. He recommended that the expanded museum be named for Gilbert Maxwell, a well-known Southwestern Indian trader who authored the book *Navajo Rugs: Past, Present and Future*. Maxwell and his wife Dorothy Maxwell were philanthropists and the major financial contributor to the museum.³² The museum collections include musical instruments and archaeological and anthropological materials from around the world.

The Alfonso Ortiz Center for Intercultural Studies³³

The Alfonso Ortiz Center for Intercultural Studies, located within the Anthropology Building, was named for the late UNM Anthropology professor Alfonso Ortiz.³⁴ Professor Ortiz, a native of San Juan Pueblo, was born in 1939. He received his undergraduate degree in sociology from UNM and his master's and doctorate from the University of Chicago. He was awarded a Guggenheim Fellowship in 1975 and became a MacArthur Fellow in 1982. "He believed Anthropology is a mirror of humanity, and that the barriers between the University and world communities must be eliminated," according to the Ortiz Center's promotional brochure. He published a landmark study "The Tewa World: Space, Time, Being and Becoming in a Pueblo Society." Later, he was an adviser for the documentary "Surviving Columbus: The Story of the Pueblo People," which received a Peabody Award in 1993. Prof. Ortiz died in 1997. The Ortiz Center promotes participation of community scholars, artists, healers, performers, and writers at UNM through collaborative projects with faculty, museum professionals, and students that foster exchange of ideas, creativity, and new research.

Rodey Hall³⁵

Fig. 13. Hodgin Hall – Exterior – Rear of Building with "U" Sign and Rodey Hall, circa 1920s (Center for Southwest Research, UNM Libraries).³⁶

In the original Student Union Building (SUB), the ballroom was a large open room where student dances, concerts, and dramatic performances were held. The ballroom, known as Rodey Hall, was completed in 1908 and named for Bernard S. Rodey, who has been called the "Father of the University." The 1910 UNM *Mirage* included a poem about the dances held in Rodey Hall.³⁷

After the New Mexico Union was completed in 1959, the Department of Anthropology took over the original building. The ballroom was renovated to create a 290-seat classroom, known as the Anthropology Lecture Hall. Rodey Hall was demolished in 1971. (See additional discussion of Bernard Rodey, Rodey Hall and Rodey Theater under section on the Fine Arts Center.)

The Hibben Center for Archaeological Research

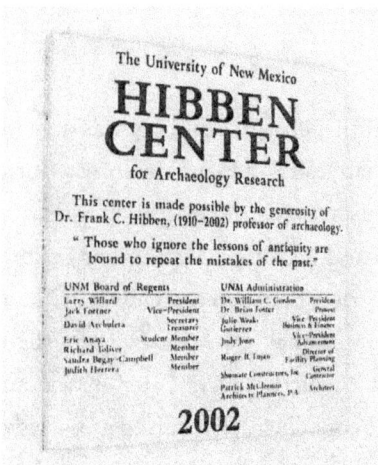

Fig. 14. Hibben Center for Archeology Research – Exterior - Dedication Plaque (Photograph by John Ralph, Center for Southwest Research, UNM Libraries).[38]

Fig. 15. Hibben Center (Photograph by Suzanne Mortier, UNM Landscape Architect, 2013).

The Hibben Center, located directly south of the Anthropology Building, contains a collection of artifacts connected with the work of Frank Cummings Hibben. Hibben was born in 1910 in Lakewood, Ohio, and received an A.B. degree from Princeton University, an M.S. from UNM, and doctorate from Harvard University. He began his career as an assistant archaeologist at the Ohio State Museum in 1928 and then moved to the Cleveland Museum of Natural History, where he worked from 1930 to 1933. Hibben came to UNM in 1936 and remained as Professor of Anthropology and Director of the Maxwell Museum. He received the UNM Zimmerman Award in 1994.[39]

Hibben was an active researcher and big game hunter throughout his life, writing many books and articles including *Hunting American Bears*, *Hunting in Africa*, and *Digging Up America*. When Hibben died in Albuquerque in 2002, his residence at 3005 Campus Boulevard N.E. was left to UNM and the Hibben Trust was established to provide fellowships to students of anthropology. Dennis and Douglas Lutz restored the residence as an exhibit space, education and research center available to the public, and repository for Hibben's collection of big game animal heads, mostly African.[40] The plaque on the Hibben Center for Archaeology Research reads:

> Those who ignore the lessons of antiquity
> are bound to repeat the mistakes of the past.

The Seaweed Totem Pole (Smith Family Totem Pole)

Fig. 16. The Seaweed Totem Pole (Smith Family Totem Pole) (Center for Southwest Research, UNM Libraries).[41]

In the patio of the Anthropology Building a totem pole initially known as the Seaweed Totem Pole stood from 1973 until recently. Before 1973, the totem pole had stood in isolation on the north side of Scholes Hall.

In 1941, Professor Frank Hibben obtained the 40-foot-tall, one-ton pole from Tim Seaweed, the sole survivor of the Seaweed Clan in Alaska. Hibben provided two cases of whiskey in exchange for the totem pole, one for Seaweed and one for his wife, who actually owned the totem pole.

Recent inquiry by the University revealed that Chief Smith Sewid of the Tlowitsis Nation of Canada commissioned the totem pole in 1907 on Turnour Island, British Columbia, Canada. Charlie Yakuglas James carved the pole. The University in consultation with the Smith Family has arranged for Kwakwaka'wakw carvers to restore the totem pole and place it in an interpretive setting. The University is the repository for the totem pole, which belongs to the Kwakwaka'wakw Tlowitsis Nation. Upon request by the Smith Family descendants, who are represented by the Tlowitsis Chief, the University will return the totem pole to Turnour Island. Until then, the University is creating a replica that will be placed on Turnour Island.[42]

THE SCHOOL OF ARCHITECTURE AND PLANNING

George Pearl Hall[43]

The strikingly contemporary School of Architecture and Planning building, named in memory of George Clayton Pearl,[44] was designed by local architect Antoine Predock, winner of the 2006 American Institute of Architects Gold Medal, the AIA's highest award for design. Although planning for the building began in the 1990s, the project was delayed due to a lack of funding. When funding was finally obtained, the design was adjusted to accommodate the Fine Arts Library. The building was completed in 2007. George Pearl Hall is a state-of-the-art facility and was the first new building for a school of architecture and planning in this country designed to accommodate new computerized and digital technologies.

George Clayton Pearl, born on a farm near Menard, Texas, in 1925, entered the University of Texas in 1943, but was soon drafted into the Army, where he served in the European Theater until wounded. After being discharged, Pearl returned to the University and completed his education. Pearl went to work for the Albuquerque architectural firm of Ferguson and Stevens in 1949 and soon became a partner and the chief designer. A talented artist, he worked mostly with watercolor. His fine architectural work was recognized by the AIA, which made him a Fellow in 1980. He was also committed to historic preservation. Pearl received an honorary Doctor of Fine Arts from UNM in 1996. On the University campus, Pearl designed Ortega Hall, the first addition to the Zimmerman Library, the first addition to Bratton Hall II, and the pedestrian bridge over Lomas Boulevard to UNM Hospital. More of his work can be seen throughout New Mexico. George Pearl died in 2003.

The Rainosek Gallery

Dorothy and Larry Rainosek and family, owners of the Frontier Restaurant on Central Avenue in Albuquerque, sponsored the Rainosek Gallery in the School of Architecture and Planning. The Gallery displays student work. Larry and Dorothy Rainosek came to Albuquerque from Texas in 1971 and established the Frontier Restaurant on the site of the old Chisum Drug Store, across Central Avenue from what is now George Pearl Hall. When the Frontier Restaurant opened, the School of Architecture and Planning was located next to the restaurant on the south side of Central Avenue. The Frontier became a popular hangout for architecture and other students, who enjoyed good food at good prices, particularly the Frontier's famous sweet rolls.

The Rainoseks have been generous contributors to UNM over the years, establishing scholarships in architecture, landscape architecture and planning, and contributing to the Presidential Scholarship program. They have supported the Lobo Club, golf tournaments, and even purchase of marimbas for the UNM Band. Dorothy Rainosek served on the UNM Foundation for many years. Larry and Dorothy Rainosek were honored by UNM, each with a Doctor of Humane Letters in 2014.[45]

BANDELIER EAST (ORTEGA HALL I)[46]

Fig. 17. Bandelier Hall East – Exterior – Two Young Trees, circa 1920s (Center for Southwest Research, UNM Libraries).[47]

Two buildings on the UNM Campus, Bandelier East and Bandelier West, are named for Adolph Francis Bandelier, who has been called an archaeologist by historians, while archaeologists have referred to him as a historian.

Born in Switzerland in 1846 and reared in Highland, Illinois, Bandelier had little formal education but became interested in Indian civilization. He was a prolific author, writing books and articles about American Indians. His only novel and most remembered work, *The Delight Makers,* was a romantic novel that depicted Indian life in New Mexico.

In the 1920s, the University did not have any dining facilities large enough to satisfy the growing student body. Bandelier East was designed by George Williamson and Company as the Women's Dining Hall and was built by Edward Lembke for $40,000. As time went on, the building became known as the Old Girl's Dining Hall. The building served its purpose as a dining hall until the early 1950's, when the University Bookstore used it for a short time. The building was also occupied by the Modern Languages Department. Later, the name was changed to Ortega Hall, named in honor of Joaquin Ortega, Professor of Spanish, Director of the School of Inter-American Affairs, and Editor of the *New Mexico Quarterly*. After completion of the new Ortega Hall (see discussion of Ortega Hall II), the building reverted to its original name, Bandelier East. Today, the building houses the Earth Data Analysis Center and several classrooms.

BANDELIER WEST[48]

Fig. 18. Bandelier Hall West - Snowfall (Photograph by Terry Gugliotta, Center for Southwest Research, UNM Libraries).[49]

Bandelier West was designed by John Gaw Meem to be a men's dormitory. After Mesa Vista Dormitory was completed, Bandelier West became faculty offices.

The building now houses the Geography Department and several Anthropology research offices. Bandelier West was completed in 1941 by the University Buildings and Grounds Department and has not changed much since.

The Van Dorn Hooker III Rose Garden

Fig. 19. Bandelier Hall East - Van Dorn Hooker III Memorial Garden (Photograph by Kate Nash, Center for Southwest Research, UNM Libraries).[50]

Fig. 20. Van Dorn Hooker III Marker (Photograph by Ann Clarke).

This beautiful rose garden at the north end of the Terrace Boulevard pedestrian mall and adjacent to Bandelier West was named for Van Dorn (Chip) Hooker III, who was the eldest son of the author Van Dorn Hooker, Jr.

Hooker, born in Santa Fe in 1954 and a graduate of Albuquerque Academy, was an accomplished artist who had attended Earlham College and the Kansas City Art Institute. In 1976, he had been accepted by Brown University, but before he could attend, he died in a motorcycle accident. This unofficial naming came about with the support of the staff of the Office of the University Architect. A collection of his art and essays was published as *The Wind Waits for Me*.

CARLISLE GYMNASIUM[51]

Fig. 21. Carlisle Gymnasium – Exterior – Looking Southwest, circa 1920s (Center for Southwest Research, UNM Libraries).[52]

In 1927, the University Board of Regents, with Mrs. Reed Holloman as President, issued bonds for several capital projects, including what would become the Carlisle Gymnasium. The exterior appears much the same as when the building was completed.

An article in the January 1930 *New Mexico Alumnus* by Professor Lynn B. Mitchell describes the dedication of the gymnasium:

> On the night of Armistice Day, the Gymnasium was dedicated to the memory of Hugh A. Carlisle '15, student, athlete, and one of the University's Gold Star Men, in exercises held under the joint auspices of the University and the local post of the American Legion. Hugh A. Carlisle attended the University from 1911 to 1914. He was a star athlete in his day, playing end on the football team, and engaging in other forms of athletics. He was well known for other sterling qualities of manhood as well as for high standards of sportsmanship. He enlisted early after the United States entered the war, but died [of pneumonia] while crossing the ocean. Hugh Carlisle was buried at sea.

In September 1968, Mercedes Gugisberg, a Professor Emeritus of Physical Education, wrote an open letter to Carlisle Gymnasium entitled *Happenings, Milestones and Believe It or Not*. In a loving tribute to an old building and its namesake, Gugisberg wrote:

> For many years it was the largest facility in Albuquerque, and events of any size and of every kind were scheduled therein. In addition to the usual physical education programs…intramurals, sports days, varsity athletics for men, there were Albuquerque Symphony concerts, band concerts, dances, Cattlemen's Conventions with livestock on the hoof…banquets served with flies, Commencement Exercises on rainy nights with its leaking roof dampening the caps, hoods, and gowns of the Board of Regents…

Carlisle Gymnasium is listed on both the National and State Registers of Historic Places.[53]

Elizabeth Waters Center for Dance at Carlisle Gym[54]

Elizabeth Waters, born in 1910 in Salem, Oregon, left home in 1929 to study at the Parry-Mansfield School of Dance in Steamboat Springs, Colorado. In 1934, Waters began studies with modern dance pioneer Hanya Holm and traveled the country with Holm's company. In 1940, she started her own touring company called Dancers En Route during World War II. When she reached Albuquerque, she took a job welding at Kirtland Air Force Base. In 1942, Waters began teaching the first dance classes at UNM. She was given a 10-foot-wide strip of space along the basketball court in Carlisle Gymnasium. Waters developed a dance minor in 1961, and the University transferred the dance program to the College of Fine Arts. Waters taught at UNM through 1979. She died in her home in Echo Canyon, New Mexico, in 1993. The University Naming Committee approved naming the dance floor at Carlisle Gymnasium in 2012 the Elizabeth Waters Center for Dance at Carlisle Gymnasium.[55]

The Korber Radio Station[56]

Fig. 22. Carlisle Gymnasium – Exterior – Electric Tower, 1928 (Center for Southwest Research, UNM Libraries).[57]

In 1921, Mrs. Jacob Korber and her son A.P. Korber gave $550 to the University of New Mexico for equipping a radio station in connection with the Electrical Engineering Department. According to the *Albuquerque Morning Journal* of Thursday, August 4, 1921, the station was able to transmit 700 to 1,000 miles and receive powerful stations in Washington D.C., France, and the Pacific Islands. Korber Wireless Station was considered a means to perpetuate the good name of Jacob Korber, a well-known Albuquerque businessman. Two small frame buildings and two steel towers were erected on the west side of Carlisle Gymnasium. The radio station was later moved, and the two buildings became part of Carlisle Gymnasium.

CASTETTER HALL (BIOLOGY)[58]

Fig. 23. Castetter Hall – Looking Northwest, circa 1950s (Center for Southwest Research, UNM Libraries).[59]

Castetter Hall is one of the several science buildings erected in the early 1950s, all designed by Edward Holien of Meem, Zehner, Holien, and Associates. A recent addition provided better access to the building and the basement was remodeled to accommodate teaching labs, offices and classrooms.

In 1968, the Board of Regents named the building for Professor Edward F. Castetter, who came to UNM in 1928 to teach biology. He was known for his expertise in ethnobiology. He chaired the Biology Department from 1932 until 1948 when he was appointed Dean of the Graduate School. In 1956, Castetter gave the UNM Research Lecture. He continued as a professor until 1957, when he became Academic Vice President of the University. Castetter retired in 1973 and died on February 10, 1978, having made outstanding contributions to the University during his 45-year tenure.

The Castetter Garden

Fig. 24. Library – Zimmerman – Exterior – Cactus Garden in Snow (Castetter Garden) (Photograph by Terry Gugliotta, Center for Southwest Research, UNM Libraries).[60]

When Zimmerman Library was built in 1938, the main entrance was on the west side where Professor Edward Castetter, then chair of the Department of Biology, installed a native plant garden, which was still thriving 70 years later. A century plant flowered a few years ago, much to the surprise of everyone.

Castetter has another garden named for him, which is not on the UNM campus, but is located immediately west of the Sandia Tramway lower parking lot. Called the Castetter Botanical Garden, it was dedicated on May 26, 1967.

Loren Potter Wing

Fig. 25. Castetter Hall – Potter Wing, 1967 (Photograph by Jerry Goffe, Center for Southwest Research, UNM Libraries).[61]

The first addition to Castetter Hall, completed in 1967 was named for Loren D. Potter,[62] Chair of the Department of Biology from 1959 to 1972. Potter was primarily a botanist and entomologist who planned the beautiful greenhouse that is part of the Potter Wing.

Loren Potter, from Fargo, North Dakota, obtained his bachelor's degree from North Dakota State University, his M.S. from Oberlin College, and his doctorate from the University of Minnesota. He taught botany and plant management at North Dakota State for 14 years before coming to UNM in 1958. Potter received 46 research grants and wrote 49 articles and four books on biology and plant ecology. One of his greatest achievements was developing land reclamation procedures for mining companies, which procedures are still in use today. Potter served as a United States Agency for International Development (USAID) consultant in India in 1965 and 1968 and Director of the National Science Foundation (NSF)-Atomic Energy Commission (AEC) Radiation Biology Institutes for Secondary and College School Teachers from 1960 to 1965. He was the Vice President for Research in the Eisenhower Consortium for Western Forestry Research from 1972 to 1983 and served as President in 1984. Potter did research for the Bureau of Land Management, the Forest Service, and the National Park Service. Potter retired in 1985 after 27 years of service to the University and died in 2016.

CENTENNIAL ENGINEERING CENTER[63]

Fig. 26. Engineering - Centennial Under Construction; Mechanical Also Shown, 2008 (Center for Southwest Research, UNM Libraries).[64]

Fig. 27. Centennial Engineering, 2013 (Photograph by Suzanne Mortier, UNM Landscape Architect).

The large structure known as Centennial Engineering Center, which was completed in 2008 and is located on Redondo Drive West, is a major addition to the Central Campus.[65]

The name Centennial Engineering Center commemorates the 100th anniversary of the founding of the

College of Engineering in 1906. The naming of spaces in the building followed then new Board of Regents' regulations.

The Robert J. Stamm Commons

The large area on the first floor of the Centennial Engineering Center was named for Robert "Bob" J. Stamm,[66] who was born in Albuquerque on November 17, 1921. He received his B.S. in civil engineering from UNM in 1942, and did graduate work at the United States Naval Academy in 1943. After World War II, he returned to New Mexico and worked for the O.G. Bradbury Construction Company. He became a partner and the firm was renamed Bradbury Stamm. Bradbury Stamm became one of the largest firms in the state. It built many major buildings, several on the UNM campuses, including the Centennial Engineering Center, which when it opened in 2008, was the largest construction project at UNM.

Stamm was noted for his personal involvement in many philanthropic organizations, having served on the boards of the UNM Foundation, the New Mexico Commission of Higher Education, the United Way, the New Mexico Museum of Natural History, Boy Scouts, Girl Scouts, and the Presbyterian Hospital Center Foundation among others. The UNM Board of Regents honored him with their Recognition Award in 1986[67] and the UNM Alumni Association honored him with the Zimmerman Award in 1989.[68] Stamm also received an honorary Doctorate in Engineering from UNM in 2009.[69] In 2001, he received the Albuquerque Samaritan Counseling Center Award for Ethics in Business. He has been honored by the Associated General Contractors and is in the Albuquerque Senior Citizens Hall of Fame.

CLARK HALL (CHEMISTRY)[70]

Fig. 28. Clark Hall – Chemistry Building (Center for Southwest Research, UNM Libraries).[71]

The present chemistry building, occupied in 1952, was designed by Edward Holien of the Meem, Zehner, and Holien architectural firm. In 1951, the Board of Regents approved naming the building for Professor John Dustin Clark.[72] The façade of the building has remained unchanged.

Clark arrived in Albuquerque in 1907, having been hired as a professor of chemistry at UNM. President George William Tight soon put him to work helping with painting, plumbing and carpentry since there was no money to hire people for maintenance work. Clark served as a professor and as the first Chair of the Department of Chemistry from 1933 to 1946. He also performed many services beyond the campus, including surveying the 200,000 acres of University-owned land and testing milk for the state. Clark was an advisor and confidant to several UNM presidents, in particular President David Ross Boyd who served from 1912 to 1919. Visiting Clark in his office, the two would smoke cigars and discuss the problems of the University.

Dorothy Hughes, author of *Pueblo on the Mesa*, wrote in 1939:

> For about a third of a century, he [Clark] has been an important assistant to most of the presidents. He served in innumerable capacities, including that of Dean of the Graduate School, Dean of Students, later Dean of Men; there are few if any students during almost the entire life of the University who do not know Dr. Clark. He is one of whom we may say: the University would not be what it is, and as it is, if his name were not a part of the history.

The Jesse E. Riebsomer Wing[73]

A major addition made to the south side of the original chemistry building in 1969 consisted almost entirely of laboratories. This wing, designed by George Pearl, was named for Jesse E. Riebsomer.[74] The two monumental stairs on the south side were constructed to conserve space that could be better used for laboratories.

Riebsomer came to UNM in 1946 as a professor of chemistry and later served as Chair of the Chemistry Department from 1949 to 1964. He earned a B.S from DePauw University in 1928 and a doctorate from Cornell University in 1932. Riebsomer served as President of the New Mexico Chapter of the American Chemical Society in 1955.

In *A Short History of the Department of Chemistry*, William M. Litchman wrote: "Professor Riebsomer, born in Indiana in 1905, grew up on a farm there. His research effort was in the field of fats, oils, and nitroparaffins. Professor Riebsomer was a good teacher, giving great effort to the process of teaching and emphasizing the need for professors to remain accessible to students." Riebsomer died in 1967.

CIVIL ENGINEERING - WAGNER HALL[75]

Fig. 29. Engineering - Wagner Hall – Exterior – Civil Engineering, circa 1950s (Center for Southwest Research, UNM Libraries).[76]

The building known as Wagner Hall was located on the far west side of the campus. Wagner Hall, the Civil Engineering building, and Tapy Hall were razed in 2006 to make way for the Centennial Engineering Center.

Wagner Hall contained various laboratories such as material testing, soil mechanics, a drafting room, classrooms, and faculty offices. In 1969, the building was named for William Chauncy Wagner. Wagner, born in South Dakota, received his B.S. in civil engineering from the South Dakota School of Mines and Technology in 1926, received his master's degree from Iowa State College in 1927, and came to UNM in 1929 as an instructor in civil engineering. Wagner became Chair of the Civil Engineering Department in 1943, retired in 1962, and died at his home near campus on July 31, 1976, at the age of 76.

At their meeting on September 21, 1976, the Faculty Senate adopted a memorial to Professor Wagner, which read in part:

> ...his warm regard for his students and his genuine concern for others made him admired and respected by the University community. An outstanding teacher, demanding taskmaster, a national authority in his area of construction materials...
>
> -- Bill was friend, counselor, champion and father confessor to generations of civil engineering students.....Bill Wagner was an institution at this University.

COMMUNICATION AND JOURNALISM[77]

Fig. 30. Communication and Journalism Building – View from Central Avenue, 1963 (Center for Southwest Research, UNM Libraries).[78]

The Will Harrison Grove

An ill-defined grove of trees on the northeast side of the Journalism Building was named for Will Harrison, the late writer for the *Santa Fe New Mexican*. Prior to the recent renovation of the building, a plaque mounted next to the north entrance denoted the naming of the grove. Harrison began his thirty-one-year career in journalism in the early 1930s as an unpaid reporter on the *Gallup Independent*. To make a living, he and his brother John had a dance band in which Will played clarinet. The band played for dances, proms, and nightclubs from New Mexico to California. After several years, he joined the Associated Press in Albuquerque and Santa Fe. Harrison became a reporter for the *Santa Fe New Mexican*, and in 1947 was made editor.

Harrison left the *New Mexican* in 1952 and started a syndicated column carried by many in-state newspapers. After his death in 1965, an *Albuquerque Journal* article stated, "The noted political columnist had been one of the outstanding newsmen in New Mexico for three decades. His column, Will Harrison's *Inside the Capitol*, was the most widely read in the state."

UNM President Tom Popejoy was quoted as saying, "I think everybody interested in good government has lost a valued friend in the passing of Will Harrison....he always came out in the open and everybody knew where he stood." Governor Jack Campbell was quoted in the *Albuquerque Journal* as saying that Harrison had "... become a legend in his own time and was probably New Mexico's best-known citizen at the time of his death."

The Tony Hillerman Memorial Plaque

Fig. 31. Hillerman Plaque (Photograph by Suzanne Mortier, UNM Landscape Architect, 2013).

On the wall of the entrance to the lobby of the Communication and Journalism Building, etched in a memorial plaque of clear plastic is a quotation by Tony Hillerman:[79]

> "A writer is like a bag lady going through life collecting interesting stuff and interesting characters."
> Tony Hillerman, Writer, Journalist, Professor and Department Chairman

Anthony "Tony" Grove Hillerman was born in Sacred Heart, Oklahoma, on May 27, 1925. After graduating from high school, he joined the Army in 1943 and served in the European Theater. He received the Silver Star Medal, the Bronze Medal with two Oak Leaf Clusters, and a Purple Heart Medal. After recovering from severe wounds suffered in combat, Hillerman was discharged and entered the University of Oklahoma, receiving his B.A. in 1948.

Hillerman worked as a newspaper reporter in Texas and Oklahoma until 1952, when he became the United Press Santa Fe Bureau Manager. In 1954, he joined the staff of the *Santa Fe New Mexican* as a political reporter and later became editor. Hillerman came to UNM in 1963 to work on a master's degree in English, which he completed in 1965. At the same time, Hillerman was an assistant to UNM President Tom Popejoy. Hillerman joined the Journalism Department faculty in 1965 and taught until he retired in 1987. He chaired the department from 1966 to 1974. He served as an assistant to UNM President William "Bud" Davis from 1975 to 1977.

Hillerman was widely known for his series of Navajo detective novels, four of which have been made into movies. His characters, Joe Leaphorn and Jim Chee, gained him international fame. He received the Edgar Allan Poe Award in 1974 for his novel *Dance Hall of the Dead*. He was President of the Mystery Writers of America and received their Grand Master writing award in 1991. Hillerman was added to the Oklahoma Hall of Fame in 1997.[80] The Navajo Tribe gave him their Special Friend of the Dineh Award.[81] In 1990, UNM awarded Hillerman an honorary Doctor in Literature, and in 1995, he received the Zimmerman Award from the UNM Alumni Association.[82] Tony Hillerman died on October 26, 2008, at his home in Los Ranchos de Albuquerque.[83]

The Keen Rafferty Reading Room

Some evidence suggests that at one time a reading room named for Keen Rafferty existed in the original Journalism Building. Rafferty came to New Mexico for his health in 1942 and became the Director of the UNM News Service and Secretary of the Alumni Association.

Rafferty was born in Robinson, Illinois, in 1902. In the February 1939 issue of *New Mexico Magazine,* he wrote the following autobiography: "As the son, grandson, brother and nephew of doctors, he was supposed to be one himself in his native town of Robinson, Illinois, but went astray after attending the University of Illinois, and became a reporter in Terre Haute."

Rafferty went from the *Terre Haute Star* to work at the *Evansville Indiana Press,* and later the *Baltimore Evening Sun.* He stayed with the *Sun* for eleven years supervising the work of copy editors until he moved his family to Roswell, New Mexico. In 1940, he was appointed Chair of the Journalism Department and Director of Publications at Eastern New Mexico University. In 1943, Rafferty came to UNM as an English instructor and received his B.A. in English from UNM in 1944.

At that time, journalism courses were taught in the English Department. In 1947, the Department of Journalism became a semi-autonomous division of the English Department. Rafferty wrote President Tom Popejoy recommending that a separate department should be established for journalism. His recommendation was accepted and in 1949 the Journalism Building was completed. In addition to the Journalism Department, the building housed the Printing Plant, the Post Office, and UNM Press.

Rafferty stood in the vanguard of journalism professors, insisting that students receive a broad education by requiring them to complete 75 percent of their course work in arts and sciences and 25 percent in journalism. He wrote numerous articles on the subject for the *Saturday Review of Literature,* the *Christian Science Monitor,* and journals and newspapers.

Rafferty remained as Chair until 1967, when he retired. He continued to serve as Secretary-Manager of the New Mexico Press Association and edited *Shop Talk,* their official publication. He also served as co-editor of the newsletter for the American Association of Teachers of Journalism, now the Association for Education in Journalism and Mass Communication (AEJMC). Rafferty passed away at 86 on August 21, 1988, in Sun City, Arizona. The *Albuquerque Journal* reported that in 1978, Rafferty had received the Dan Burrows Award for "continuing outstanding contribution to journalism in New Mexico" from the New Mexico Chapter of the Society of Professional Journalists. The award was named for Dan Burrows, the former editor of the *Albuquerque Tribune,* who had established the award in 1971 by bequest.

COUNSELING, ASSISTANCE, AND REFERRAL SERVICE (CARS)

Maria Palacios Memorial Tree

Fig. 32. Maria Palacios Tree (Source unknown).

Maria Palacios, the Director and Senior Clinical Psychologist for CARS, obtained degrees in sociology, Spanish, and counseling and a doctorate in clinical psychology. She worked in a variety of offices on campus, all of which involved helping people. On August 5, 2006, Dr. Palacios passed away at age 49. Her obituary in the *Albuquerque Journal* read:

When once asked how she would most like to be remembered, Maria said,

> "As a person who left situations, places, and things better than she found them. I made a difference when I passed through life." There is no better way to describe and remember her, her life.[84]

A Chinese pistache was planted in her memory and dedicated on the afternoon of June 21, 2007, at CARS, 1800 Mesa Vista Rd. N.E.[85]

DORMITORIES and DINING HALLS

Coronado Hall[86]

Fig. 33. Dormitory – Coronado Hall – Looking East Across Dirt Lot, 1964 (Center for Southwest Research, UNM Libraries).[87]

In 1540, Francisco Vasquez de Coronado, a young aristocratic governor of Nueva Galicia, now known as Jalisco, Mexico, led an ill-fated expedition into western New Mexico in search of the fabled Seven Cities of Cibola. Expecting to find well-developed cities of gold, he discovered the Pueblo of Zuni. Coronado returned to Mexico City in 1542. Though he did not find gold, he gained much knowledge about the area. Coronado Hall was completed in 1859 as a dormitory. The building was designed by Shafer and Merrell of Clovis.

DeVargas Hall and Laguna Hall[88]

Fig. 34. Dormitory - DeVargas Hall – Upper Story Windows, 1970 (Center for Southwest Research, UNM Libraries).[89]

The dormitory and dining hall complex, known as the DeVargas Complex, was completed in 1969. One of the dormitory units was named for the Laguna Pueblo and the other for Don Diego de Vargas.[90]

Don Diego de Vargas Zapata y Lujan Ponce de Leon y Contreras was appointed Governor of New Mexico by the Spanish Crown in 1688. He came from a noble Spanish family and had studied at the University of Valladolid before coming to New Spain and joining the administration of the Spanish regime. He led the colonists in El Paso who fled the Pueblo Revolt of 1680 back into New Mexico in 1693. The re-conquest of New Mexico was successful, and De Vargas served as Governor until he died in a campaign against the Apaches in 1703. For more information regarding De Vargas, see *The Vargas Papers*, edited by former UNM professor John Kessell.

La Posada Dining Hall and Howard Mathany Room

Fig. 35. Dining Hall - La Posada – Exterior – Building Sign, circa 1970s (Center for Southwest Research, UNM Libraries).[91]

Located within the DeVargas Complex, La Posada serves as the dining hall for all dormitory residents. Within La Posada Dining Hall was the Howard Mathany Room.

The dedication plaque reads:

> Dedicated in honor of Howard W. Mathany,
> for 22 years of Outstanding Service
> with The University of New Mexico.

Mathany served as a professor of mathematics from 1947 to 1965, Dean of Men from 1947 to 1968, and Dean of Students from 1968 to 1969.[92] He also served as an advisor to the Senior men's national honorary organization Blue Key, the Junior men's honorary organization Chakaa, and the Sophomore men's honorary organization Vigilantes, as well as the campus Greek fraternities and Circle K. Mathany served as Co-advisor of Student Scholarships and Financial Aid, Administrative Advisor to the Student Standards Committee, and Administrator of the Athletics Grants-in-Aid Program.

Mathias Lambert Custers Cottage ("Ladies Cottage")

Originally, the Mathias Lambert Custers Cottage was a private residence. The building was demolished long ago. The cottage and the man for whom it was named comprise an interesting story. Mathias Lambert Custers was a Civil War veteran who came to New Mexico with his family for health reasons and began working for an Albuquerque newspaper. When the University opened in 1889, he became the first custodian of the new University.

Custers had a great knowledge of math and surveying and was soon offered a faculty position teaching surveying and trigonometry. He became the University's first librarian when the library was a small room in the Main Building, now named Hodgin Hall. Custers and his family lived in the house until he obtained permission to finance and build a small house northeast of the Main Building. The family lived there until Custers was dismissed by the Regents due to his failing eyesight. In 1968, a story appeared in Ripley's *"Believe It Or Not"* describing how Custers rose from janitor to faculty member at the University of New Mexico.

After the Custers family vacated the cottage, the Regents paid off the mortgage and made it into the first campus dining hall, with women's dormitory facilities on the second floor. Informally, the cottage became known as the "Ladies Cottage."

Hokona Hall I[93]

Fig. 36. Dormitory - Hokona I – View Across Lawn, circa 1910s (Center for Southwest Research, UNM Libraries).[94]

Fig. 37. Hokona I (Center for Southwest Research, UNM Libraries).

The original Hokona Hall was located on the south side of the campus where the current Marron Hall and Castetter Hall are located. Hokona I was built in 1906 as the Girls or Women's Dormitory. According to the information from the expedition of Jesse Walter Fewkes in the late 1800s, Hokona meant "butterfly maiden" in an Indian language. Hokona Hall I was demolished in 1952.

Hokona Hall II

Fig. 38. Dormitory - Hokona II – South Entrance, 1997-98 (Photograph by Terry Gugliotta, Center for Southwest Research, UNM Libraries).[95]

Fig. 39. Dormitory - Hokona II - Aerial View Looking Northeast, 1964 (showing the two 5-sided wings: Hokona-Zia and Hokona-Zuni) (Center for Southwest Research, UNM Libraries).[96]

Hokona Hall II is the second dormitory to bear the name Hokona on the UNM campus. Hokona Hall II was designed to provide rooms for 400 female students. The two five-sided wings, known as Hokona-Zia and Hokona-Zuni, were named for the Zia and Zuni Pueblos. The wings are connected by a section that contained offices, a student lounge, study space, a large dining room, and a kitchen. The dining room and kitchen are located at the north end of the building. In effect, the plan resembled a woman's brassier and was called such by the students. The dining facilities were discontinued after La Posada was constructed, but the space continues to be used for on campus events. Today, part of the building is occupied by the College of Education, the Religious Studies Program, the *Colonial Latin American Historical Review*, Asian Studies, and other functions.

Lena C. Clauve Lounge

Fig. 40. Faculty Housing – 1925 Las Lomas Road - Lena Clauve's House, 1995 (Center for Southwest Research, UNM Libraries).[97]

The large lounge in the center of Hokona II was named for Lena C. Clauve, the first Dean of Women at UNM. Clauve served in that position from 1929 to 1961. Born in Wabash, Indiana, on August 10, 1895, she attended schools in Indiana and taught music and art in high schools. She moved to Albuquerque in 1923 to live with her ailing mother and enrolled in the summer session at UNM. Clauve received her bachelor's degree in 1925, majoring in piano. She returned to Indiana to teach in the public school system until 1929 when President Zimmerman asked her to become the first UNM Dean of Women. She served in this position with distinction until retiring at age 65. Clauve received the UNM Lobo Award in 1954, the Rodey Award in 1974, and the Fergusson Award in 1981.[98]

Clauve also served as a professor of music. One of her many contributions to UNM was writing the music for the University fight song, "Hail, New Mexico."[99] George St. Clair, Chair of the English Department, wrote the lyrics. Clauve remained active in many philanthropic organizations until she died in her nineties. Her home is now used as faculty housing.

The Conrado Gutierrez, Patrick McNamara, and Joyce Rogers Room

On the fourth level of Hokona-Zuni is one room. Now occupied by the office of the Director of Religious Studies, the room is known as the Conrado Gutierrez, Patrick McNamara and Joyce Rogers Room.

Conrado Gutierrez, a chemist by profession, was born in Socorro, New Mexico, in 1919. He graduated from Menaul School in Albuquerque after having served in the Civilian Conservation Corps during the Great Depression of the 1930s. Gutierrez received a B.S. in chemistry from UNM and worked for Anaconda Copper Company in Mexico until he was called into service in World War II. After attending officer training, Gutierrez was commissioned as a lieutenant and assigned to the U.S. forces occupying Japan. After the war, Gutierrez became a research and development chemist at Los Alamos National Laboratory for 29 years. He then spent seven years as an Equal Employment Opportunity officer, before retiring to Albuquerque and serving as Interim President of the Menaul School. Gutierrez was very involved in the affairs of the Presbyterian Church and the Religious Studies Program at UNM. He contributed regularly to the program and is recognized for his generosity. Throughout his life, Gutierrez was active in community, civic, and Presbyterian Church affairs. He died in 2003 at 84.[100]

Patrick McNamara, a California native and Professor of Sociology, completed a bachelor's degree at Santa Clara University, a master's degree at St. Louis University, and doctorate in sociology from the University of California at Los Angeles. He began studying for the priesthood as a member of the California Order of the Society of Jesus. He left the Society of Jesus and taught at the University of Texas in El Paso for two years. In 1970, McNamara came to UNM in 1970 as an assistant professor and remained in that position until he retired in 1998.

McNamara taught Sociology 101 classes of 600 or more students in Woodward Hall, where he became famous for his innovative teaching techniques. Some examples included a class in which he and his teaching assistants presented themselves as monks carrying candles. In another class he dressed as an old man of the 19th century, and in yet another, McNamara wore a hard-hat and boots to represent an ironworker building a skyscraper. In his smaller classes, he knew each student by name.

In 1985, McNamara was voted UNM Outstanding Teacher of the Year[101] and received the Student Service Award. In 1987, he was named Sociology Faculty Member of the Year. Princeton University honored him in 1993 with the Advancing the Frontiers of Research Award. During the latter part of his career, McNamara received two sizeable grants from the Lilly Endowment to study church giving and stewardship.

During his time at UNM, McNamara wrote eight books, more than 30 articles on sociology and religion, and five research monographs. He presented 39 papers and spoke at many meetings around the country.

Professor McNamara helped the community and the University in many ways, including being a consultant to various city departments and University committees, including the Faculty Senate, Athletic Council, and Academic and Tenure Committee. McNamara retired after a brilliant teaching career and 28 years of service to the University. He died shortly after his retirement in 1998. He bequeathed his library to the Division of Religious Studies, which is housed in Hokona-Zuni.[102]

Joyce Rogers Memorial Religious Studies Library

The Joyce Rogers Memorial Religious Studies Library is a collection of religious publications located in the west wing of Hokona-Zuni. Joyce Rogers was an associate professor at UNM when she died in 1994. She was born in 1933, and received her bachelor's and master's degrees at Texas Christian University. She received her doctorate in English from UNM in 1969.

Professor Rogers, a popular teacher, taught several courses including Spanish Mysticism, Medieval English Mystics, Religion and the Arts, and Introduction to Academics. She also taught a class on C.S. Lewis, and in 1990, she was a scholar-in-residence at his home in Oxford, England. She wrote several books, including *Louis Martin, Father of a Saint, Shakespeare's Will in a New Light,* and *A Process Approach to Writing*. Rogers published several poems as well as critical essays on mysticism and theological aesthetics, and wrote and produced a local radio program entitled *The Glory of Man*. In addition to her literary work, Rogers was a talented musician who played the organ for her church. Her religious devotion was exemplified by her service as a leader of both the national and state associations for the Lay Order of Carmelites.

Kwataka Hall[103]

Fig. 41. Dormitory - Kwataka Hall – Exterior, circa 1920s (Center for Southwest Research, UNM Libraries).[104]

Built in 1906, Kwataka Hall was a men's dormitory (also known as the "Boy's Dormitory"). Kwataka is an Indian name meaning "man-eagle" based on the Sikyatki or Tuscayan names found in the Fewkes Expedition Report. Kwataka was believed to be a powerful bird and was worshiped for its strength, alertness, and swiftness. In other interpretations, he was known as "a voracious monster who abode in the sky and whose chief pleasure was to plague the children of men." The University later used the building as office space before demolishing it in 1957.

Alvarado Hall[105]

Alvarado Hall was constructed as a men's dormitory[106] and named after the Spanish explorer Hernando de Alvarado. Alvarado was a captain during the expedition of Francisco Vasquez Coronado to New Mexico in 1540. He persuaded Coronado to winter on the banks of the Rio Grande near Santa Ana Pueblo. Alvarado led an exploratory journey following the river northward as far as Taos. He also led the first contingent to visit Acoma Pueblo. On a related note, the venerable Alvarado Hotel in downtown Albuquerque, which was built in 1902, was also named for this explorer. The hotel, the early site of many UNM social events such as dances and dinners, was demolished in the early 1970s.

Santa Ana[107] and Santa Clara[108] Dormitories

Fig. 42. Dormitory - Santa Ana Hall – Looking Northwest, circa 1960s (Center for Southwest Research, UNM Libraries).[109]

Fig. 43. Dormitory - Santa Clara Hall – Looking North Over Hill, 1979 (Center for Southwest Research, UNM Libraries).[110]

Santa Ana and Santa Clara dormitories were built to house women students and named for Santa Ana Pueblo and Santa Clara Pueblo.

Oñate Hall[111]

Fig. 44. Dormitory - Oñate Hall – White Metal Fence, circa 1970s (Center for Southwest Research, UNM Libraries).[112]

In 1595, Juan de Oñate of Zacatecas[113] won a contract with the Viceroy of New Spain to pacify and settle New Mexico. He assembled a group of settlers that included soldiers, women, children, and slaves as well as livestock. After a difficult journey northward, the group stopped in the Indian village of Ohkay Owingeh, which they named San Juan Bautista and later named Pueblo de San Juan de los Caballeros. The Spaniards soon built a church and established a villa, which they named San Gabriel de Yungé and which became New Mexico's first capital. Oñate was made Governor of New Mexico and served from 1598 to 1608. He explored the region, but found no gold or silver and returned to Mexico. There, he was tried and convicted of many crimes. Oñate Hall houses KUNM radio station.

Solon Rose Cottage

The Solon Rose Cottage was a small house, which stood where the contemporary Humanities Building stands today. Solon Rose was a rancher and merchant who bought the land under the Desert Land Act and built an adobe home. He died in 1893. In 1904, the University rented the property. The cottage was used as a men's dormitory until 1907, when the land, house, and outbuildings were acquired by the Methodist Church and used as a sanatorium. Thomas Bell, the first Rhodes Scholar from UNM, lived in Solon Rose Cottage as a student. The University purchased the property in 1917, remodeled the cottage, and established a women's dormitory. In 1934, the cottage was demolished when the construction of Zimmerman Library began nearby.

Yatoka Hall[114]

Fig. 45. Dormitory - Yatoka Hall – Cars Parked in Front, circa 1920s (Center for Southwest Research, UNM Libraries).[115]

Yatoka Hall, constructed as a men's dormitory in 1928, was converted into offices and classrooms after World War II. Yatoka is an Indian word meaning "sun." In 1974, the University razed Yatoka Hall to install the UNM Duck Pond.[116]

EARL'S GROTTO[117]

In 1936, Professor John D. Clark noted that in the early days of the University no businesses existed on the east side of Broadway Avenue. In 1915, an enterprising student named Earl Gerhardt received permission to establish a store in one of the cottages that surrounded the men's dormitory, Kwataka Hall. Earl's Grotto, as he named the place, became a popular student hangout where students bought candy and soda pop and played cards. Tobacco, which was prohibited on campus, was also bootlegged at the store. It may have been the University's first bookstore. The store became an early predecessor to the Student Union when the University took over management and renamed it the Varsity Store.[118]

BRATTON HALL I (ECONOMICS)[119]

Fig. 46. Bratton Hall I – Economics, 1967 (Photograph by Tyler Dingee, Center for Southwest Research, UNM Libraries).[120]

Bratton Hall I was built in 1951-52 to house the School of Law, which was located in the old Stadium Building prior to that time. Named in honor of Judge Samuel Gilbert Bratton of the Tenth Circuit Court of Appeals, the dedication ceremony took place on October 4, 1952. U.S. Supreme Court Justice Hugo Black was the keynote speaker. UNM Board of Regents President Paul Larrazolo was the master of ceremonies.

Judge Bratton was born on August 19, 1888, in Kosse, Texas. After being admitted to the bar, he moved his law practice to Clovis, N.M., in 1915. He served as a state district court judge from 1919 to 1923, after which he became an associate of the N.M. Supreme Court. He resigned in 1924 to run for the U.S. Senate. Upon being elected, he served as a U.S. Senator until 1933, when he was appointed to the U.S. Court of Appeals for the Tenth Circuit. He served on the Tenth Circuit until 1961. He died on September 22, 1963.[121]

Bratton Hall I now houses the Department of Economics. The exterior of the building, which was designed by Meem's firm in the Spanish-Pueblo Revival style, has not been altered since the building was completed in 1952. (For information on Bratton Hall II, which was named for Judge Sam Bratton's son Judge Howard Bratton, see the North Campus section.)

COLLEGE OF EDUCATION COMPLEX[122]

Some of the spaces in the College of Education Complex were named for particular people, but unless one has reason to enter the complex, these named places would go unnoticed by most. Nonetheless, no other complex of buildings since John Gaw Meem's work in the 1930s has had so much influence in shaping campus buildings or generated as much discussion about design appropriateness as this creation by Max Flatow and his chief designer William Jette. The concept of an enclosed complex, which included several separate buildings with different functions, represented a modern architectural perspective. The interiors of the buildings include glass curtain walls that enclose courtyards and landscaped areas, while the massive sloping windowless walls that form the exterior create the impression of a fortress or compound that shelters the occupants.

Herman Goldman designed a fountain on the south side of the building, which he dubbed *A Desert Thing*. The fountain, which incorporated brown fiberglass embedded with marble chips, included a central spout. The cascading water served as a focal point for entering the complex. Seldom used and painted blue, the fountain remains part of the University's landscape.[123]

Frank Angel Latin American Program in Education (LAPE) Conference Room

Within the College of Education Complex is the Frank Angel Latin American Program in Education (LAPE) Conference Room. Frank Angel, a native of Las Vegas, New Mexico, was born in 1914. He graduated from East Las Vegas High School and attended the New Mexico Normal School. Angel became an elementary school teacher, teaching classes in one and two room schools in rural New Mexico from 1932 to 1937. He then taught at Nambe Experimental Community School until the beginning of World War II, when he enlisted in the Army Air Force. Angel piloted a B-24 in the Asiatic Pacific Theater, rose to the rank of captain, and received the Distinguished Flying Cross and the Air Medal with seven oak leaf clusters.

After the war, Angel returned to school and completed his bachelor's degree in education from UNM, a master's degree in rural education from the University of Wisconsin, and in 1955 his Doctor of Education from the University of California-Berkeley. The following year, Angel returned to UNM as a professor and taught until 1971, when he became the President of New Mexico Highlands University. He was known as the first Hispanic president of a public university. Through the years, Frank Angel received many honors and awards for his contributions to higher education, including an honorary degree of Doctor of Humane Letters for literature from UNM in 1982.[124] Angel died in Porto Alegre, Brazil, at the age of 92 on May 29, 2005, during a family visit.[125] Dean David Darling wrote in his 1979 memorandum of support for naming this room for Frank Angel:

> Dr. Frank Angel, Founder of the Latin American Program in Education (LAPE),
> is a distinguished and recognized scholar who has made a name in education for
> the University of New Mexico throughout Latin America. He began the LAPE in
> 1965 with a Paraguayan participant training program. With the impetus of this first

program, Dr. Angel moved LAPE and the College of Education to a multitude of successful projects in almost every country in South America. As a result of his efforts, LAPE and the University of New Mexico have become known throughout Latin America for the quality of educational programs and technical assistance.

The Richard E. Lawrence Courtyard

The University named the courtyard, or patio, in the center for the Faculty Office Building (now demolished) within the Education Complex for Richard E. Lawrence, Dean of the College of Education from 1969 to 1974.[126] Lawrence was born on August 10, 1920, in St. Paul, Minnesota, and received his bachelor's degree from the University of Minnesota in 1942. During World War II he served in the U.S. Navy as a mine disposal officer. Lawrence earned his master's degree in 1946 and his Doctor of Education in 1953 from the Teachers College at Columbia University.

Lawrence served as Associate Executive Director of the American Association of Colleges for Teacher Education until he came to UNM in 1960 to become Dean of the College of Education. He served as Dean until 1973 when he left to teach educational administration. Lawrence retired from teaching in 1983 and passed away on November 10, 1987. Vice President for Administration Joel Jones wrote, "As a dean, Professor Lawrence always impressed me as an individual of high integrity and incisive intelligence." Dean David Colton wrote of Lawrence, "He brought to the college deeply held convictions about the need to transform teaching, to make schools more humane places to help educators make things better."

Manzanita Center[127]

Fig. 47. College of Education - Manzanita Center – Interior – Children with Wooden Toys, circa 1960s (Center for Southwest Research, UNM Libraries).[128]

The Manzanita Center, located within the College of Education, was designed originally as a learning center for students studying teaching methods for small children. Manzanita is a Spanish word meaning "Little Apple." The center is now used for the Counselor Education Program.[129]

Masley Hall and Gallery[130]

In 1982, the UNM Regents named the Art Education Building and gallery for Alexander S. Masley, the long time professor of art education who also served as Department Chair from 1969 to 1978. The gallery provides exhibition space for faculty and student artwork.

Masley was born in Akeley, Minnesota, and was the son of Czechoslovakian immigrants. As a young student at the Minneapolis School of Art, he won a scholarship to study at the London School of Arts and Crafts and the Hans Hoffman School of Art in Munich, Germany. Masley taught at the University of Texas, the University of Montana, the University of Wyoming, and Columbia University before coming to UNM in 1947 to establish the art education program.

Alexander Masley's work has been exhibited in the Museum of Fine Arts in Santa Fe, the Dallas Museum of Fine Arts, the Chicago Art Institute, the New York Metropolitan Museum of Art, and the Minneapolis Museum of Art. His abstract paintings are held in several national museums, including the National Museum of American Art, the Smithsonian Institute, and the San Francisco Museum of Modern Art. Masley died at the age of 93 on January 2, 1997.

Simpson Hall (Home Economics)[131]

Fig. 48. College of Education - Simpson Hall – Exterior – Blue Tarp on Building Sign (Mrs. Simpson (right)), 1989 (Center for Southwest Research, UNM Libraries).[132]

Simpson Hall was named for Elizabeth Parkinson Simpson, former Chair of the Department of Home Economics and Director of Dining Facilities on campus from 1933 to 1953. Home Economics was originally housed in Sara Raynolds Hall until the construction of Simpson Hall. The bronze plaque from Sara Raynolds Hall, now installed at Simpson Hall, reads:

> Dedicated to the Women and Children
> of the State of New Mexico by
> Citizens and Friends of Albuquerque 1920.

Elizabeth P. Simpson was born on July 7, 1888, on a farm near Yale, Michigan. She received her diploma from Michigan State Normal in 1912 and began teaching in a one-room schoolhouse at a nine-month salary of $360. She came to UNM in 1918 as acting head of the home economics program. The next year she became manager of the UNM dining hall.

The UNM dining hall included tables reserved for faculty. Librarian Wilma Loy Shelton recalled, "As we gathered around these tables where we felt the best and cheapest food in town was served, our hearty appetites were satisfied and a lot of social chitchat and banter indulged in."

While serving as head of the department, Simpson continued her education, receiving her bachelor's degree in home economics from UNM in 1928. Taking a leave of absence from UNM, she received her master's in food and nutrition from Iowa State University in 1932 and completed additional graduate work at Columbia University. She taught at UNM for thirty-four years, during which time she was President of the Faculty Senate and faculty sponsor of Chi Omega sorority. She was a member of Mortar Board and many other organizations.

In 1955, Elizabeth Simpson was awarded the UNM Alumni Association's Lobo Award for outstanding service to the University.[133] She celebrated her 100th birthday in 1986 as Queen of the University Centennial Ball. She died at 103. Betty Huning Hinton's book *Elizabeth P. Simpson: Menu for Success* written with Ms. Simpson provides more historical information.

Travelstead Hall[134]

Fig. 49. College of Education - Travelstead Hall – John Tatschl and Stained Glass Window (Center for Southwest Research, UNM Libraries).[135]

Fig. 50. Travelstead Hall (Photograph by Suzanne Mortier, UNM Landscape Architect, 2013).

Within the College of Education, Travelstead Hall houses administrative offices and was named for Chester Coleman Travelstead in 2003. The west side of Travelstead Hall features a beautiful faceted glass wall designed by Professor of Art, John Tatschl. Travelstead, a Kentucky native, started teaching when he was 17 years old. He received his bachelor's degree from Western Kentucky University, his master's degree in music from Northwestern University in 1947, and his doctorate from the University of Kentucky. Travelstead served as a communications officer in the U.S. Navy during World War II.

Travelstead was Dean of the Colleges of Education at the University of Georgia and the University of South Carolina. Fired from the University of South Carolina for his outspoken support for racial integration, Travelstead was hired by UNM President Tom Popejoy, who considered Travelstead's stance on the topic a positive recommendation as to Travelstead's character. Travelstead was Dean of the College of Education from 1956 to 1969, Academic Vice President from 1969 to 1970, Vice President for Academic Affairs from 1970 to 1977, and Provost from 1977 to 1979. During his time as Dean, he created a doctoral program in education and improved the overall quality of teaching at the University. In 1977, he received the Bernard S. Rodey Award from the UNM Alumni Association for having contributed significantly to the field of education.[136] In 1980, he was awarded an honorary Doctor of Humane Letters from UNM.[137] He also received honorary degrees from two Argentinean universities.

Travelstead, a trumpet player, was instrumental in starting the Youth Symphony Orchestra at Western Kentucky University. He was also an ardent supporter of the Albuquerque Symphony, serving as a long-time member of the Board of Directors and twice as President. He died in December 2006 at the age of 95 and was buried in his hometown of Franklin, Kentucky.[138]

Tireman Learning Materials Center

The Tireman Learning Materials Center is the College of Education library of material related to teaching the field of education. The Center was named for Loyd Spencer Tireman, who chaired the Department of Elementary Education from 1933 to 1960.

Tireman was born in 1896 in Orchard, Iowa. He attended Upper Iowa State University, graduating in 1917 with his bachelor's degree and immediately going into military service during World War I. After the war, he taught in various high schools in Iowa and then continued his education, receiving his master's and a doctorate from the University of Iowa, the latter in 1927. He died in Albuquerque at the age of 63 in 1959.

Tireman was known for his dedication and drive. At UNM, he constantly involved himself in experimental programs. In his book *Educational Reform in New Mexico*, David L. Bachelor wrote:

> [Tireman] came to the University of New Mexico in 1927 and, as a professor of elementary education, spent thirty-two years working on the problems of teaching reading, bicultural education, and school-community relations. His calling was a strenuous, demanding one that resulted in limited recognition while he lived, and obscurity after he died.

The Simon P. Nanninga Conference Room

Within the Tireman Learning Materials Center of Travelstead Hall is the Nanninga Conference Room. The conference room was named for Simon Peter Nanninga, the first dean of the College of Education. Nanninga served as Dean from the formation of the College in 1928 until 1954.

Born in Yates County, Kansas, on January 21, 1891, Simon P. Nanninga received his bachelor's degree from the Kansas State Teachers College in 1916, his master's degree from Stanford University, and his doctorate from the University of California-Berkeley. Nanninga began teaching in rural schools in 1911 and was superintendent of a high school in 1917, when he entered the U.S. Army, where he served as a lieutenant in the 341st Machine Battalion, 89th Division and was wounded in action. Nanninga, a member of General Pershing's Army of Occupation from 1919 to 1921, was the interpreter for General Pershing. After being discharged from the Army, he became a high school principal in California. Nanninga came to UNM as an associate professor of education in 1925. Nanninga's greatest interest was in educational administration. He wrote several books and articles in educational journals and taught courses on the subject. During his tenure as Dean, the College of Education grew steadily, providing teachers to New Mexico. Mondragon and Stapleton, in their book *Public Education in New Mexico*, noted:

> Nanninga may have had a special affinity for a course that meant teaching pupils about the humane treatment of animals and that developed in students a spirit of kindness, humanity and tolerance toward others. Described as a 'farmer at heart,' it is even reported that when he died he was irrigating his land; his pet dog guarded him when others tried to minister to him.

The Anita Osuna Carr Library

Anita Carr was the first Hispanic woman to become a faculty member at UNM. Professor Carr was born in Albuquerque and received her bachelor's degree from UNM in 1921. She received her master's degree from Stanford University in 1922 and taught at Middlebury College before coming to UNM to teach French and Spanish. Carr was the first director of the International Alliance of Pan American Round Tables from 1946 to 1948. She served on the board of the Los Lunas Training School and was Vice President of the UNM Alumni Association from 1945 to 1946. Anita Carr died on November 19, 1968, leaving her personal collection of educational materials to the College of Education.[139]

THE ESTUFA[140]

Fig. 51. The Estufa – Looking Northeast at Door on Side, 1932 (Center for Southwest Research, UNM Libraries).[141]

The small adobe building known today as "The Estufa" is owned by the Pi Kappa Alpha Fraternity and is on land leased from UNM at the southeast corner of University and Dr. Martin Luther King Jr. Drive. The fraternity maintains the building and holds meetings there.

President Tight built the Estufa with the help of UNM students in 1906. The building was originally named "The Kiva," but due to objections by Pueblo Indian groups, the name was changed to "The Estufa," meaning "stove, steam room or hot-house" in Spanish. The Estufa was the first meeting place for the Yum Yum boys, a UNM group. Alpha Alpha Alpha, a local fraternity that later affiliated with the national Pi Kappa Alpha fraternity, took over ownership and became the first Greek organization on campus. The Estufa is listed on the New Mexico State Register of Cultural Properties and the National Register of Historic Places.

FARRIS ENGINEERING CENTER[142]

Fig. 52. Engineering – Farris – Looking West from Regener Hall Plaza, circa 1970s (Center for Southwest Research, UNM Libraries).[143]

The Farris Engineering Center, named for Marshall E. "Mike" Farris, was designed to provide offices for the faculty and college administration, research and teaching laboratories, and classrooms. Farris was born in Cabool, Missouri, on August 16, 1895. He received his bachelor's degree from Purdue University in 1922 and his master's from the University of Texas in 1925. Farris was a sergeant first class during World War I. He taught at the University of Texas, Texas Technological College, and the University of Arkansas before coming to New Mexico in 1931.

At UNM, he became Dean of the College of Engineering as well as Chair of the Department of Mechanical Engineering. In 1942, Farris arranged the first flight training for 1,600 Navy pilot trainees during World War II. He retired as Dean in 1960 to become the first director of the Sandia Technical Development Program. Farris died on Dec. 8, 1973, at the age of 78.[144]

THE FINE ARTS CENTER[145]

Fig. 53. Fine Arts Center – Exterior –North Doors, circa 1970s (Center for Southwest Research, UNM Libraries).[146]

The Fine Arts Center[147] was designed as a single unit by Edward Holien. Due to funding problems when the Center was completed in 1964, the Center included space for only the Department of Music, the Fine Arts Library, and the Art Museum. Additional spaces were added later, including, for example, Popejoy Hall, named for former UNM President Thomas Lafayette Popejoy, and Rodey Hall, named for Bernard Shandon Rodey, a delegate from the New Mexico Territory.

UNM Art Museum[148]

The UNM Art Museum was founded in 1963 and as of this writing has more than 27,000 pieces in the collection, comprising the largest collection of art in New Mexico. The collection includes old masters' paintings and sculpture, Spanish colonial works, and works from the 1800s and 1900s. Within the UNM Art Museum is the Clinton Adams Gallery. The gallery is located in two rooms on the third floor and in association with the Beaumont Newhall Study Room, the Enyeart/Malone Library and Archive, and other named resources.

Clinton Adams Gallery[149]

Clinton Adams[150] was the former Dean of the College of Fine Arts and University Provost.[151] Adams was born in Glendale, California, on December 11, 1918. He attended the University of California-Los Angeles (UCLA), where he received his bachelor's degree in 1940 and his master's degree in 1942. Adams served in World War II in a camouflage unit. After the war, he was hired as an instructor at UCLA from 1946 to 1948 and made an associate professor in 1948.

In 1954, Adams was hired as a professor at the University of Kentucky, where he headed the art department and served as Director of the University Art Gallery. He moved to the University of Florida in 1957, serving as Professor and Chair of the Art Department. Hired as Dean of the College of Fine Arts, he came to UNM in 1961. In 1976, Adams was made Associate Provost. He also served as Interim Provost. Adams received the UNM Research Lecture award that year. In 1985, Adams was awarded the UNM Regents' Meritorious Service Medal, and in 1998, he received the Fergusson Award. President William Davis wrote of Adams, "Certainly one of the best academic administrators I have ever known or worked with. He was known as one who did not suffer fools gladly." Adams' paintings are included in the permanent collections of the Chicago Art Institute, the Brooklyn Museum of Art, the British Museum, the Australian National Gallery, and the Museum of Modern Art to name a few. He wrote many books about art and art history, and in 1985 he received the Governor's Award for Outstanding Contributions to the Arts of New Mexico. Adams continued painting until his death on May 13, 2002, in Albuquerque at age 83.[152]

Beaumont Newhall Study Room

Beaumont Newhall[153] was a renowned professor of photography and known as the "father of the history of photography." He was born in 1908 in Lynn, Massachusetts, and received his undergraduate and graduate degrees in art history and museum studies from Harvard. After continuing his studies in Paris and London, he joined the Museum of Modern Art (MOMA) in New York as a librarian. At MOMA, he continued his interest in photography and curated a major show on the history of photography from 1839-1937. He was also an excellent writer and his textbook *The History of Photography*, which resulted from the 1937 show, eventually went into five editions. In 1940, he became the first curator of MOMA's Department of Photography. Soon after, in 1942, he was drafted into the Army to further the military's aerial photography effort.

After WWII, Newhall became Director of the International Museum of Photography in 1948 and a decade later became Director of the George Eastman House, today known as the International Museum of Photography. He left Eastman House in 1971 to lead the History of Prints and Photography program in the Art History Department at UNM.

Before retiring in 1984, Newhall was recognized as a MacArthur Fellow for his exceptional talent.[154] The International Photography Hall of Fame and Museum recognized Newhall as a pioneer in the field. Newhall was an engaging professor, prolific author and photographer in his own right. The Beaumont Newhall Study Room at UNM, where the University's extensive print and photography collections can be studied, was named in his honor.[155] Newhall died at his home in Santa Fe in 1993.[156]

Enyeart/Malone Library and Archive

The Enyeart/Malone Library and Archive, located on the third floor of the UNM Art Museum, was named after James Enyeart and his wife, Roxanne Malone, who were widely recognized photography scholars and artists.[157] James Enyeart, like Beaumont Newhall, worked at various institutions including the Eastman House, and Roxanne Malone was associated with the College of Santa Fe. The Library and Archive named in their honor include many of their books and articles on the history of photography along with other materials.[158]

Bunting Visual Resources Library[159]

The Bunting Visual Resources Library is on the third floor of the Art Building and was named for Bainbridge Bunting, Professor of Art and Architectural History.[160] The collection holds more than 350,000 items and 35,000 digital images and is widely used by researchers and faculty. The commemorative plaque reads:

> In appreciation of Bainbridge Bunting, teacher, author, and preservationist, and his signal contributions to the study of the architecture of New Mexico and to historical preservation in New Mexico, this plaque has been placed by the Historic Preservation Program of the State of New Mexico.

Bunting was born in Kansas City, Missouri, in 1913. He came to the University of New Mexico in 1948 after serving with the American Friends Service Committee during World War II. He received his doctoral degree in art and the history of architecture from Harvard University. Bunting wrote several books including *Taos Adobes* (1964), *Of Earth and Timbers Made* (1974), and *The Early Architecture of New Mexico* (1976), as well as many articles in various publications. He received the Governor's Award for Excellence in the Arts in 1978. At the time of his death in February 1981, he had completed a history of architecture on the Harvard campus as well as a *Survey of Architectural History in Cambridge* and *Houses of Boston's Back Bay: An Architectural History, 1840-1917*.

Lannan Reading Room

The Lannan Reading Room, dedicated in 2015, was named in honor of the Lannan Foundation[161] for its support, especially of the Land Arts of the American West and the Arts and Ecology programs in the Department of Art and Art History at UNM. The Lannan Reading Room includes a major collection of books on the arts and the environment donated by the Lannan Foundation.[162]

Van Deren Coke Photography Gallery[163] and Van Deren and Joan Coke Library

The UNM Art Museum also includes a photography gallery named for Frank Van Deren Coke,[164] founder and Director of the University Art Museum, Professor of Art, and Chair of the Art and Art History Department from 1966 to 1979. An authority on the history of photography, Coke wrote extensively on the topic.

Born in Lexington, Kentucky, on July 4, 1921, Frank Van Deren Coke received his bachelor's degree from the University of Kentucky in 1956 and master's degree in fine arts from Indiana University in 1958. He did additional graduate work at Harvard University in 1958 and 1960 to 1961. He taught at both the University of Florida and Arizona State University before coming to UNM in 1962 and gave lectures at St. Martin's School of Art in London, the Universities of California at Berkeley and Davis, and many other institutions.

In 1979, Coke left UNM to become the Director of the San Francisco Museum's Department of Photography. In 1986 Coke received the Governor's Award for Excellence in the Arts. After retiring in 1987, he moved to Santa Fe, where he died on July 11, 2004. Linda Bahn, Director of the UNM Art Museum, was quoted by a *Daily Lobo* reporter as saying, "He [Coke] put us on the map to becoming probably the best university collection of photography." She also noted that Coke was a "tireless historian." Over the years, Coke gave more than 1,600 items to the University. The University dedicated the gallery in his honor on Friday, March 21, 1986.

The Kurt Frederick Rehearsal Hall

Fig. 54. John Donald Robb with Kurt Frederick (right) (Photograph by John D. Robb, Center for Southwest Research, UNM Libraries).[165]

Within the Fine Arts Center is the Kurt Frederick Rehearsal Hall. Kurt Frederick, a native of Vienna, Austria, came to the United States in 1938 after the Nazi regime invaded his country. In 1930, he had graduated from the Vienna State College of Music. In New York, he played with the New Friends of the Orchestra. Frederick said, "I got into a rut playing in an orchestra. I had given up hope of doing what I wanted to do -- conduct. Ever since I was a boy of 14 in Vienna -- that is what I wanted to do."

Upon moving to Albuquerque in 1942, Frederick was appointed Professor of Music at UNM where he pursued conducting and his interest in oratorio. In addition to teaching violin, he led the University Mixed Chorus. He also organized the University Symphony, the UNM Opera Workshop, the UNM Madrigal Singers, and was the founding conductor of the Albuquerque Youth Symphony. Frederick also conducted the Albuquerque Civic Symphony and founded the Albuquerque Choral Association. In 1977, he received the Governor's Award for Excellence in the Arts for his contributions to music.[166] Frederick also received an honorary degree of Doctor of Music from UNM in 1979. He died in Falls Church, Virginia, in 1997 at 90.[167]

Keller Recital Hall[168]

Fig. 55. Fine Arts Center - Keller Hall – Set for "The Magic Flute," 1964 (Center for Southwest Research, UNM Libraries).[169]

Opening into the main lobby of the Fine Arts Center on the north side of the building is Keller Hall, a recital hall named in 1971 for Professor of Music Walter Keller.[170] Keller died in 1970 while on sabbatical in Portugal and was buried in Lisbon. He was serving as Chair of the Department of Music at the time of his death. Keller graduated from the Julliard School of Music and received his Ph.D. from Harvard University. He came to UNM in 1938 to teach temporarily, and he remained for 32 years, taking leave during World War II to serve in the Coast Guard.

Keller founded the Albuquerque Chamber Music Society and served as President of the Albuquerque Symphony Orchestra Board of Directors. Dr. Kurt Frederick, who taught and directed the UNM Symphony Orchestra for many years, was quoted by the *Albuquerque Journal* as saying, "He [Keller] was a wonderful person, one of the most respected and beloved members of our faculty."

Keller Hall is used for musical events, lectures and meetings of large groups. The 1967 Holtkamp pipe organ, an instrument of both physical and musical beauty, is used for teaching, recitals, and concerts.

Mattox Sculpture Center

Fig. 56. Maddox Sculpture Center (Source unknown).

Associated with the Fine Arts Center is the Mattox Sculpture Center,[171] named for Professor of Art Emeritus Charles Mattox. The Mattox Sculpture Center is located at 1524 Copper N.E., in a former automobile repair and paint shop. When the University acquired the property from Galles Motors, Mattox thought it would be ideal for the sculpture program, as the building was composed of concrete floors, no ceiling, and bare walls.

Charles Mattox,[172] sculptor and educator, was born in Bronson, Kansas, in 1910. He studied art at the Kansas City Art Institute with Arshile Gorky from 1934 to 1935 and worked on a federal art project with noted sculptor David Smith and others in the 1930s. To support himself, Mattox worked as a molder and tool and instrument designer in many parts of the United States and on special effects and set design in Hollywood from 1942 to 1950. Mattox taught at many institutions, including the Karn Art Institute in Los Angeles, the University of California at Berkeley, the San Francisco Art Institute, and the University of New Mexico. His sculpture reflected his interests in geometric shapes and machinery. A pioneer in the development of kinetic sculpture, Mattox also took an early interest in the application of computer graphics to art. Mattox's work has been displayed in a variety of solo artist shows, as well as group exhibits mainly in New Mexico and California. Many of his pieces are housed in various art museums in California, British Columbia, Washington D.C., and New Mexico, as well as in many private collections. Mattox also published many articles in art journals such as *Leonardo, Artform, Art News, Art International,* and *Art in America.* His papers are housed in the Center for Southwest Research in the UNM Zimmerman Library.

Popejoy Hall[173]

Fig. 57. Fine Arts Center - Popejoy Hall – Interior – Orchestra on Stage, 1973 (Center for Southwest Research, UNM Libraries).[174]

Popejoy Hall, named for former UNM President Thomas Lafayette Popejoy, was the first addition to the Fine Arts Center. The hall was started in 1965, just after completion of the first elements of the complex. Designed as a symphony hall, it has moveable walls onstage that reduce the stage for small musical groups. In an article in the *New York Times*, Howard Taubman called Popejoy Hall an outstanding, acoustically near perfect, performance center. It has since been remodeled and new seating installed. George Izenour, an internationally recognized theater designer and historian of theater design, designed the hall. Holien and Buckley were the architects.

Tom Popejoy[175] was born on a ranch in Colfax County, New Mexico, on December 2, 1902. After graduating from Raton High School, he and his bride, Bess Kimball, entered the University of New Mexico in 1921. Popejoy became an outstanding athlete and lettered in football three years, one of his favorite stories being how he dropkicked a field goal that defeated the University of Arizona 3-0. In 1989, Popejoy was posthumously inducted into the UNM Athletics Hall of Honor.[176]

Popejoy worked his way up the University ladder with various jobs and became Comptroller in 1937 and then Assistant to Presidents Zimmerman and Wernette. He succeeded Wernette and became the first president of UNM born in New Mexico. Popejoy was active in the 1930s in obtaining funds from the Works Progress Administration and the Public Works Administration and oversaw the construction of buildings including Scholes Hall and Zimmerman Library as well as the UNM Golf Course. Under his presidency, enrollment grew rapidly and the campus expanded to meet the challenge. When Popejoy retired, a new law school was bring planned, the Medical School's first building was completed, and a new football stadium and basketball arena were built on the South Campus. Popejoy received the Zimmerman Award from the UNM Alumni Association in 1968[177] and was awarded an honorary degree of Doctor of Law and Letters from UNM in 1969 for serving as University President from 1948-68.[178]

Before Popejoy retired, Vice President Sherman Smith asked Popejoy if he would like the football stadium named for him. Popejoy replied that he had rather the new symphony hall in the Fine Arts Complex be his namesake. The University approved, and bestowed this fitting honor to a man who gave most of his life to the betterment of the University, from being a star athlete to the longest serving President the institution has had to date. More about his career can be found in former University President William E. "Bud" Davis' book

Miracle on the Mesa.

The Popejoy Trees

Fig. 58. The Popejoy Trees (Source unknown).

The Popejoy Trees are in a grove on the south side of Popejoy Hall. The trees were brought to the campus from the birthplace of Thomas Lafayette Popejoy, former UNM President. A plaque on the wall that, while difficult to read, says:

> The ponderosa pines nearby this marker came from the ranch twenty miles east of Raton, New Mexico, where Tom L. Popejoy was born. Planted May 6, 1970.

Robb Archive of Southwestern Folk Music[179]

John Donald Robb was Dean of the College of Fine Arts as well as a composer, folklorist, and attorney. In 1911, he entered Yale University to study English literature and the history of music. During World War I, Robb commanded an artillery battalion in France. Following the end of the war, he studied law at Harvard University and the University of Minnesota. He became a lawyer specializing in corporate bond law and moved to New York City.

As a young man, Robb pursued music composition while living in Minneapolis and maintained contact with musicians and composers in this country and abroad. His love of music led him to give up law in 1941 and take the position of Acting Dean of the College of Fine Arts at UNM, resulting in a tremendous cut in income. In 1942, Robb was made the permanent dean and served as such until 1957. During his tenure, Robb added many well-known musicians to the faculty, which led to a dramatic increase in enrollment. He also established the UNM Symphony Orchestra. Robb created some 100 works, including symphonies, chamber music, stage and other types of pieces, and was an early experimenter with the MOOG synthesizer.

John Robb was especially interested in the music of the Southwest and researched and recorded more than 3,000 songs and dances. He wrote *Hispanic Folk Music of New Mexico and the Southwest,* a classic compilation. The Center for Southwest Research in the UNM Zimmerman Library contains his personal papers and photographs as well as the John Donald Robb Archive of Southwestern Folk Music. The Archive has grown to more than 30,000 titles and 1,200 hours of recordings. In 1983, Robb received the UNM Rodey Award,[180] and was awarded an honorary Doctor of Music in 1986.[181] Robb died in Albuquerque in 1988 at the age of 96.[182]

Rodey Hall and Rodey Theater[183]

Fig. 59. Hodgin Hall – Exterior – Rear of Building with "U" Sign and Rodey Hall, circa 1920s (Center for Southwest Research, UNM Libraries).[184]

As mentioned in an earlier section, Rodey Hall was a small assembly hall built as an addition to the main building, Hodgin Hall, around 1908 as part of President Tight's remodeling. Rodey Hall was described in the *UNM Weekly* of that time:

> It [Rodey Hall] is cross shaped, the platform occupying the shorter arm of the cross. The ceiling is quite high and a balcony is being constructed in the upper part of the longer arm of the cross. Large rough pine logs are used for rafters, joists, and pillars in both this and the Administration Building. The walls and corners are heavily buttressed and the general effect of this building is that of an old Pueblo church.

Rodey Hall was demolished in 1971 after it had been condemned by the State Fire Marshal and to make way for construction of Redondo Drive. The next year, in 1972, a new Rodey Theater[185] was constructed as part of the addition to the Fine Arts Center. The Rodey family made a substantial contribution to the project and it was named for Bernard Shandon Rodey and his son Pierce C. Rodey.

Bernard Rodey, born in County Mayo, Ireland, on March 1, 1856, moved with his family to Sherbrooke, Quebec, in 1862. He had little formal education and was self-taught until he moved to Boston to study law. Rodey came to New Mexico in 1881 and held the job of private Secretary to the General Manager of the Atlantic and Pacific Railroad. He worked as a court reporter for a time, and in 1883, was admitted to the Bar and became City Attorney for the City of Albuquerque from 1887 to 1888.

Rodey served one term as a member of the Territorial Senate in 1909 and wrote the bill, known as the Rodey Act, establishing the University of New Mexico, thus earning the sobriquet "Father of the University."[186] Rodey was elected to the 57th and 58th Congresses (1901 to 1905), but lost his bid for reelection. There followed appointment as a federal judge in Puerto Rico and later as the United States Attorney for Alaska. Bernard Rodey died in Albuquerque on March 10, 1927.[187] (See also discussion of Rodey Hall in the Anthropology Building section.)

Pierce Rodey,[188] who was born on Nov. 8, 1889, received his B.A. from Harvard in 1912 and his Bachelor of Law also from Harvard in 1915, and joined his father Bernard Rodey in the practice of law in Albuquerque. Upon his father's death in 1927, he became the senior partner in what became one of the largest law firms in the New Mexico. He retired in 1957, a year before he died. Pierce Rodey was a distinguished lawyer and public-spirited citizen. One of his greatest achievements was the organization of the Middle Rio Grande Conservancy District.[189]

The John Sommers Gallery[190]

The John Sommers Gallery, located on the second floor of the Art Building, was named for the former Master Printer, John Sommers. The gallery is used to display student works.[191] Sommers was born in 1927 in Michigan and trained as a Master Printer at the Tamarind Institute in Los Angeles. Clinton Adams and Garo Antresian were responsible for the relocation of the Tamarind Institute to the University in New Mexico in 1970.

Sommers transferred to New Mexico, initially as the Studio Manager and Master Printer of the Institute, where he oversaw the Printer Training Program. From 1975 to 1983, he was the Technical Director of the Institute and a lecturer in lithography in the Department of Art and Art History. While at the Institute, he worked with notable artists such as Judy Chicago. He died in 1987 in Albuquerque.[192]

Tamarind Institute[193]

Fig. 60. Tamarind Institute, circa 1970 (Center for Southwest Research, UNM Libraries).[194]

Fig. 61. Tamarind Institute, 2013 (Photograph by Suzanne Mortier, UNM Landscape Architect).

The Tamarind Institute is renowned worldwide for excellent instruction in the art of lithography. The institute was originally located on Tamarind Street in Los Angeles, and bears the name of that location. The Institute's facility has since been relocated to a building at 2500 Central S.E., which was remodeled to accommodate the Institute.[195]

Hartung Hall[196]

Associated with the Fine Arts Center is Hartung Hall, named for Robert Hartung. Robert Hartung, born in Mt. Vernon, Iowa, on March 6, 1917, became involved in acting and theater work when 19 years of age. He received his undergraduate degree in speech from Cornell University in 1939 and M.F.A. from Yale in 1942. He joined the Theo Irvine Studio in 1944, where he staged many plays and became a director there in 1949.

From 1950 to 1954, Hartung travelled the country as a guest director at many theaters and entered the world of television as the Associate Director of the Sid Caeser and the Lucky Strike Hit Parade shows. In 1955, he became Director of the Hallmark Hall of Fame and received three Emmy Awards, three Writers Guild Awards, and four Directors Guild Awards.[197] Hollywood beckoned and in 1968, Hartung moved to Hollywood and stayed until 1972, when he came to UNM as Chair of the Theater Arts Department.

Hartung breathed life into the UNM program and directed many plays on campus. He wanted more time to teach, and in 1978, he stepped down as Chair and taught and directed plays until he retired at age 73 in 1991.

The students loved Bob and called him "Daddy Bob." Former student Mike Ross founded a theater on Sunset Boulevard and named it the Robert Hartung Theater. Hartung Hall at UNM as of this writing houses portions of the Interdisciplinary Film & Digital Media Program[198] and the Department of Theatre and Dance.[199] Robert Hartung died on March 9, 1999, at age 81.

FORD UTILITIES CENTER[200]

Fig. 62. Ford Utilities Center – Snow on Ground, circa 1950s (Center for Southwest Research, UNM Libraries).[201]

Fig. 63. Ford Utilities Center, 2013 (Photograph by Suzanne Mortier, UNM Landscape Architect).

The Ford Utilities Center is the University's main generating plant for steam and chilled water on the campus. Several additions to the building have been made over the years, including an expanded mechanical plant, cooling towers, and office space. As of this writing, the latest expansions occurred in 2005, increasing the capacity and function of the Ford Utilities Center.

The utility center was named for Professor Albert D. "Pop" Ford. Ford was born in Iowa and moved with his family to Montana at an early age. He received a B.S. in mechanical engineering from Montana State College in 1929 and his M.S. in 1938. After working for Anaconda Copper and The Texas Company, Ford came to UNM in 1936 to be the superintendent of the new power plant then under construction. Ford was made a professor and appointed Chair of the Department of Mechanical Engineering in 1942, serving in that capacity until 1953. During World War II, Ford chaired the University building committee, which planned development projects that would occur when the war ended.

"Pop" Ford, as the students called him, retired from teaching in 1960 but served as a consulting engineer for several years. The UNM Board of Regents named the newly built utility center for Ford on September 27, 1969, a decision celebrated at a gala dedication dinner on November 4 at the Elks Club. The event was attended by hundreds of friends of Ford, and the Montana State University Alumni Association presented him with their Distinguished Alumni Award. Ford gave 33 years of dedicated service to UNM, retiring in 1969. Today, the Ford Utilities Center continues to showcase innovation in energy management.[202]

CAMP FUNSTON[203]

On April 6, 1917, Congress declared war on Germany and its allies. Most of the men on campus enlisted immediately, causing a total disruption of University life. That summer, the Board of Regents leased land east of the city reservoir for a mobilization training camp for the 1,500 members of Battery A of the New Mexico National Guard. The camp was named for General Frederick Funston, a hero of the Philippine War, which followed the Spanish American War, and as the man who as Brigadier General of the Presidio saved San Francisco after the 1906 earthquake. Twelve wood-framed barracks buildings with pitched roofs were built along with a Red Cross hospital, a mess hall, a YMCA building, and horse stables. When the Guard was called up, the camp housed students enlisted in the Student Army Training Corps until the end of WWI.

HADLEY HALL I[204]

Fig. 64. Hadley Hall I – Front Entrance and Young Trees, circa 1890s (Center for Southwest Research, UNM Libraries).[205]

Fig. 65. Hadley Hall I – Building in Ruins after Fire, circa 1910 (Center for Southwest Research, UNM Libraries).[206]

The second major building to be erected on the campus was largely the gift of friends of the University and Alice Coates (Paxson)Hadley, whose father-in-law, Hiram Hadley, held the office of Vice President of the University and later President of the New Mexico Agricultural and Mechanical College. Mrs. Hadley gave $10,000, a significant amount in 1899, toward the erection of a science building in memory of her deceased husband, Walter Carpenter Hadley, who died on February 15, 1896. Walter Hadley was a health seeker who came to New Mexico and built a considerable fortune as a mining engineer. A mining camp, Hadley, N.M., was named for him.[207] He studied at Haverford College and the University of Chicago.

Architect Edward B. Cristy designed the two-story brick structure, which was completed in 1899 and used as a climatology lab. The building, now known as Hadley Hall I or Hadley Climatological Laboratory, was totally destroyed by fire on May 23, 1910.[208] The geological collection of UNM President Clarence Luther Herrick (1897–1901), the ethnological museum, a botanical collection, and the entire mineralogical collection, which had been exhibited at the 1904 St. Louis World Fair, were lost in the fire.

HADLEY HALL II[209]

Fig. 66. Engineering - Hadley Hall II – Car Parked in Front, 1920 (Center for Southwest Research, UNM Libraries).[210]

A second building named Hadley Hall II or Mechanical Arts Engineering Building was completed in 1919. An explosion in 1949 destroyed most of Hadley Hall II. What remained is now part of the Chemical Engineering Laboratory.[211]

HODGIN HALL ("MAIN BUILDING")[212]

Fig. 67. Left, University of New Mexico Building: Hodgin Hall under construction, 1892 (Center for Southwest Research, UNM Libraries).[213] Fig. 68. Center, Hodgin Hall – Exterior – View from Redondo Road, 1980 (during restoration) (Center for Southwest Research, UNM Libraries).[214] Fig. 69. Right, Hodgin Hall, 2013 (Photograph by Suzanne Mortier, UNM Landscape Architect).

The Main Building, as it was called, held almost all of the functions of the University when it was completed in 1892. An entire volume could be written about the first building built on the UNM campus and the man for which it was named, Charles Elkanah Hodgin.[215] The following is excerpted from *Only In New Mexico*:

> The University's Main Building (later named the Administration Building, and then Hodgin Hall) was red brick with a light colored stone trim, typical of Midwestern school architecture and was designed by architect Jesse M. Wheelock.

Charles Hodgin later recalled what the University was like when the building was occupied in 1892:

> Visualize if you can: without a tree, with no houses between it and the town, and none between it and the mountains, and no street leading to the mesa except the extension of Railroad Avenue, by the mere scratching of the gravel over the undulating and ungraded foothills. The only approaches for vehicles were two sandy arroyos, one coming up at the north line of the campus and one several blocks south.

By 1908 it became apparent that the roof trusses were failing and had to be replaced. William George Tight[216] who had become president in 1901 and architect Edward Buxton Cristy installed a flat roof supported by vigas with parapets and stuccoed the walls thus introducing the Pueblo Style architecture to the campus and restoring its use in New Mexico. In 1989, a small addition was made on the southeast corner. The space was named the Alumni Lettermen's Room and houses numerous trophies and photographs from all the sports.

Charles Elkanah Hodgin, born in Indiana in 1858, graduated from Indiana State Normal School and taught school in the state for six years. In 1885, he brought his wife, Sallie B. Overman, to Albuquerque to seek recovery from her tuberculosis. He taught at the Albuquerque Academy (no relation to the present Albuquerque Academy) from 1886 until 1890 when he became the principal. In 1891 he became the first superintendent of the Albuquerque Public School system. Hodgin received a Bachelor of Pedagogy from UNM in 1894, as a member of the first graduating class. In 1897, he became head of the University's Normal Department, the forerunner of the College of Education, which position he held for over 28 years. By 1903, his duties included being the Registrar and later Dean of the University, a position he held for twenty years. After he retired in 1925, he became the Editor of the New Mexico School Review and Chairman of the Rhodes Scholarship Trust. UNM, in 1927, bestowed on him a Doctorate of Law and Letters, the first honorary degree given by UNM. He died in August 1934 and two years later the Board of Regents named the building for him.

Hodgin Hall is listed on both the State Register of Cultural Properties and National Register of Historic Places.[217]

The Charles Hodgin Elm and Hodgin Grove

While Charles E. Hodgin was still alive, an elm tree was planted and named for him, but it died. Hodgin quipped that the name was too much for the tree to bear. In the Biennial Report for 1927-29, President James F. Zimmerman noted that Judge C.M. Botts of Albuquerque had provided a fund to establish two groves on Central Avenue between University and Cornell Avenues, one to honor Miss Josephine Parsons and the other to honor Dr. C.E. Hodgin, Professor Emeritus. Zimmerman wrote that the City planted the Hodgin Grove since it was close to the reservoir and would be maintained by the City. This area is now known as Yale Park. The marker that identified Hodgin Grove has been relocated to the north side of the Art Annex Building, which was the first campus library.

Parsons Grove

The second grove of trees funded by Judge C.M. Botts was planted at the northwest corner of Central Avenue and Yale Boulevard and named in memory of Josephine Parsons. The identifying marker has been moved to the front of the Art Annex Building, but the grove's location can be identified based on President Zimmerman's report for 1927-29. For more information about Josephine Parsons, see discussion under Parsons Hall.

The Irma Bobo Room[218]

Fig. 70. Irma Bobo Room, Hodgin Hall (Source unknown).

The third floor of Hodgin Hall was named the Bobo Room in honor of Irma Bobo, a long time elementary school teacher in the Albuquerque Public Schools. Caswell Silver, Class of 1940 and a tenant of Ms. Bobo's while he attended school, provided funding to renovate the room. The room contains paintings donated by Dr. Scott Adler and his wife Barbara, a pottery collection donated by Dr. Alfred Lopez and his wife Eppie, and a piano, which was a gift from Calvin Horn, a former University Regent. The chandeliers were locally made and hung in the old Student Union, now the Anthropology Building. The room is open during business hours and is used for meetings, receptions, and other events.

The Glenn Emmons Room[219]

Dorothy Emmons donated funds to renovate a room in Hodgin Hall in 1977 in honor of her husband Glenn L. Emmons, UNM Class of 1919. Born in Alabama, Glenn Emmons and came to New Mexico as a child in 1905. He served in the "Air Service" in World War I as a first lieutenant and after the war lived in Gallup where he became a banker. Emmons was with the Gallup State Bank, President of the New Mexico Bankers Association, and Treasurer of the American Banking Association. He was President of the Gallup Chamber of Commerce and served with the Intertribal Indian Association. During the Eisenhower administration, he served as Commissioner of Indian Affairs for eight years. It was said of him by the tribes, "…you are the most human commissioner we have ever had, by that is meant friendliness, warmth and a personal interest in people."

Glenn Emmons was a UNM Regent from 1931 to 1933 and President of the UNM Alumni Association from 1946 to 1949.[220] In 1977, he received the Alumni Zimmerman Medal for outstanding service to UNM.[221] That same year, he was awarded an honorary Doctor of Law and Letters from UNM.[222] Mrs. Emmons also donated a bronze bust of Emmons by sculptor Felix de Welden, which is displayed in Hodgin Hall.

The Gazebo[223]

Fig. 71. Hodgin Hall – Gazebo Construction with Snow, 1991 (Center for Southwest Research, UNM Libraries).[224]

The commemorative plaques on the Gazebo are in Spanish and English and read:

> Donated by the Government of Mexico To
> the University of New Mexico Architect.
> Dagdug Kalife, Undersecretary of Foreign Affairs of
> Mexico Javier Barros, and President Peck.

Through efforts of Gwynn "Bub" Henry, Director of Alumni Relations, the Mexican government gave the University this attractive gazebo near Hodgin Hall. Henry had initiated talks with the local Mexican Consul Dona Galindo Saroz about a gazebo on the campus honoring the friendship between New Mexico and Mexico. The structure was dedicated in 1991.

The Dorothy and Ray Hickman Parlor[225]

Dorothy and Ray Hickman of Birmingham, Alabama, UNM Class of 1925, donated funds for the restoration of the parlor in Hodgin Hall. The Hickman Parlor houses the George Washington portrait, Zimmerman Award plaques and photographs, and Hickman memorabilia. The portrait of President Washington by Gilbert Stuart was given to the University by Donn and Henrietta Davies of Cimarron, New Mexico, and had been in their family since 1928. The portrait itself is more than 200 years old.

The Huggett-Heald Tree and Plaque

Lillian (also sometimes spelled "Lilian") G. Huggett and Clarence E. Heald planted a tree on Arbor Day in 1903 on the west side of the Main Building, now known as Hodgin Hall. In a letter from Myron Fifield to Winifred Reiter dated February 5, 1965, Fifield states that the tree died and the plaque was taken to the Physical Plant Department for safekeeping. He suggested that the two may have been commemorating a campus romance, but it is more likely they were important members of the student body.

Lillian Huggett, born on March 10, 1881, in London, England, moved with her father, a Methodist minister, and family to New Mexico. While a student at UNM, Huggett edited the *Mirage* (1903-04)[226] and *UNM Weekly* (1903-05).[227] Huggett was President of her Junior Class, the Athletic Association, and the Estrella Literary Society. She tied with Clarence Heald in an oratorical contest.

Huggett became the first woman to earn a four-year degree from UNM. After graduation, Huggett taught Latin and German at UNM for two years and obtained an M.A. from Northwestern University in 1909. She then became a teacher in the El Paso public schools where she remained for 42 years teaching math and

English. She regularly attended Homecoming festivities at UNM, and in 1947 and 1951, was the Guest of Honor, becoming an "Honorary Lobo" at the 1951 event. Lillian Huggett died in El Paso on June 30, 1958.[228]

Clarence Heald managed the *UNM Weekly*, (1903-04).[229] He was also an outstanding athlete and is listed as an "All-Time Letterman" in basketball (1903, 1908) and football (1903, 1906).[230] He later became one of the youngest men to become a major in the Army during World War I. Heald commanded the 56th A.T. Coast Artillery Corps Ammunition Train at Camp Eustis in Virginia, and just two days before the Armistice was signed, he had readied the command for deployment overseas.[231]

The Lettermen's Wing and John C. "Luke" Luksich Foyer

In 1988, an addition was made to the southeast corner of Hodgin Hall for a Lobo Athletics Lettermen's Memorial Wing. The inner rooms contain trophies, photographs, and newspaper and magazine clippings about UNM men and women's sports. In the lobby, there is a framed list of all lettermen killed in the two World Wars and the Vietnam War. These names also appear in the Alumni Memorial Chapel memorial list of war dead.

The foyer of this wing was named the John G. "Luke" Luksich Foyer to honor this UNM alumnus who contributed generously to UNM, including initiating the endowment program for the Alumni Lettermen's Association and the scholarship endowment to the Lobo Club's Football Program. While playing football at UNM, Luksich was named to the All Border Conference First Team in 1940 and 1941. In 1998, Luksich was named to the UNM Athletics Hall of Honor for distinguished service.[232] He was also an honor student.

Luksich, who was born in Indiana, Pennsylvania, on June 19, 1914. Luksich worked for the Crucible Steel Company as a chemical analyst for 43 years, and is credited with improving the performance of ball bearings, a major industrial achievement. Luksich died in Beaver, Pennsylvania, on June 26, 2001.[233] All of the memorabilia has been moved to the basketball arena, known as "The Pit."

The Horace F. McKay Lobby

Fig. 72. Horace F. McKay Lobby (Source unknown).

Elmyra and Horace F. McKay Jr. donated funds for the decoration and renovation of the second floor lobby. The lobby was finished in "mission or art-craft with accessories reflecting art noveau influences," according to a brochure from the UNM Alumni Association.[234]

Horace McKay, Jr., was born in Fayetteville, Tennessee, on June 4, 1920, and died in Albuquerque on February 21, 2008. He attended UNM from 1939 to 1942. McKay was very active in real estate in the city and was a pioneer in the oil and gas industry in New Mexico. He supported many charitable organizations and served on the Board of Directors of Bataan Memorial Methodist Hospital, which became Lovelace Hospital. McKay also served on the Lovelace Foundation for Medical Research and the Board of Directors of the American Bank of Commerce.[235]

The Faulhaber Stained Glass Window

The stained glass window, designed by Donna Walton Faulhaber, was donated by Jack and Jane Walton (UNM classes of 1934 and 1940 respectively) and installed in Hodgin Hall on August 29, 1985. The artist, UNM class of 1972 alumna Donna Walton Faulhaber, is their daughter.[236]

John D. Robb Bust and Rodey Awards

The bronze bust of Dean John D. Robb, Sr., and the display of Rodey Award recipients were donated by Pricilla Robb McDonnell of St. Louis, Missouri, who was the daughter of Dean Robb. More information about Dean Robb can be found in the section on the College of Fine Arts. More information about Bernard S. Rodey, for whom the Rodey Awards are named, can be found in the sections on Rodey Hall and Rodey Theater.

Wall Plaques

Many alumni and friends have recognized friends, family members, professors and employees of the University and themselves by adding names to the first foyer wall of Hodgin Hall, the stair risers of the main stairway on the east side of the building and on bricks in the main walkway leading to the building. The latter are part of the "Brick Brigade" created by Alumni Association in recognition of UNM's 100th anniversary.[237]

The Memorial Concrete Benches and Kiwanis Fountain

Fig. 73. Class of 1921 Bench (Source unknown).

On the east side of Hodgin Hall are several uncomfortable concrete benches erected by classes from the early days of the University, including the Class of 1921. These benches were relocated to a Courtyard of Classes.[238]

In 1985, the Albuquerque Kiwanis Club built a fountain centered on the north entrance of the Art Annex and the east entrance to Hodgin Hall. The fountain is a replica of an old fountain from the southwest part of the campus that was removed to make way for new construction. According to legend, graduating engineering students were dunked in the old pool by their fellow classmates.

Dr. Karen Abraham Courtyard

The Alumni Center Plaza at Hodgin Hall has been renamed the Dr. Karen Abraham Courtyard in recognition of Dr. Abraham's service to UNM as Associate Vice President of Alumni Relations and Executive Director of the UNM Alumni Association.[239] Abraham earned her B.S. in 1967, master's in 1968, and D.Ed. in 1971, all from UNM.

Tight Grove[240]

 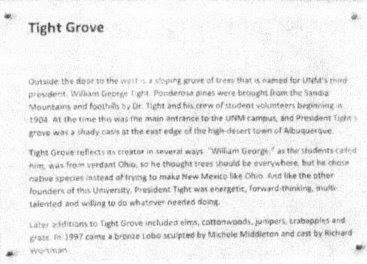

Fig. 74. Hodgin Hall – exterior – winter in Tight Grove, circa 1909 (Center for Southwest Research, UNM Libraries).[241]

Fig. 75. Tight Grove plaque (Photograph by Suzanne Mortier, UNM Landscape Architect, 2013).

Tight Grove, named in honor of President Tight, is located near Hodgin Hall at the northeast corner of University Boulevard and Central Avenue. According to an article regarding the more than 5,000 trees currently on campus:

> The oldest trees on campus are the Ponderosa Pines located in Tight Grove on University and Central. It is believed that some of these trees are over 100 years old, and were planted after the construction of Hodgin Hall, and may also be some of the earliest Arbor Day plantings to occur on campus.[242]

William George Tight was called the "Human Dynamo" because in his eight years as President from 1901 to 1909 he brought new life to the University and took actions that continue to affect the campus even to this day.

Tight was born on March 12, 1865, to George and Thalia (French) Tighton on a farm near Granville, Ohio, where he attended public schools. After graduating, he received a B.S. in 1886 and M.S. in 1887 from Denison University, and a Ph.D. from the University of Chicago in 1901. He studied at Harvard several summers and was an Assistant Professor of Geology and Biology at Denison. Tight authored several scientific articles. He was a charter member of the American Association for the Advancement of Science and a member and Secretary of the Ohio State Academy of Science. In 1901, he was appointed President of the Territorial University of New Mexico and Chair of Geology.

President Clarence Herrick, who was forced to retire due to health reasons and who knew Tight from Ohio, recommended Tight for the presidency. When Tight arrived in Albuquerque in June 1901, he was immediately impressed with the uniqueness of the state and became very interested in the architecture of the Indian pueblos. He saw a chance to bring that architecture to the UNM campus when the Main Building (now known as Hodgin Hall), which had been built between 1890 and 1892 as the first building at the University, had to be remodeled because of structural problems. With architect Edward Buxton Christy, Tight transformed the Richardson Romanesque designed red brick building into a stucco building in the Pueblo style. Christy designed other buildings on campus in this style during Tight's tenure as President.

Tight also took a great interest in landscaping and made Arbor Day a holiday from classes to allow students to go into the mountains to bring out trees and plant them on campus, and in 1908 the trees placed in the area now known as Tight Grove were planted.

In 1909, Tight was removed as President for various reasons, but remained in New Mexico for a short time as President of the Territorial Fair. Tight died on January 15, 1910, some say of a broken heart. Tight Grove in association with Hodgin Hall is listed on the National Register of Historic Places. The NRHP nomination form notes that Christy "might be called Albuquerque's first architect" and that Tight "deserves recognition as the first New Mexican to envision the Spanish-Pueblo tradition as a fitting architectural expression for this region."[243]

Lobo Sculpture

Fig. 76. Lobo sculpture by Michelle Middleton located in Tight Grove (Center for Southwest Research, UNM Libraries).

One of several lobo sculptures located on the UNM campus is a sculpture by Michele Middleton located within Tight Grove in 1997 and facing the entrance to UNM at Central and University Avenues. This statue was a gift by the Alumni Association to commemorate the University's 100th year.[244]

Lobo Head

Fig. 77. Hodgin Hall – Tatschl Lobo Head and Logan Hall, 1991 (Center for Southwest Research, UNM Libraries).[245]

In front of Hodgin Hall is a sculpture of a lobo head by John Tatschl. The Mexican lobo is the mascot of the University. For additional information about lobo sculptures at UNM, see sections on Lobo Statue, Lobo Sculpture, and "Spirit of the Lobos."

HUMANITIES BUILDING[246] and SMITH PLAZA[247]

Fig. 78. Humanities Building – Looking Southeast across Smith Plaza, circa 1970s (Center for Southwest Research, UNM Libraries).[248]

The Humanities Building is a large building that forms the south edge of Smith Plaza, named for former Vice President Sherman Smith, and is one of the most photographed buildings on the Central Campus. Based on studies made by campus planner Robert Riley, it was apparent that a building of this mass was necessary to balance the plaza against the size of Zimmerman Library on the north side and Ortega Hall on the west. The design architect, Robert Krueger, said that he was influenced by the forms of Taos Pueblo in creating the building. The name of the building recalls the departments located in the building at the time of construction: English, Philosophy, and Mathematics.

Sherman E. Smith Plaza

Fig. 79. Homecoming – Vendors on Smith Plaza, 1972 (Center for Southwest Research, UNM Libraries).[249]

As Chair of the Campus Planning Committee, Vice President Sherman E. Smith described this space as, "the main central plaza of the ultimate campus." Earlier plans had indicated a grassed area south of Zimmerman Library with winding walks through it, but Smith felt the space must be paved due to the amount of student traffic through it each day.

Lighting proved to be a challenge, however. Landscape architect Garrett Eckbo specified low fixtures to light the floor of the plaza, but these were quickly vandalized. The Plaza is, as of this writing, lit with only the parapet lights on the surrounding buildings illuminating the space. Nonetheless, Smith Plaza serves as a significant gathering place regardless of the time of day.

Sherman Smith was born in Custer, South Dakota on April 10, 1909. He earned his undergraduate degree in chemical engineering from the South Dakota School of Mines in 1931 and his Ph.D. in Chemistry from Ohio State University in 1935. After working for Dupont and teaching at the University of North Carolina, Smith came to UNM as Chairman of the Chemistry Department in 1945. In 1949, he was made Director of Student Affairs and began representing the University before the legislature. Smith became Dean of Students and Administrative Vice President in 1965, later becoming Vice President for Administration and Development in 1970.

Smith was considered a Renaissance man given his wide range of interests including in campus planning and development,[250] hence his extraordinary accomplishment as Chair of the Campus Planning Committee in steering the University's capital development program across diverse disciplines during a period of rapid campus expansion following World War II.[251]

Smith died on October 4, 1973. Then President Ferrel Heady wrote: "The death of Sherman Smith is a tragic loss to the University. He was not only a man of many talents whose record of accomplishments for the University is unexcelled, but he represented the highest type of faculty member and administrator."

An *Albuquerque Journal* editorial noted: "He was a man of so many talents that they were outnumbered only by his wide range of interests, music, architecture, legislation, disadvantaged children and – most of all – people." At Smith's urging, the Warneke Plan was prepared, which guided campus development for many years, thus, it is quite fitting that this great plaza in the heart of campus bears his name.

The Franklin Dickey Memorial Theater

At the March 1979 meeting of the Board of Regents, the Regents approved naming the Humanities Theater for Franklin Dickey,[252] Professor of English, who died at a young age in 1976. Dickey received his B.A. from the University of Wisconsin in 1942 and his doctorate from the University of California-Los Angeles in 1954. He taught at the University of Michigan from 1950 to 1955 and at the University of Oregon from 1955 to 1958. Dickey came to UNM in 1958, joining the English Department. Dickey chaired the Department from 1963 to 1976. He received a Guggenheim Fellowship and published many scholarly books and essays.

The *Memorial Minute* passed by the UNM Faculty on September 21, 1976, concluded with this paragraph:

> There are no means by which one adequately measures the achievement of a brilliant teacher. No statistics can reveal the great and good influence he had on his students and colleagues. I can only say that he led the life of the mind and that he made that life seem the best possible life one could ever have. He was a scholar and a true gentleman whose death diminishes and whose memory cheers the lives of his many friends.

The Leon Howard Library and Conference Room

Leon Howard was a professor at the University of California-Los Angeles before coming to UNM. A library and conference room are named for him. The *Albuquerque Tribune* of December 22, 1982, carried the following story about Professor Leon Howard:

> Leon Howard, a distinguished scholar of literature, author, and visiting professor of English at the University of New Mexico since 1968, died Tuesday in an Albuquerque hospital. He was 79.
>
> Howard taught a graduate course in American romantic literature despite failing health. He wrote five books and dozens of articles, pamphlets and reviews, many of which have been translated into several languages. In 1974, Howard received the Jay B. Hubbell Medal, the highest award of the Modern Language Association. Recognizing a lifetime of research and teaching, the award citation singled out

Howard's works on Melville, James Russell Lowell, Wright Morris, and other American writers. In 1978 he was a consultant for a biographical film about Herman Melville. In 1979, the UNM regents named a library in the English department in honor of Howard. He later became a member of the UNM Foundation's Tom Popejoy Society and established an endowment for the library.

A native of Alabama, Howard attended Birmingham South College, the University of Chicago, and Johns Hopkins University.

JOHNSON CENTER and GYM[253] and JOHNSON FIELD

Fig. 80. Left, Commencement – Ceremony in Johnson Gym, circa 1961 (Center for Southwest Research, UNM Libraries).[254]

Fig. 81. Right, Aerial Photo – Looking West across Johnson Field, 1971 (Center for Southwest Research, UNM Libraries).[255]

Fig. 82. Left, Johnson Field (Photograph by Suzanne Mortier, UNM Landscape Architect, 2013).

Fig. 83. Right, Johnson Center – Exterior – West Entrance, 1974 (Center for Southwest Research, UNM Libraries).[256]

The Board of Regents, meeting on May 6, 1957, named the University's new gymnasium for Roy William Johnson, known as the "Father of UNM Athletics."[257] Designed to accommodate a basketball court that could seat 2,500 spectators, Johnson Gymnasium also included a swimming pool, Department of Athletics offices, classrooms, training rooms, and locker facilities. As years went by, many athletic functions were moved to the South Campus and the gym was used for teaching, student recreation, and intramural sports.

Johnson was born in Grand Rapids, Michigan, on September 6, 1892. His father died when Johnson was seven, forcing young Johnson to work early in life to help support his family. He attended the University of Michigan and made the football team in 1915, where he was known as "Old Iron Head." Johnson joined the Michigan National Guard and fought in France in World War I. He served as a first lieutenant and was engaged in several major battles including the Marne, Chateau Theirry, and Meuse-Argonne. Johnson received a Purple Heart medal and the Croix de Guerre from the French government. He was wounded three times and severely gassed. While recuperating, he attended the University of Poitiers and received a degree in dramatics.

After WW I, Johnson earned a degree in theater production from Michigan and played another year of football. Due to the gassing he experienced during the war and his continued breathing problems, he moved to New Mexico seeking relief. Johnson joined the UNM faculty in 1920 and set about building a physical education program, coaching almost every sport and overseeing the construction of Carlisle Gymnasium, one of the oldest buildings on campus. Under his guidance, UNM teams were brought into the new Border Conference. He also helped organize the New Mexico High School Athletic Association.

Johnson became Chair of the Department of Physical Education from 1926 to 1935. Remaining true to his early education, Johnson also formed a drama club on campus and helped start the Albuquerque Little Theater. During World War II, he served stateside as a major. Johnson retired from UNM in 1959. In 1986, he was inducted into the UNM Athletics Hall of Honor.[258] He died in 1989 at the age of 97.[259]

The open field between the dormitories and Johnson Center is referred to as Johnson Field since it is next to Johnson Center. It was part of the first golf course that stretched from the corner of Girard and Central into what is now the North Campus. As buildings intruded on the course, the University moved it to the North Campus, leaving the open space, known as Johnson Field, available for intramural games, kite flying, Frisbee throwing, and other activities. Lights have been installed to allow more night use of the facilities.

Lobo Statue

Fig. 84. Landscaping – Sculpture – Lobo Statue by John Tatschl, 1965 (Center for Southwest Research, UNM Libraries).[260]

Fig. 85. Landscaping – Sculptures – Lobo Statue at Stanford Entrance, circa 1950s (Photograph by Harvey Caplin, Center for Southwest Research, UNM Libraries).[261]

The famous Lobo statue by sculptor John Tatschl stands on the south side of Johnson Center.[262] The adoption of the lobo, the Mexican gray wolf, as the UNM mascot came in 1920 shortly after Roy Johnson arrived to create the athletic department. According to Bud Davis' history of UNM, *Miracle on the Mesa*, using the lobo as the mascot was suggested by George S. Bryan, editor of the *UNM Weekly* and manager of the football team. However, as late as 1939 in *Pueblo on the Mesa* by Dorothy Hughes, the lobo was still only mentioned in the context of the student newspaper. Van Dorn Hooker, University Architect Emeritus, remembered:

In June 1947 when my new bride and I were on our honeymoon and were staying in Albuquerque trying to get hotel accommodations in Santa Fe, one day we took the city bus up the hill to the campus. We got off at the Terrace Boulevard stop and as we walked up the deserted campus, through a window I saw this fellow working on the lobo statue in the basement of what is now called the Art Annex, so we went in to ask directions. John Tatschl, the first person I ever met on the UNM campus, had been commissioned to do the lobo sculpture and was working on it that day. John told us a lot about the University and his work and gave us directions to the student union where we could get a cup of coffee. It was a very pleasant introduction to the University.

For an immobile object, the lobo sculpture has been moved around quite a bit. The sculpture, which was commissioned by the Inter-Fraternity Council and completed in 1947, was first erected in front of the old stadium building and included a bronze plaque, which reads:

> Dedicated to those students of the University of New Mexico who gave their lives in World War I and World War II. This edifice was erected by the fraternities and sororities of UNM. John Tatschl, Sculptor.

With the completion of Johnson Gymnasium, the sculpture, which features a standing Mexican wolf leaning forward, fur raised, and mouth open,[263] in a post World War II Streamline Moderne style, was moved during a howling windstorm by the Physical Plant Department to the west side of the gym. Later, it was moved to the south side of the gym so that it faced the entrance to the campus at Stanford. Additions were made to the gym in 1987-88, and the sculpture was moved again. When an access road to the new parking structure was installed, the "Lobo" got a new base and was moved to its present location at the corner of Stanford and Redondo Drive. Another lobo statue by Tatschl recognizing the University's mascot is the Lobo Head located at Hodgin Hall.[264] Tatschl was born in Austria in 1906. He came to UNM in 1946, where he had a long career as a professor of art. Several of his other works are displayed on the UNM campus, such as "History of Writing."[265] John Tatschl died in 1982.[266]

"Spirit Of The Lobos"

In addition to the two lobo sculptures by Tatschl and the one in Tight Grove by Middleton, lobo sculptures have been placed around the University as part of the "Spirit of the Lobos" fundraising campaign by the UNM Athletics Department. As of 2014, a seated lobo sculpture, for example, sits on a rock by Johnson Gymnasium, a pair of lobos are located at the President's House, and others can be found at Zimmerman Library, the Duck Pond, Scholes Hall, and the "Pit."[267]

Vivian H. Heyward Exercise Physiology Teaching Laboratory

Within Johnson Center is the Vivian H. Heyward Exercise Physiology Teaching Laboratory. In his letter recommending that a teaching laboratory be named for Vivian H. Heyward, David Scott, Chair of Health, Exercise and Sports Sciences, wrote: "Professor Emeritus Vivian H. Heyward has rendered extraordinary service to UNM. She is recognized by her peers at the University and throughout institutions of higher learning in the U.S. and abroad with exceptional distinction for her research and writings."

Vivian Heyward developed several degree programs at UNM relating to exercise science and wrote many books and articles on the subject. Heyward also revised the M.S. and Ph.D. degree programs in the Exercise Science Program. A textbook she wrote on the subject has been translated into six languages.

Heyward received many awards, including distinguished alumni awards from the University of Illinois and SUNY-Cortland, and several awards from related societies and organizations, such as Sigma Xi. In 1979, she received the UNM Outstanding Teacher Award. In 1980, she was listed as an Outstanding Young Woman in America. In 1993, she received the UNM Alumni Association Faculty Recognition Award. Howard retired from UNM in 2000 as a Regents Professor Emeritus of Exercise Science. Since retiring, she has remained active.[268]

Seidler Natatorium

Fig. 86. Johnson Center – Interior - Seidler Natatorium, circa 2000 (Center for Southwest Research, UNM Libraries).[269]

Named for Armand H. Seidler, the natatorium was added to Johnson Gymnasium in 1972 and includes an Olympic-size pool, supplanting the smaller swimming pool constructed with the original building. Armand H. Seidler graduated from the University of Illinois where he received a master's and doctorate. He was a coach and athletic director in high schools in Iowa and Illinois before returning to the University of Illinois as an assistant professor from 1947 to 1955. In 1955, he took the position of Director of the Department of Health and Physical Education at Highlands University.

Seidler came to UNM in 1958, serving as Chair of the Department of Physical Education for Men from 1958 to 1960 and then as Chair of the Department of Health and Physical Education and Recreation for Men from 1960 to 1963. He has been credited with inventing a new method of bayonet training using pugil sticks, which was adopted by the Marine Corps and is generally acknowledged as superior to the earlier methods taught by the armed forces. Seidler retired in 1990 and passed away in 2017 at age 97.[270]

JONSON GALLERY

Fig. 87. Jonson Gallery – Looking Southeast, circa 1970s (Photograph by Tyler Dingee, Center for Southwest Research, UNM Libraries).[271]

Jonson Gallery[272] was the first art gallery on campus and provided a display gallery, studio space, and living quarters for Raymond Jonson and his family. Constructed with funds given by Mr. and Mrs. Frank Rand Jr. and Miss Amelia White of Santa Fe, it was with the understanding that the building would become University property when Jonson and his wife died. Jonson Gallery was thus the second building at UNM funded entirely through private money, the first being Sara Raynolds Hall. The living quarters have been remodeled and now house the Robert Wood Johnson Foundation (no known relation to Raymond Jonson). The original gallery is located on the lower level.

Raymond Jonson was born on July 18, 1891, on an Iowa farm to Swedish immigrant parents. The family changed their name from Jonsson to Johnson, though Raymond later changed it to Jonson. Jonson's father was a minister, and constant moves make it difficult to recount Jonson's early education. At age seventeen, he enrolled in the Portland Art Museum School in Oregon to pursue his dream of being an artist. In 1910, the family moved to Chicago and Jonson entered the Chicago Academy of Fine Arts where he began producing oil paintings. For several years, he created stage designs and taught at the Academy. In 1922, he spent four months in Santa Fe. After exhibiting around the country, he returned to live in Santa Fe in 1924. Jonson joined eight other New Mexico artists to form the well-known "Transcendental Painting Group."[273]

Jonson began teaching at UNM in 1949 and opened the Jonson Gallery in 1950. Although he retired from teaching in 1954, he remained the Director of the gallery. In 1974, the University conferred on him an honorary Doctor of Humane Letters[274] and stated, "… his life and works are a celebration of the human spirit, a triumphant assertion of the power of contemporary ideas in art." Jonson continued to paint, exhibit, and win honors for his work until he died in 1982.

The Robert Wood Johnson Foundation

The Robert Wood Johnson Foundation now occupies the former living quarters within the same building as the Jonson Gallery. Robert Wood Johnson (no known relation to Raymond Jonson) founded the Johnson & Johnson Company. Johnson was a politician, writer, sailor, pilot, activist and philanthropist. During World War II, he was appointed Brigadier General by President Roosevelt and chaired the Smaller War Plants Commission, became Vice Chair of the War Production Board and was in charge of the New York Ordinance District. After the war, Johnson established the Robert Wood Johnson Foundation in an effort to improve the quality of health care delivery and funding in the United States. The Foundation provides significant funding to UNM and other schools to aid medical education and the teaching of hospital administration.

LOGAN HALL[275]

Fig. 88. Logan Hall – Psychology – Looking Southwest, 1972 (Center for Southwest Research, UNM Libraries).[276]

Shortly after this building was completed, it was named for Professor Frank Anderson Logan. Logan, born on July 22, 1924, in Palaka, Florida, enrolled at the College of William and Mary in 1941, but transferred to the University of Iowa. He served three years in the military during World War II and then returned to Iowa, receiving his bachelor's, master's and doctorate by 1951. Learning theory became his specialty in the field of psychology, a specialization that developed international recognition.

Logan taught at Yale University from 1951 to 1964 before coming to UNM. While at UNM, he became the Chair of the Psychology Department. He developed a master's program focused on the experimental psychology of learning. Logan taught the basic introductory course in psychology at UNM, which was the most popular single course on campus, attracting 1,800 students. By 1970, Logan had initiated a strong research department, which continues today. He authored many books and articles that were influential in the area of learning motivation research. He is listed as one of the top five learning theorists in contemporary psychology. Logan received many professional honors, serving as a charter member and member of the governing council of the American Psychology Association (APA) and was elected President of the APA's Division of Experimental Psychology. He chaired the governing board of the Psychonomics Society and was President of the Southwestern Psychological Association. Logan gave the APA Annual Research Lecture in 1974, entitled "Learning Theory and Higher Education." That same year, he gave the UNM Research Lecture. Logan died in Albuquerque on November 18, 2004.[277]

MARRON HALL[278]

Fig. 89. Marron Hall – Looking across Redondo Road, 1998 (Photograph by Van Dorn Hooker, Center for Southwest Research, UNM Libraries).[279]

Marron Hall, which was completed in 1941, was built on the east side of old Hokona Hall and named for Frances Halloran Marron. Frances Halloran Marron was born in Old Town Albuquerque in 1881 and graduated from UNM in 1901. She married Owen N. Marron, a prominent businessman who became the mayor of Albuquerque. Francis Halloran Marron served from 1933 to 1935 as one of the first women on the UNM Board of Regents and was very active in the UNM Alumni Association.[280] The architectural history of what remains of the complex of women's residence halls is hard to come by. The original north-south wing of the original Hokona Hall[281] was combined with another wing that was added to the south side of the area, leaving architectural remnants dating to 1941. In 1966, the north hall was demolished to make way for the Loren Potter Wing addition to Castetter Hall and the building that is left has been used for offices for many years, including for the *Daily Lobo* student newspaper.

MESA VISTA HALL I[282]

Mesa Vista Hall I was built as a cooperative men's dormitory known as the Co-Op Dormitory. This building is the only adobe structure on the UNM campus. It was designed by John Gaw Meem in the Pueblo Style[283] and built by the Physical Plant Department in 1941. After World War II, the building became a student infirmary and was used as such until the present Student Health Center was completed in 1968. It is now the Naval Sciences Building (see discussion under "Naval Sciences Building").[284]

Mesa Vista Hall[285]

Fig. 90. Mesa Vista Hall – Exterior – Looking East from Cornell Mall, circa 1990s (Center for Southwest Research, UNM Libraries).[286]

The present Mesa Vista Hall was originally called the "400-Man Dormitory" or "New Dorm," until President Popejoy demanded it be named something else.[287] "Mesa Vista" was decided on and made the official name. In the early 1970s, the University converted the building for use as office space.

The John W. "Wolfie" Smeltzer Garden

Fig. 91. The John W. Smeltzer Garden (Source unknown).

John "Wolfie" Smeltzer was an alumnus of UNM who died in Barcelona, Spain, on June 13, 2008, at the age of 24. A Chicago native, he graduated from Albuquerque's Highland High School and enrolled at UNM. While travelling through Spain to attend the Graduate Institute of International Development Studies in Geneva, Smeltzer and a group of students were climbing the Mountain of Steps in the Olympic Village when he suffered a massive heart attack.[288] An unsigned tribute reads:

A memorial is dedicated to celebrate someone's life and contributions to the community where the memorial is placed. There is no memory more deserving than that of John W. Smeltzer. John was a dedicated student deceased just weeks after receiving his Bachelor of Arts degree in Political Science, French, Spanish and European Studies with a minor in Economics at the University of New Mexico. John was an incredible and passionate student, whose desire to learn was fueled [by] ambitious goals of making a real difference in the world.

John was the best and brightest UNM had to offer to the world. He would leave UNM with a generous scholarship to pursue his graduate studies at the Graduate Institute of International Studies in Geneva, Switzerland. At UNM he held more extracurricular memberships than even the most outstanding students he served with.

Listed on the memorial are ten organizations in which Smeltzer served as an officer, including the UNM World Affairs Delegation, the UNM Honor Student Advisory Council, the Golden Key International Honor Society and the Lambda Iota Tau Literature Honor Society. He was also awarded a Fulbright Scholarship for studies in Canada in 2008, received the Lena Clauve Outstanding Senior Award in 2007, the University Honors Outstanding Student Award, and was published in UNM Student's Best Essays.

When the proposal to create a garden in memory of John Smeltzer was to go to the Board of Regents, several letters were offered in support. For example, Steven I. Bishop, Assistant Professor of French and Director of European Studies wrote in support of the World Affairs Delegation's desire to plant a tree in Smeltzer's memory:

> In my ten years here at UNM, I have never encountered a student who led a more full and successful academic career and who at the same time participated in the establishment, growth, and flourishing of multiple organizations and activities on campus and who still found the time, generosity, and good humor to touch so many other people's lives in a consistently positive manner. He was quite literally a student who exemplified everything that the university would like to see it its graduates. John was the best and brightest UNM had to offer the world.

Ellen Grigsby of the Department of Political Science wrote:

> I have taught at UNM for eighteen years and I have known no one – student, faculty, staff or community supporter – who cared more about UNM or who represented UNM's best qualities as completely as John. He was intelligent, hard working, talented, skilled, high-energy, open to the world but deeply grounded, ambitious but also welcoming and hospitable.

A memorial service was held in the Student Union Ballroom where hundreds packed the room. A desert willow was planted in John Smelter's memory in the small flower garden named for him on the west side of one of the patios at Mesa Vista Hall.

———

MITCHELL HALL (CLASSROOM BUILDING)[289]

Fig. 92. Mitchell Hall – Exterior – Snowfall, 1997 (Center for Southwest Research, UNM Libraries).[290]

Mitchell Hall, first known as the Classroom Building, was dedicated on September 9, 1951, and named for Lynn Boal Mitchell. A small handout printed for attendees had the following description of the building:

> Mitchell Hall is the first building on campus to be designed exclusively for classroom teaching. The building houses no offices, and provides no space for laboratories or specialized workshops. The capacity of the building at a single hour is 1,900 students.

In 2010, extensive remodeling on the building was completed, incorporating digital technology in every classroom and establishing a common study area for students.

Lynn Boal Mitchell, a graduate of Cornell University, came to UNM in 1912 to teach Latin and Greek, and soon the students were calling him "The Old Roman." Mitchell became the administrative assistant to President David Ross Boyd. In an effort to improve "Town and Gown" relations, Boyd placed Mitchell in charge of University affairs locally, while he set out to improve statewide relations. Mitchell served as the University Registrar from 1917 to 1919, when he became Dean of the College of Arts, Philosophy and Science, in which capacity he served until 1932. Mitchell was President of the Foreign Language Section of the New Mexico Education Association. He taught until his retirement in 1950. The handout provided at the dedication ceremony added:

> At the suggestion of a committee of the Faculty, the Regents of the University have named this building Mitchell Hall in grateful appreciation of the thirty-eight years of devoted service of Lynn Boal Mitchell, Professor Emeritus of Classics. Through the years from 1912 until his retirement in 1950, Dr. Mitchell served the University in many administrative capacities. His insistence on high standards of scholarship was matched by teaching of a quality, which inspired scholars. His wise and kindly counsel was a source of strength and guidance for his colleagues and for generations of students.

Mitchell also established the first University Golf Course. With the help of Professor Asa Weese, Mitchell cleared and leveled land about where the Anthropology Building now stands to create a short golf course using sand and gravel for the greens and fairways and tin cans for the holes. This early effort prompted the establishment of the Albuquerque Country Club and the Country Club Addition in the area west of University Boulevard.[291]

NAVAL SCIENCES BUILDING[292]

Fig. 93. Naval Sciences Building – Looking Southeast across Dirt Lot, 1941 (Center for Southwest Research, UNM Libraries).[293]

The Naval Sciences Building, constructed by the Physical Plant Department in 1941, was originally named Mesa Vista Hall, a men's dormitory and later a student infirmary. Today, the building houses the Department of Naval Science and Navy Reserve Officers Training Corps (ROTC).

The Hank Willis Library

Fig. 94. Hank Willis Plaque (Photograph by Suzanne Mortier, UNM Landscape Architect, 2013).

The plaque inscription reads:

> This library is dedicated to CDR Henry M. "Hank" Willis, USNR (Ret.), Class of '45, whose commitment contributed to the preservation of the NROTC Unit at UNM.

The Hank Willis Library in the Naval Sciences Building was named for Henry McDonald "Hank" Willis, who retired from the U.S. Naval Reserves in 1972 as Commander of the Naval Reserves in New Mexico. Willis was born in Fayetteville, Tennessee, in 1925 and died in Albuquerque on March 29, 2009. After enlisting in the U.S. Navy at the start of World War II, he wound up at UNM, where he remained until transferred to the Pacific Theater in 1945. After the war he enrolled at New Mexico State University, graduating in business administration. Willis was employed at Sandia Laboratories for 36 years, retiring in 1986. When the Navy announced the closing of the UNM Naval ROTC Unit in 1991, Willis was instrumental in efforts to retain the program.[294]

Hank Willis was involved in many civic and charitable organizations including the UNM Alumni Association, the UNM Naval ROTC Alumni Association, the YMCA, the United Way, the New Mexico Heart Foundation, and the UNM Presidential Scholarship program. He was President of the Albuquerque Public Schools Board of Education for six years and a member of the Hearing Committee for the New Mexico Supreme Court Discipline Board.

NORTHROP HALL (GEOLOGY)[295]

Fig. 95. Geology - Northrup Hall – Looking across Yale Boulevard, 1953 (Center for Southwest Research, UNM Libraries).[296]

Northrop Hall was completed in 1953 after several delays in receiving structural steel during the Korean War. The exterior of the building is virtually unchanged except for a third floor addition over the north wing in 1972. The building was designed by Edward Holien to house the Department of Geology, now called the Department of Earth and Planetary Sciences, and the second and third floors were rented to the U.S. Department of the Interior Geological Survey and the U.S.D.A. Soil Conservation Service. The Institute of Meteoritics, founded by Lincoln LaPaz, opened the Meteorite Museum in 1974 in Northrup Hall. The Meteorite Museum features an exhibit of meteorites, including one of the largest stony meteorites in the world, and samples collected from space missions.[297]

In 1969, the Regents named the building for Professor Stuart Alvord Northrop. Northrop was born in Danbury, Connecticut, on March 14, 1904, and attended Robert College in Istanbul, Turkey, before obtaining his bachelor's and doctorate from Yale University. He came to UNM in 1928 and became first the acting and then the permanent Chair of the Department of Geology, a position he held until 1961. While Chair, he established the Department's master's and doctoral degree programs and created the Geology Museum. After serving as Dean of the Graduate School for one year from 1961 to 1962, Northrup returned to the Geology Department as a research professor until he retired in 1969.

Northrop was an authority on paleontology, New Mexico minerals, and its earthquake history. He wrote several books and articles including *Turquoise* (1973) published by UNM Press. He also co-authored *Minerals of New Mexico* and *Bibliography of New Mexico Paleontology*. In 1964, he wrote *UNM's Contribution in Geology 1892-1964*. Northrop gave the UNM Annual Research Lecture in 1961 with the topic *New Mexico's Fossil Record*. Northrop died in Albuquerque in 1994 at the age of 89.[298]

The Silver Family Geology Museum[299]

The Silver Family Geology Museum was named in honor of the contributions of the Silver family, beginning with those of Caswell "Cas" Silver,[300] who received his B.S. from UNM in 1940 and his master's degree in 1946. Born in New York City in 1916 and raised in Waterbury, Connecticut, Silver began his college education at the University of Connecticut in 1934. Ongoing problems with asthma caused him to move west to New Mexico. He entered the UNM geology program in 1936. In 1942, he joined the Photo Interpretation Branch of the U.S. Navy, serving until 1945. By 1949, Silver began working as an independent oil and gas exploration consultant in Albuquerque. He moved his family to Denver in 1959 and purchased a controlling interest in Sundance

Oil Company. Silver became President of the company and over the course of 24 years built it into a model independent exploration company. Sundance acquired substantial holdings in Colorado, Nebraska, and Alberta, Canada. When Sundance Oil Company was sold, Silver established a privately held exploration company named The Argentia Corporation headquartered in Colorado.

Silver, a Fellow in the Geological Society of America and its Secretary in 1956, was also a member of the Society of Economic Geologists and the American Association of Petroleum Geologists. He wrote several articles and books on petroleum geology including *Geology of Caballo Mountain* in 1952 and *Entrapment of Petroleum in Isolated Porous Bodies* in 1973.

The Caswell Silver Foundation, started in 1981, has funded many projects in UNM's Department of Earth and Planetary Sciences, including graduate fellowships and an endowed chair that is filled for one or two years by an internationally known earth scientist. The Foundation also provides funds to invite distinguished earth scientists to present talks and interact with faculty and students, allow students to travel to professional meetings, and recognize faculty who have distinguished themselves.

Caswell Silver received an honorary Doctor of Science from UNM in 1981.[301] He died in Santa Fe, N.M., on October 18, 1988. The Foundation continues under the guidance of Silver's brother Leon and a distinguished Board of Directors. Silver also contributed to the restoration of Hodgin Hall, particularly its Irma Bobo Room, named in honor of Irma Bobo, an Albuquerque elementary school teacher and Caswell Silver's former landlady.[302] (For more information on the Irma Bobo Room, see section on Hodgin Hall.)

ORTEGA HALL II[303]

Fig. 96. Ortega Hall and the Center of the Universe, 1998 (Photograph by Terry Gugliotta, Center for Southwest Research, UNM Libraries).[304]

Ortega Hall (also known as Ortega Hall II)[305] was named for Joaquin Ortega. It forms the west wall of Smith Plaza. The building is mostly devoted to the teaching of foreign languages with classrooms, faculty offices and audio-visual laboratories. The first building named for Joaquin Ortega, the remodeled dining hall, is now called Bandelier East.[306]

Professor Joaquin Ortega was born in 1892 in the lovely hill town of Ronda, Spain, and died there on August 23, 1955. From 1909 to 1915, Ortega worked as a journalist serving as correspondent for Argentinian newspapers. He studied economics and in 1915 received a government scholarship to study at the University of Michigan. Transferring to the University of Wisconsin, Ortega received a master's degree in 1917. From 1917 to 1930, he did research in the United States and in the Historical Archives of the National Library of Spain. He became a U.S. citizen in 1936. During this time, Ortega taught Spanish and Portuguese at the University of Wisconsin until coming to UNM in 1941. Ortega served at UNM for seven years as Director of the School of Inter-American Affairs and from 1948 to 1951 as editor of the *New Mexico Quarterly*. Ill health forced his retirement from active duty in 1954. He died in Ronda, Spain, on August 25, 1955.

Ortega was deeply involved in many civic affairs, wrote many articles and was recognized as an outstanding teacher, researcher, and person. UNM awarded him an honorary Doctor of Literature in 1941.[307]

The commemorative citation noted:

> Joaquin Ortega, native of Spain, distinguished American citizen and scholar, contributor to literary journals, founder and dynamic leader of a progressive department of Spanish and Portuguese in a great American university, literary critic, profound student and interpreter of the life and thought of all the Americas, and pioneer in fundamental planning for the advancement of the spiritual and cultural solidarity of the western hemisphere….

The Robert Manly Duncan Reading Room

Within Ortega Hall is the Robert Duncan Reading Room.[308] Robert Manly Duncan[309] was born in Estelline, Texas, in 1903 and grew up in New Mexico, graduating from Farmington High School. He graduated from Oberlin College in 1926 and received his doctorate from the University of Wisconsin in 1936. Soon after, he joined the UNM faculty and spent his entire professional life at UNM, retiring in 1969. He served as Acting Chair of the Department of Modern and Classical Languages (M&CL) during World War II while the then current Chair, Francis M. Kercheville, served in the armed forces. Duncan chaired the Department from 1952 to 1964. Dick Gerdes wrote in his history of the Department for the UNM Centennial History:

> ….the Duncan years saw M&CL move to new quarters on campus, strengthen its teaching capabilities with new language laboratory systems, give greater importance to research and publication, tap federal granting agencies for the development of important teaching training programs and new graduate study programs, and solidify the dominance and leadership of the Spanish faculty vis-à-vis the other languages.

Duncan chaired the Language Section of the American Association of Teachers of Spanish and Portuguese and in 1961 became its president. He was President of the Rocky Mountain Modern Language Association, Secretary of the Phonetics Section of the Modern Language Association and the UNM Chapter of the New Mexico Education Association. He was noted for playing an important role in establishing the New Mexico Public Employees Retirement Act. Duncan died in 1998.

PARSONS HALL and PARSONS GROVE

Fig. 97. Parsons Hall, 1928 (Center for Southwest Research, UNM Libraries).[310]

Parsons Hall was designed to accommodate the Biology Department.[311] The Board of Regents entered into a contract for construction in November 1927, naming the building for Josephine S. Parsons at that time. A grove of trees, also named for Josephine Parsons, was planted at the northwest corner of Central Avenue and Yale Boulevard (discussed under Hodgin Hall). After a new biology building was built in 1952, Parsons Hall became the home of the fledgling Department of Architecture.

Architecture moved out in the early 1960s and the building was used by the Art Department in conjunction with the adjacent Crafts Annex. When it became necessary to build the Centennial Library and Electrical and Computer Engineering Center in 1984, Parsons Hall was demolished. A plaque was placed near the original location of the building with information about the building and Parsons.

"Miss Josie," as students fondly called her, came to UNM in 1893 or 1894 to take over the Commercial Department. She taught stenography, typing, bookkeeping, and mathematics. From 1909 to 1911, she held the position of Faculty Secretary and in 1912 she was made Secretary of the University and Faculty, Associate Professor of Modern Languages, and University Registrar. Parsons was a professor of Romance languages from 1916 to 1919 when she became the Financial Secretary of the University, holding that position until she died on June 21, 1927.

Remembrance Wakes was a ceremony held yearly in the early days of UNM to "… recognize various persons no longer living – regents and administrative officers and instructors who contributed to the growth, success, and prestige of UNM." The University during the 1941 ceremony eulogized Parsons and President James F. Zimmerman said of her, "The University task was always first in her mind, so completely was her interest and her life dedicated to this institution."

THE JOHN AND JUNE PEROVICH BUSINESS CENTER

Fig. 98. John and June Perovich Business Center (Source unknown).

The John and June Perovich Business Center stands on the southeast corner of Lomas and University Boulevards. Many of UNM's business functions are housed in the Center. In 2009, it was named for John Perovich, former Vice President and later the twelfth President of UNM and his wife June. John Perovich, appointed Interim President in 1982 for one year, reluctantly agreed to serve two more years while the Board of Regents sought a new president. The following is from William E. Davis' history of UNM, *Miracle on the Mesa*:[312]

> Perovich was born near Raton [in Van Houten] in 1924. Like his mentor, Tom Popejoy, he grew up in that small coal mining community and set his sights on attending the University of New Mexico. He entered UNM in 1942. During World War II, he served with the Army Air Force as a navigator. Following the war, Perovich married his hometown sweetheart, June Brewer. He also returned to his studies at UNM on the GI Bill, graduating in 1948 with a bachelor's degree in business. A year later he earned a master's in business administration while also working in the University's business office. Perovich rapidly rose through the ranks as administrative assistant to the comptroller, chief financial officer, and finally, vice president for business and finance. Fifty-eight years old at the time of his appointment, Perovich had served under three UNM presidents, Popejoy, Heady, and Davis. He was often credited with much of the University's success with the legislature and praised for his outstanding management of the institution's fiscal affairs, which included real-estate transactions, bond issues for capital improvements, contracts and grants, and creation and management of foundations and complex service centers like the UNM medical facilities. Regarded as a person of 'unquestionable integrity and commitment to the well being of UNM,' Perovich was warmly hailed from all quarters. Described as modest and low-keyed, Perovich was a task-oriented administrator and like Tom Popejoy was respected as a man who could get things done.

Perovich received many awards, including an honorary Doctor of Law from Dickinson College, the UNM Regents Meritorious Service Medal in 1979,[313] the Fergusson Award in 1999, the Lobo Award in 2002,[314] and an honorary Doctor of Humane Letters in 2006.[315] He served as Director and President of the Sandia and Woodward Foundations, Director of the UNM Foundation, and Trustee of the Hibben Charitable Trust, and was a commissioner to the Western Interstate Commission for Higher Education (WICHE). He also served as Director of the New Mexico Medical Foundation and the Albuquerque YMCA and as a member of countless other charitable and philanthropic organizations. John Perovich retired in 1985. June Perovich died March 20, 2019.

SARA RAYNOLDS HALL[316]

Fig. 99. Sara Raynolds Hall – Exterior – Looking North, 1921 (Center for Southwest Research, UNM Libraries).[317]

As early as 1919, concern was voiced by citizens about the lack of adequate facilities for teaching home economics. President David Spence Hill appointed a committee consisting of George Kaseman, A.B. McMillin, Frank Hubbell, Horace B. Hening, and M.L. Fox to plan a new building. Construction money came from private contributions. The largest donation, $5,000, was given by Joshua Raynolds, a local banker. In return, President Hill agreed to name the building for Raynolds's mother, Sara Raynolds.

The building was dedicated, "To the Women and Children of New Mexico "on Mother's Day, May 6, 1921, in a ceremony open to the public and honoring all of the 100 or so donors. The Albuquerque Indian School band played and several people made speeches. Mrs. Rupert F. Apslund, member of the Board of Regents, accepted keys to the building. Refreshments were served and one source says a baseball game was played between teams of the Kiwanis and Rotary clubs.

Until the completion of the College of Education in 1963, the Home Economics program occupied the building, after which Sara Raynolds Hall became a classroom facility. The building was remodeled again in 1988, although the exterior remained unchanged. Sara Raynolds Hall is listed on the National Register of Historic Places and the N.M. State Register of Cultural Properties.[318]

REGENER HALL[319]

Fig. 100. Physics Lab and Lecture Hall - Regener Hall - Exterior, 1972 (Center for Southwest Research, UNM Libraries).[320]

Regener Hall, an undergraduate physics teaching facility, was proposed to be located between Logan Hall and Farris Engineering Center. The architect, Jesse Pacheco, decided to build the building below grade with a walking deck on top. The design left an open space between the two large buildings, preventing the area from seeming too crowded. In 1986, a food facility for faculty, staff and students was added to the deck.

Regener Hall contains laboratories and classrooms as well as one large lecture hall. There are two sculptures on the deck, *Static Motion* and *Ripple*, by artist John Keyser. The former sculpture was produced after Keyser won a competition, and the latter has been on extended loan from the sculptor. Both works are made from various types of steel and include painted elements.

Victor Regener, for whom the Regents named the building, was born in Berlin, Germany, in 1913. Earning his doctorate in engineering physics from the Institute for Technology in Stuttgart in 1938, he immediately left Germany to accept a research position at the University of Padua. He then moved to the United States, taking a position at the University of Chicago. In 1946, he was hired as an associate professor at UNM. The following year, he became Chair of the Physics Department. When, in 1963, the Department was reorganized and renamed to include Astronomy, he continued as Chair until he retired in 1979.

Regener presented the UNM Research Lecture in 1960 with the subject, "Science in Space." His research covered a number of interests including the study of cosmic rays. He also built cosmic ray detection devices, which he installed in a Bolivian mine, a mine near Socorro, and a cave in the Sandia Mountains. Regener built Capilla Peak Observatory in the Manzano Mountains and there did astronomical studies including studies of ozone in the atmosphere. When he retired from UNM, he built his own laboratory in the Journal Center.

In 1979, Regener received the UNM Board of Regents' Meritorious Service Medal.[321] Tony Hillerman wrote this dedication:

> As a scientist, Victor Regener brought this university international respect. As a brilliant teacher, he endowed a legion of his students with a love of the demanding discipline of physics. As a leader of faculty thought, he improved a thousand faculty debates with his keen intelligence, his humanism, and his good-natured wit. For 33 years, he has given this community a model of what a university professor should be.

Victor Regener died on January 20, 2006, at age 92.[322]

SCHOLES HALL

Fig. 101. Scholes Hall, 1939 (Center for Southwest Research, UNM Libraries).[323]

The building, later named for France Vinton Scholes, was the first building at UNM designed by John Gaw Meem. It started as a multipurpose facility called the Administration-Classroom Building, housing the administration, the Anthropology Department and its museum, classrooms and laboratories, the telephone operators, and other administrative functions. The building was financed in part by Public Works Administration funds that were matched with state funds. Meem's design was based on early mission church architecture, particularly the San Esteban del Rey Church at Acoma that Meem had helped restore in the 1920s. The building was placed on the State Register of Historic Places on June 20, 1975, and on the National Register of Historic Places on September 22, 1988.

The building was completed in 1936, and in more than 70 years of its existence, it has seen many changes to its interior as occupants and functions have changed. Today, it is fully dedicated to the University's top administration. Until recently, the exterior had remained unchanged. However, in 2001, the blue door and window trim color and the naturally colored beams and corbels selected by Meem were painted a dark brown.

France Vinton Scholes, born in Bradford, Illinois, on January 26, 1897, served in a cavalry unit in World War I. Following the war, he received his B.A. and M.A. from Harvard University in 1921. As happened to other World War I veterans such as John Gaw Meem, Scholes developed tuberculosis and moved to New Mexico in 1921 for the curative climate.

In 1925, Scholes joined the UNM faculty to teach history part time for a salary of $45 per month. Scholes began to regain his health and became a full time professor, conducting invaluable research on Latin American history. With Eleanor Adams, he wrote extensively on the subject. As the University Research Lecturer in 1957, Scholes examined the life of Hernando Cortez. Scholes was appointed Academic Vice President in 1949 and served as such until 1957. Scholes was awarded an honorary Doctor of Humane Letters from UNM in 1972. He retired in 1962 and died in 1979.[324]

President Popejoy wrote about Scholes, "His vision has helped to shape the university and set its standards, his selfless loyalty has ever served the best interests of the institution; his devotion to research has been marked by a warm sharing of its opportunities and deep satisfaction with students and colleagues alike. These, too, are the fruits of scholarship."

Thomas Reaser Roberts Room

Fig. 102. Thomas Reaser Roberts Plaque (Photograph by Suzanne Mortier, UNM Landscape Architect, 2013).

A new meeting room for the Board of Regents was created on the second floor of Scholes Hall sometime during the period 1974 to 1975 and named the Thomas Reaser Roberts Room. Thomas Reaser Roberts, a Los Alamos scientist, was appointed to the Board by Governor Edwin Mechem in 1961 and reappointed by Governor David Cargo in 1967. At the time of his untimely death in 1968, Roberts was President of the Board.[325] Roberts, born in Minneapolis, Minnesota, obtained an A.B. degree in chemistry from Harvard in 1943.

During World War II, he served in the United States Navy until 1946. After the war, he received an M.A. and Ph.D. from the University of Minnesota. Roberts began his tenure at the Los Alamos National Laboratories in 1951 as a low temperature scientist and served as the representative of Los Alamos County in the state legislature from 1957 to 1960.

The commemorative plaque in the room reads:

> The Roberts Room, in recognition of the distinguished
> and dedicated service of Thomas Reaser Roberts
> as Member, Vice President and President
> of the Regents of the University, 1961-1968.

The north wall of the room holds a framed resolution by the Board of Regents expressing "…their deepest sympathy and deep sense of love" to the family of Thomas Roberts, dated March 9, 1968.

After the room was established, Roberts's widow, the former Carol Naus, and their three children donated a large oiled walnut table, a small side-table and chairs made by Max Chaves to honor Roberts' soutstanding service to UNM. The table was so large it had to be partially dismantled to move it into the room. In 2003, the Regents moved their meetings back to the recently renovated Student Union Building. The Roberts Room is used as a general use meeting room for University organizations.

DANE SMITH HALL

Fig. 103. *Dane Smith Hall – Exterior – Cyclist on Path, 2001 (Center for Southwest Research, UNM Libraries).*[326]

Dane Smith Hall,[327] built in 1997, was the first general instruction facility built on the main campus since Mitchell Hall was constructed in 1950. The building has three levels with the lowest level partially below grade. The building includes classrooms, instructional television rooms, and lecture halls. The classrooms were equipped with the latest in teaching equipment and the building can seat up to 2,000 students at one time. A large atrium brings natural light to all floors. The first level includes a food court, copy center, and student lounge. The building is a contemporary adaptation of the Pueblo style. The main entrance is on the east side of the building and offers an inviting appearance to the structure.

Dane Farnsworth Smith, born in Mobile, Alabama, in 1895, graduated from Vanderbilt University in 1917. During World War I, he served with the 114th Field Artillery in the battles of St. Michel and Argonne Forest. After the war, Smith earned M.A. and Ph.D. degrees from Harvard University. He taught at Harvard, DePauw University, Carnegie Institute of Technology, and Texas A&M before coming to UNM in 1934. Smith, an authority on English drama, wrote two books and many articles on the subject. He retired in 1960 and died in 1968. Dane Smith and his wife, Candace, lived in a house on Roma N.E. in Albuquerque, which they gave to the University with the understanding that they could live in the house until their deaths. The site of the house formed part of the footprint of Dane Smith Hall.

The Student Grove

The Student Grove is a small grove that sits on the south side of Dane Smith Hall and commemorates the opening of the building on October 9, 1998. The grove includes a plaque listing the names of those who contributed to establishing the grove.

STUDENT HEALTH CENTER and UNDERGRADUATE STUDIES[328]

Student Health Center[329]

Fig. 104. Student Health Center (Photograph by Suzanne Mortier, UNM Landscape Architect, 2013).

The Student Health Center, located at 300 Cornell N.E., was designed by Holien and Buckley and completed in 1983. The Student Health Service is located on the upper two floors and the University College was located on the lower floor. Subsequently, the University College was relocated to the former Student Services Center building at 400 Cornell N.E.[330] The vacated space now houses the Dudley Wynn Honors Center.

Dudley Wynn Honors Center

Professor Dudley Wynn founded UNM's Honors Program in 1957. Honors courses were first offered in a World War II barracks building. In 1967, the University moved the program to the new east wing of Zimmerman Library. At their meeting on April 12, 1988, the Regents designated the west wing ground floor of the Humanities building as the Dudley Wynn Honors Center.[331] In 2000, the University renovated the ground floor of the Student Health Center to include the Dudley Wynn Honors Center.

Dudley Wynn was born in Cooper, Texas, in 1925. He received a bachelor's degree from the University of Texas and a master's and doctorate from New York University and was a member of Phi Beta Kappa. He taught at the University of Colorado from 1947 until 1953, when he came to UNM. Wynn served as Dean of the College of Arts and Sciences until 1961, when he was appointed to establish the Honors Program, which he headed until 1971.

Wynn was a founder and Chair of the New Mexico Council for the Humanities. He helped found the National Collegiate Honors Council in 1966 and served as its first president. Wynn was also active in the Modern Language Association of America, Common Cause, the New Mexico Symphony, and the American Association of University Professors.

Wynn died in 1989 and his ashes, along with his wife's, are interred under a marker on the patio on the southwest side of Zimmerman Library in the Raul Dominguez Memorial Garden. In an *Albuquerque Tribune* article dated November 17, 1989, V.B. Price wrote:[332]

> New Mexico lost one its greatest citizens this week, Dudley Wynn – beloved for his kindness, cherished for his integrity, and admired for his fierce defense of democratic ideas and compassionate social values – died in Overland, Kansas, at age 85...

For many years, Dudley Wynn gave UNM a gentle but passionate moral gravity, a deep commitment to students, equity and freedom of speech. His presence filled the school with a wonderful enthusiasm for learning and an empowering belief in the intelligence of his students. Dudley always spoke his mind, and never pulled his punches, but somehow he was never cruel, even if his prose was often biting.

Lawrence R. Klausen Memorial Park

Fig. 105. Lawrence R. Klausen Memorial Park (Source unknown).

Fig. 106. Lawrence R. Klausen Memorial Plaque (Photograph by Suzanne Mortier, UNM Landscape Architect, 2013).

Lawrence R. Klausen was a 1971 UNM graduate who died of cancer. Terry Gugliotta, UNM Archivist, supplied the following information in a column called *Ask Ms. Scholes* in a University publication:

> During the early 1970s, People's Parks were springing up around the country – especially at universities. Many universities, including Berkeley, did not permit such parks, but UNM did. The park was developed during the spring and summer of 1971 entirely with volunteer labor by students, the Physical Plant and contributors. Lawrence R. Klausen graduated from the College of Education in January 1971. Together with Stephen I. Wilkes and Gordon Andrews of the Architecture faculty, Klausen shared the total responsibility for carrying out the project, often with little help. Lawrence Klausen died from cancer in January 1972. Some of his friends and coworkers on the park suggested that it be named for him.

At its February 2, 1972 meeting, the Board of Regents approved naming a small park to the south of the University College and Student Health Center for Klausen. The Regents recognized Klausen as one of the proponents of the park and for his diligent efforts in completing the park.[333]

The plaque reads:

> Named in memory of Lawrence R. Klausen
> Class of 1971 whose personal efforts helped
> make this project a reality to be shared by all

STUDENT SERVICES CENTER BUILDING
(UNIVERSITY ADVISEMENT AND ENRICHMENT CENTER)

Fig. 107. Student Services Center – Exterior – Looking North across Courtyard, 1984 (Center for Southwest Research, UNM Libraries).[334]

The Student Services Center building, now known as the University Advisement and Enrichment Center and which also houses the University College, is located at 400 Cornell N.E. to the north of Johnson Gym and northeast of Mesa Vista Hall.

The building was completed in 1984 and initially contained space for most of the student administrative services, including the Registrar, Cashier, Admissions, Records and Registration, University College, various advisement offices, and the Office of the Dean of Students. The idea to locate this facility as near to the areas of student activity as possible led to the creation of a "zaguan," or pedestrian way, through Mesa Vista Hall. In 2007, an Enrollment Management One-Stop Student Services Center was created in Mesa Vista Hall and a new Student Support and Services Center was built on the South Campus.

The Karen Glaser Conference Room

The Karen Glaser Conference Room, located in the former Student Services Center building on the Central Campus, was named for the former Dean of Students who served in that capacity and as Associate Vice President from 1970 until her retirement in 1997. Glaser, from Wichita, Kansas, received her Bachelor of Music degree from Lindenwood College in 1960, and her M.S. in education at Indiana University in 1962. She came to UNM that same year, beginning her career as a personnel coordinator in Hokona Hall. By 1965, she had become Associate Dean of Women and later, Dean of Students. She was Dean of Students from 1972 to 1999.[335] Glasser received the UNM Regents' Meritorious Service Medal in 1996 and the UNM Rodey Award in 2001.[336]

THE NEW MEXICO STUDENT UNION BUILDING[337]

The first Student Union Building (SUB) on the main campus was dedicated in 1937. The Department of Anthropology and the Maxwell Museum now occupy that building. The current Student Union (today's SUB) is also known the New Mexico Student Union. The current SUB was built in 1959 and extensively remodeled in 2003-04.

Esther Thompson Gallery

The Esther Thompson Gallery was a part of the current Student Union Building for many years, beginning in 1984 until the space was converted to other uses when the SUB was remodeled. The gallery was established to honor Esther Thompson, who directed the Student Union for 22 years from 1937 until she retired in 1959. The gallery displayed student works of art and other items of interest to students. Originally from Lebanon, Indiana, Thompson or "Mrs T" as she was called on campus came to Albuquerque in 1924 with her husband James, who was a member of the Department of Biology faculty. In 1960, Mrs. T received the UNM Alumni Association's Lobo Award for her outstanding contributions to UNM.[338]

TAPY HALL[339]

Fig. 108. Engineering – Civil - Tapy Hall – Front Lawn, circa 1950s (Center for Southwest Research, UNM Libraries).[340]

Tapy Hall was planned for the instruction of electrical engineering students who would join the profession in the early 1950s, a profession that was significantly different from what it is today. Edward Holien of the firm of Meem, Zehner, and Holien designed the building. Van Dorn Hooker, Jr., later the University Architect, did working drawings of the building and recalled a lab with a high ceiling at the south end of the building that contained nothing but electrical generators and switchgear. In 1972, former students petitioned the Regents to name the building for former Department Chair and Professor Ralph W. Tapy, which the Regents did.[341] The exterior of the building remained unchanged through the years until it was demolished in 2006 to make way for the Centennial Engineering facility.

Tapy was born on September 17, 1902, in Terre Haute, Indiana, and received two engineering degrees from Rose Polytechnic Institute in 1927 and 1937. He also held a master's and doctorate from Michigan State University. Tapy served as Chair of the Department of Electrical Engineering from 1939 to 1960, when he took a leave of absence to establish an electrical engineering program at the University of Gadjah Mada in Jakarta, Indonesia. Tapy, a consultant to the United States Navy in San Francisco from 1957 to 1970 was also a Fellow in the International Society of Electrical Engineers. Tapy died in 1980.[342]

WOODWARD HALL[343]

Fig. 109. Woodward Hall – Exterior – Walkway, circa 1970s (Center for Southwest Research, UNM Libraries).[344]

Woodward Hall, designed in 1974 to be UNM's largest lecture hall seating several hundred, was equipped with the latest in teaching equipment at the time. On the main level, north side, are two smaller lecture halls. The building was named for Hugh Beistle Woodward and Helen Kisner Woodward, the largest benefactors the University of New Mexico had ever had. Hugh Beistle Woodward was born in Clearfield, Pennsylvania, in 1885, and entered Pennsylvania State University in 1904. He graduated from Dickinson College in Carlisle, Pennsylvania, with a doctoral degree in 1908 and a master's degree and an LL.B. in 1910.

Hugh and Helen met in college and were married in 1911. Helen contracted tuberculosis and was advised to move to a drier climate. Hugh practiced law in Clearfield from 1911 to 1913. He and Helen then moved to Greeley, Colorado, and in 1915 to Clayton, New Mexico, where they ran a cattle ranch and Hugh practiced law until 1929. Elected Lieutenant Governor of New Mexico in 1928, he only served one term before being appointed U. S. Attorney for New Mexico by President Herbert Hoover. The Woodwards then moved to Albuquerque. In 1933, Woodward returned to the practice of law until he retired in 1951.

Woodward stayed involved in many civic organizations through the years. He was elected Director of the Middle Rio Grande Flood Control Authority and served from 1948 to 1961. He also served as a member of the first Albuquerque Planning Commission from 1948 to 1957. Woodward founded and was President of the Southwestern Construction Company, the New Mexico Credit Corporation, and the Southwest Loan Company. He became active nationally in many wildlife and environmental protection organizations. He and his wife received numerous awards and citations for their benevolence both locally and nationally. In 1963, he was awarded an honorary Doctor of Law and Letters from UNM and an honorary Doctor of Laws from Dickinson.[345]

Woodward died in 1960 and the Sandia Foundation became administrator of his large estate. One-half of the income from the foundation was left to his wife, while Dickinson College and UNM shared equally the remaining fifty percent of the income. Upon Helen's death, each school received half of ninety percent of the income. The astute management of the bequest by John Perovich and others has generated millions of dollars in income for both schools.

ZIMMERMAN LIBRARY[346]

Fig. 110. Library - Zimmerman – Exterior – East Side Prior to Additions, circa 1938 (Center for Southwest Research, UNM Libraries).[347]

Zimmerman Library was named for former UNM President James Fulton Zimmerman in 1961.[348] With its tall stack tower and Pueblo Revival architecture, it represents the symbolic heart and soul of the University of New Mexico. John Gaw Meem was commissioned in 1933 to design the library, now the west wing of the present complex. Construction had to wait until 1936 with completion in 1938. The University has made three major additions on the east and south sides of the building. The first addition was completed in 1966, the second in 1975, and the latest addition on the south side, which is mainly underground, in 1993.

In 1938, the main entrance was on the west side of the building and opened into a long lobby with a ceiling. The lobby contained the circulation desk and card catalog files. Across from the lobby was a large reading room. The original building, now known as the West Wing, featured an abundance of handicraft incorporated in the furnishings, the metal light fixtures, corbels, and the carved boards enclosing beams. The West Wing has been maintained much as it was originally, with some improvements to lighting, mechanical systems and flooring. The three additions to Zimmerman Library have provided more stack and study space and computer facilities.

The University Archives, which contain the history of the University, is housed in the Center for Southwest Research located in the West Wing. The Archives are available to the public for research. The Archives contain the papers of the University Presidents, the Regents' minutes and actions, thousands of photographs of people and events, and copies of many articles about the schools and colleges in the University. The Archives are a treasured record of more than 100 years of the growth and development of the University and are used heavily by historians, journalists, and other writers.

In May 2006, a disastrous fire caused much damage in the additions and destroyed books and materials in the basement of the building, but the West Wing suffered only slight smoke damage.

President Zimmerman was born in Glen Allen, Missouri, on September 11, 1887. He received his A.B. and M.A. from Vanderbilt University and became an instructor in economics and sociology there from 1917 to 1919. In 1925, he completed work on a doctoral degree from Columbia University and received offers of positions at Ohio State University and the University of New Mexico. Finding UNM the more interesting of the two, he accepted a one-year contract to teach history and never left, spending the rest of his career here. His diplomatic manner and his commitment to higher education made him the ideal successor in 1927 to President David Hill after only 18 months in New Mexico and at the young age of 39.

Zimmerman led the University through the Depression years to become a larger, more respected institution. Interested in the construction of major buildings, he utilized the resources available in the 1930s, including the Public Works Administration and Works Progress Administration as well as other federal programs. His success with the legislators led to substantial increases in the University operating budget and matching bond funds.

In 1994, Zimmerman Library was declared the Building of the Century by the New Mexico Chapter of the American Institute of Architects. Zimmerman Library was listed on the National Register of Historic Places in 2016. John Gaw Meem said it was the best building he designed in the Pueblo Revival style.

Zimmerman was such a powerful force in the development of the University that former President William E. Davis, in his book *Miracle on the Mesa*, devoted two chapters to his administration. Unfortunately, Zimmerman's health began to fail and he died on October 20, 1944, at age 57, after serving as President for seventeen years.[349]

Zimmerman Field

Fig. 111. Zimmerman Stadium and Zimmerman Library, circa 1960s (Center for Southwest Research, UNM Libraries).[350]

Old Zimmerman Field no longer exists. Until completion of the new football stadium on the South Campus in 1960, Zimmerman Field occupied the large open area south of Zimmerman Library, east of Yale Boulevard over to Cornell Boulevard and down to the water reservoir on the south.

On the west side of the field stood the stadium building with Tatschl's "Lobo" statue in front and bleachers behind. On the east side were more bleachers. Shortly after President Zimmerman died in 1954, the University named the field for him. After 1960, with the field no longer used as a football stadium, the Regents named the library in his name to assure that Zimmerman's huge contributions to the University would not be forgotten.

During its existence, the field hosted track and field events, commencements, sunrise Easter services, and 120 football games.

One of the highlights in the field's existence happened in 1937, when lights were installed for evening football games. People came from all over the city to see the "blaze of lights" as it was described in local newspapers. Van Dorn Hooker, Jr., University Architect Emeritus, recalled: "I remember sitting in the stands on the west side of the Zimmerman Field listening to the speech Robert Kennedy made on his way to California where he was assassinated on June 5, 1968."

The Raul D. Dominguez Memorial Garden/Smith Patio

Fig. 112. Library – Zimmerman – Exterior - Raul D. Dominguez Memorial Garden (Photograph by Robert Reck, Center for Southwest Research, UNM Libraries).[351]

The intimate patio garden on the south side of Zimmerman Library is designed around a fountain that Vice President Sherman E. Smith bought for the University. The fountain came from a mansion located near the Zócalo in Mexico City. It sat in a warehouse on Yale Boulevard S.E. for many years before a site for it could be found on the campus. The "pineapple" on top of the fountain is regularly stolen, and each spring the Physical Plant filled the fountain with blue colored water, which would stain the fountain as well as the flagstone below.

Around 2000, Jim and Rebecca Long gave money to refurbish the garden where they had met while students. New flagstone was laid, the fountain repaired and new benches installed. They saw the effort as a way to honor Rebecca's father, Raul Dominguez, who died in 1999. A community leader, Dominguez was an advocate for educating the underprivileged and instrumental in getting the Head Start program started in New Mexico.

The ashes of Dudley Wynn, founder of the University Honors Program, and his wife are buried under a marker in the planting bed, although the marker is obscured by vegetation.

Clinton P. Anderson Room

Fig. 113. Library – Interior – Zimmerman - Clinton P. Anderson Reading Room, 1985 (Center for Southwest Research, UNM Libraries).[352]

The Clinton P. Anderson Room was named for U.S. Senator Clinton Presba Anderson who gave his collection of more than 7,000 volumes of Western Americana to UNM and 53 large boxes of his papers. The room, part of the Center for Southwest Research, has been enlarged and is used for reading and research. Informally, the room is known as the Anderson Reading Room.

Born in 1895 in Centerville, South Dakota, Anderson came to New Mexico from South Dakota in 1917, suffering from tuberculosis. He was diagnosed when he tried to enlist in World War I. While recuperating, Anderson worked as a reporter for the *Albuquerque Herald* and later formed the Clinton P. Anderson Agency. In 1940, after heading several federal relief agencies during the Great Depression, he was elected to the U.S. House of Representatives. In 1945, President Truman appointed him Secretary of Agriculture. In 1948, he was elected to the U.S. Senate, where he served four full terms before retiring in 1972.[353] After retiring, he moved to Albuquerque and pursued his interest in collecting rare books and historic research materials. As one of the most influential champions of space exploration, he was inducted into the International Space Hall of Fame in 1977.[354]

Senator Anderson led a life of public service to New Mexico and the nation. Beyond his gift of research materials to UNM, he helped the University in many other ways and is not forgotten. He died at home on November 11, 1975.

The Anderson Spruce

Fig. 114. Anderson Spruce (Source unknown).

In March 1973, a 14-foot tall spruce tree was planted near the southwest corner of the northwest wing of Zimmerman Library in honor of Senator Clinton P. Anderson. The bronze plaque on the nearby wall reads:

> In grateful recognition of the many contributions of Senator Clinton P. Anderson to New Mexico and this University, the spruce west of this marker donated by Governor Tom Bolack was planted on March 2, 1973.

Senator Anderson is also commemorated through the Anderson Room in Zimmerman Library.

The Thomas Bell Room

The Thomas Bell Room was named for Thomas Sydney Bell, who was selected in 1906 as New Mexico's first Rhodes Scholar. The room was located on the second level of the original portion of the library and housed the rare book collection in a controlled environment. During a recent remodeling, the room was eliminated, the plaque removed, and the books dispersed into the general collection. However, Bell was a distinguished UNM alumnus who should not be forgotten. Since the closing of the Thomas Bell Room, Thomas Bell is memorialized by the American flag and painted reredos screen donated by William B. Macey and Jean Mullins Macey to the Alumni Memorial Chapel. An article in *The New Mexico Alumnus* noted:

> The class of 1905 was one of the most successful classes ever to graduate from the University. It provided New Mexico with its first Rhodes Scholar. Its scholarship had a wide range, from the classics through history, philosophy and literature. From that class came a teacher, a lawyer, an amateur botanist, a student of Spanish literature and a lumber man whose interests have extended from the top to the bottom of the North American continent. But the record of the class of 1905 was not all written in the world of scholarship and business. It was a completely athletic class, participating in football, baseball, basketball, and track. For you see, Thomas Sidney Bell was the class of 1905. He was not only the entire class, but he was the first student to graduate from the University with a college degree.

When Bell entered Oxford University,[355] he studied law and was a member of the football (soccer) and rowing teams. After completing his studies in England, he taught for a time at the University of Washington Law School and then moved to Los Angeles where he established a successful law practice. Eventually he gave up his law career to enter the lumber business, and his holdings extended from Louisiana to British Columbia and South America. Bell was awarded an honorary Doctor of Law and Letters from UNM in 1956 as a lumberman, botanist, businessman, scholar, and attorney.[356]

Thomas S. Bell lived in Pasadena, California at the time of his death in 1960 at age 80. Bell and his wife willed UNM $475,000, which was the largest bequest to that date. His wife, who had died several years earlier, left an estate of about $90,000 and bequeathed $80,000 to UNM for a scholarship in Mr. Bell's name and $10,000 to the Alumni Chapel. The *UNM Daily Lobo* quoted President Tom Popejoy as saying, "Mr. and Mrs. Bell proved in life and death to be staunch friends of the University."

The Alice S. Clark Room

The Alice S. Clark Room[357] is on the first floor of the library on the north side of the large computer room and east of the Interlibrary Loan Office. The room was named for Alice Clark, who was Associate Dean of the General Library from 1974 to 1987 and for Readers' Services in 1977. She was also a professor of library sciences. Under her leadership, the Library organized its services for all segments of the University population, including special needs faculty, staff, students, and other patrons. The University has dedicated this room for use by disabled individuals. Alice Clark retired around 1987.

The Ford Room

The Ford Motor Company contributed several million dollars to UNM to be used to establish, among other things, an Information Commons, equip a computer training room, and upgrade the library's telecommunication and technology capability.

The Sigmund and Estelle Herzstein Room

The Sigmund and Estelle Herzstein Room, also known as the Latin American Reading Room, houses the University's collection of texts on Latin America and is used extensively by historians and researchers. The commemorative plaque reads:

> The Herzstein Latin American Reading Room was supported by a contribution from Sigmund E. Herzstein Jr. and his wife Barbara Herzstein and is dedicated as a memorial to Mr. Herzstein's parents, Sigmund E. and Estelle B. Herzstein and his grandparents Sigmund and Maud Herzstein who settled in Clayton, New Mexico Territory in 1901 and resided there for fifty years.

Another plaque states that the El Paso Energy Corporation funded the purchase of electronic workstations with internet access, LIBROS terminals to access UNM's library catalog, and CD-ROM workstations. The room was previously named for Alice Clark.

The John Gaw Meem Archive of Southwestern Architecture

A part of the Center for Southwest Research, the John Gaw Meem Archive of Southwestern Architecture is a collection of drawings and papers of southwestern architects and is supported in large part by members of the Meem family. John Gaw Meem, IV, and his partners, Hugo Zehner and Edward O. Holien, were architects for some 26 UNM buildings. Meem himself designed the first seven buildings his firm built prior to WWII and oversaw the design of other buildings later. Meem, whose office was in Santa Fe, is credited with refining the Pueblo Revival style of architecture and some of his best work is illustrated in Scholes Hall and Zimmerman Library.[358] Other firms whose drawings, models and papers are housed in the collection include Harvey Hoshour; Stevens, Mallory, Pearl and Campbell; successors to Ferguson and Stevens; McHugh and Hooker; Bradley P. Kidder and Associates; W.C. Kruger and Associates; and some drawings from Flatow, Moore, Bryan and Fairburn and successors, and many other firms.

John Gaw Meem was one of the many illustrious people who came to New Mexico seeking "the cure." Meem was born on November 17, 1894, in Pelotas, Brazil, to Episcopal missionaries. After an early education in a German preparatory school, he received his bachelor's degree in civil engineering from Virginia Military Institute in 1914. After working for his uncle, James Meem, in New York City, he was called into service as an infantry captain in World War I. While stationed on Long Island, he became seriously ill with influenza and developed tuberculosis. Hearing about the healthy climate of Santa Fe, he came to the Sunmount Sanatorium in 1920.

While at Sunmount, Meem became interested in architecture as a profession. As his health permitted, he studied in Denver at an atelier taught by Burnam Hoyt. When he came back to Santa Fe, he opened an office with Cyrus McCormick in 1924. Meem's early work included several historic preservation projects. He obtained his first project with UNM in 1933, when he was hired to design what is now Zimmerman Library and several other campus buildings funded in part with Public Works Administration/Works Progress Administration money.

Meem's firm was commissioned to design all the University buildings until 1959, at which time other architects were brought in to do commissions. Meem hired Edward O. Holien in 1945 and later made him a partner, turning all of the design work over to him. The firm was very successful, designing hospitals, schools, churches and residents throughout New Mexico. Meem received many awards and honors during his lifetime including an honorary Doctor of Fine Arts from UNM in 1960[359] and a fellowship with the American Institute of Architects.

Meem retired in early 1959 and gave his drawings and papers to UNM, thereby establishing the Meem Archive of Southwestern Architecture.[360] Meem died in 1983 in Santa Fe at age 88.[361] Two biographies of Meem have been written, one by Beatrice Chauvenet and one by Bainbridge Bunting, both titled *John Gaw Meem*.

The Frank Waters Room

The Frank Waters Room is a study and conference room on the first floor of the West Wing of the library and was named for the man who was often called "The Grandfather of Southwest Literature." Frank Waters[362] was born in Colorado Springs, Colorado, in 1902, and attended Colorado College. During World War II, he worked in the Office of Inter-American Affairs and after the war he was an information advisor at Los Alamos National Laboratory.

His work as an author began in the late 1930s and is known worldwide. Waters' classic non-fiction works on the Hopi, Navajo and Pueblo cultures include *The Book of the Hopi* (1963) and *Masked Gods: Navajo and Pueblo Ceremonials* (1950). His novel, *The Man Who Killed the Deer* (1942) is his best known book. He was also Editor of *El Crepusculo* from 1950 to 1951. Waters was nominated five times for the Nobel Peace Prize in Literature, and received an honorary Doctor of Literature from UNM in 1978.[363] Living most of his life in Taos, he died there in June 1965.[364]

The Willard Reading Room

Fig. 115. Library – Zimmerman – Interior – Outside View of Willard Reading Room, 1940 (Photograph by Wyatt Davis, Center for Southwest Research, UNM Libraries).[365]

The Willard Reading Room[366] on the first floor of the West Wing of Zimmerman Library was named for Larry D. Willard, a banker, philanthropist, and former President of UNM Board of Regents. The Willard Reading Room holds two bookcases with collections of material about his mother, Billie Willard, who was a librarian, his father Edgar, who was a public school administrator in Texas and an inspiration to his son, and himself.

Larry Willard graduated from Eastern New Mexico University and did graduate work at the Universities of Colorado and Oklahoma. He started his financial services career in 1961, working with The First United Bank Group, which later merged with Wells Fargo. Having served as the Wells Fargo Bank's Regional President for New Mexico and West Texas, he retired in June 2004, after a banking career spanning 42 years. Willard served on many civic and financial organizations, including, for example, the New Mexico Bankers Association and the Greater Albuquerque Chamber of Commerce. He served on the UNM Board of Regents from 1995 to 2003, including as President when he resigned to chair the New Mexico Economic Development Corporation.

Endnotes: Section One—Central / Main Campus

1. See Van Dorn Hooker, *Only in New Mexico*, University of New Mexico Press (Albuquerque, NM) (2000), p. 308 (Building 25); see also drawings and photographs on pp. 140, 141, and 142, and Color Plate 3 (top photo).

2. http://econtent.unm.edu/cdm/ref/collection/ULPhotoImag/id/3408 (last accessed April 7, 2018).

3. See Hooker, pp. 122-123 and 272.

4. UNM Alumni Association, "Alumni Memorial Chapel," https://www.unmalumni.com/alumni-chapel.html (last accessed April 18, 2018).

5. UNM Alumni Association, "Commemorative Chapel Tiles," https://www.unmalumni.com/commemorative-tile.html (last accessed April 18, 2018).

6. http://econtent.unm.edu/cdm/ref/collection/ULPhotoImag/id/3403 (last accessed April 7, 2018); see also UNM Alumni Association, "Alumni Memorial Chapel," https://www.unmalumni.com/alumni-chapel.html (last accessed April 17, 2018).

7. See Hooker, p. 275.

8. UNM Alumni Association, "Our Fallen Veterans," https://www.unmalumni.com/our-fallen-vets.html (depicting plaques with list of fallen veterans, last accessed April 17, 2018).

9. http://econtent.unm.edu/cdm/ref/collection/ULPhotoImag/id/3423 (last accessed April 7, 2018).

10. See Hooker, pp. 180 and 181 (photographs), 311 and 312 (Buildings 76 and 87), and Color Plates 9 (bottom photograph) and 10.

11. http://econtent.unm.edu/cdm/ref/collection/ULPhotoImag/id/2802 (last accessed April 7, 2018).

12. See Hooker, p. 312 (Building 87).

13. See Hooker, p. 311 (Building 78).

14. UNM Anderson School of Management, "Robert O. Anderson (1917-2007): A Tribute to Mr. Anderson," https://www.mgt.unm.edu/about/roanderson.asp (last accessed April 17, 2018).

15. UNM Anderson School of Management, Anderson at Work, "The Largest Capital Gift Ever Received," p. 1; see also "Robert O. Anderson, 1917-2007," p. 5, https://www.mgt.unm.edu/news/pdf/newsletter/Spring2008.pdf (last accessed April 17, 2018).

16. See UNM Newsroom, "ASM Jackson Student Center," http://news.unm.edu/file?fid=5491c1f4fe058b20df13930f&id=51e01ff529371a5699003745 (last accessed April 17, 2018).

17. American Sociological Society, *Footnotes*, vol. 15, n. 7, p. 14 (October 1987), http://www.asanet.org/sites/default/files/savvy/footnotes/1987/ASA.07.1987.pdf (last accessed April 17, 2018).

18. UNM Libraries, "About Parish Library," https://elibrary.unm.edu/about/wjparish.php (last accessed April 17, 2018).

19. UNM Anderson Newsroom Press Release, "Anderson School Opens New Student Event Center: Center Houses Student Financial Services Center, Pillmore Room for Ethics, Radosevich Room for Management of Technology & Entrepreneurship" (Jan. 26, 2007), https://www.mgt.unm.edu/news/details.asp?PR=378 (last accessed April 17, 2018), and https://sites.google.com/site/unmgame/clickable-map/anderson-school-of-management-1 (last accessed Jan. 26, 2017).

20. Wall Street Journal, "Rebuilding trust after a crisis: Eric Pillmore, former Tyco governance executive" (Aug. 1, 2016), https://deloitte.wsj.com/riskandcompliance/2016/08/01/rebuilding-trust-after-a-crisis-eric-pillmore-former-tyco-governance-executive (last accessed Oct. 22, 2018).

21. UNM Anderson Events, "Hall of Fame: Previous Honorees," https://www.mgt.unm.edu/events/hall-of-fame/previous-honorees.asp?y=2004 (last accessed April 17, 2018).

22　UNM Alumni Association, "Zimmerman Award," https://www.unmalumni.com/zimmerman-past.html (last accessed April 17, 2018).

23　UNM Anderson Newsroom Press Release, "Anderson School Opens New Student Event Center: Center Houses Student Financial Services Center, Pillmore Room for Ethics, Radosevich Room for Management of Technology & Entrepreneurship" (Jan. 26, 2007), https://www.mgt.unm.edu/news/details.asp?PR=378 (last accessed April 17, 2018).

24　See UNM Newsroom, "McKinnon Center for Management groundbreaking set for Monday, Jan. 30" (Jan. 23, 2007), https://news.unm.edu/news/mckinnon-center-for-management-groundbreaking-set-for-monday-jan-30. See also Mara Kerkez, UNM Newsroom, "Sonnet and Ian McKinnon Give $7.5 Million to UNM's Anderson School and Lobo Athletics Programs" (July 22, 2011), https://news.unm.edu/news/sonnet-and-ian-mckinnon-give-7-5-million-to-unm-e2-80-99s-anderson-school-and-lobo-athletics-programs (last accessed April 17, 2018), and UNM *Mirage*, vol. 37, n. 2, p. 8 (Fall 2017), https://issuu.com/unm-alumni-association/docs/mirage_f17 (last accessed April 17, 2018).

25　http://econtent.unm.edu/cdm/ref/collection/ULPhotoImag/id/73 (last accessed April 17, 2018). See also Hooker, pp. 193 (bottom photograph) and 307 (Building 11).

26　See UNM Anthropology Department, "UNM Anthropology," https://anthropology.unm.edu, and UNM Maxwell Museum of Anthropology, http://maxwellmuseum.unm.edu/collections/archives (last accessed April 17, 2018).

27　Arizona Archives Online, "W. W. (Willard Williams) "Nibs" Hill collection, 1898-1909," http://azarchivesonline.org/xtf/view?docid=ead/mna/MNA_MS271_Hill.xml, and Phillip K. Bock, "Anthropology at UNM, 1928-1968: A Trial Formulation" (1988), http://digitalrepository.unm.edu/unm_hx_essays/1 (last accessed April 16, 2018). See also Charles H. Lange, "W.W. "Nibs" Hill, 1902-1974," *American Anthropologist*, vol. 78, pp. 87-88 (1976).

28　See UNM Maxwell Museum of Anthropology, https://maxwellmuseum.unm.edu (last accessed April 17, 2018) and https://sites.google.com/site/unmgame/clickable-map/anthropology-building (last accessed Jan. 26, 2017).

29　http://econtent.unm.edu/cdm/ref/collection/ULPhotoImag/id/3528 (last accessed April 7, 2018).

30　http://econtent.unm.edu/cdm/ref/collection/ULPhotoImag/id/2823 (last accessed April 7, 2018).

31　UNM Anthropology, Departmental News, "The Department reports the passing of Dr. John Martin "Jack" Campbell on May 28, 2013 after a brief illness" (June 3, 2013), https://anthropology.unm.edu/news-events/news/item/the-department-reports-the-passing-of-dr.-john-martin-jack-campbell.html (last accessed April 17, 2018).

32　https://en.wikipedia.org/wiki/Maxwell_Museum_of_Anthropology (last accessed Jan. 25, 2017).

33　See UNM Alfonso Ortiz Center for Intercultural Studies, "Our Mission," http://www.unm.edu/~ortizctr/old/index.html (last accessed April 17, 2018).

34　George Johnson, "Alfonso Ortiz, 57, Anthropologist of the Pueblo, Dies," *New York Times* (Jan. 31, 1997), http://www.nytimes.com/1997/01/31/us/alfonso-ortiz-57-anthropologist-of-the-pueblo-dies.html (last accessed April 17, 2018).

35　See Hooker, p. 23. See also UNM Alumni Association, "Hodgin Hall Alumni Center: The Heart and Soul of UNM," https://www.unmalumni.com/uploads/images/hodgin/pdf/hodgin-hall-walking-tour.pdf (describing history of original Rodey Hall, the fire and subsequent demolition), available at https://www.unmalumni.com/hodgin-hall.html (last accessed April 17, 2018).

36　http://econtent.unm.edu/cdm/ref/collection/ULPhotoImag/id/1757 (last accessed April 7, 2018).

37　University of New Mexico, *The Mirage, 1910* (1910), http://digitalrepository.unm.edu/unm_yearbooks/17 (last accessed April 17, 2018).

38　http://econtent.unm.edu/cdm/ref/collection/ULPhotoImag/id/2851 (last accessed April 7, 2018).

39　UNM Alumni Association, "Zimmerman Award," https://www.unmalumni.com/zimmerman-past.html (last accessed April 17, 2018).

40　See J.A. Ueckert, "When the world knew of Sandia Cave," *Sandoval Signpost* (Jan. 2014) (reprinted from The Independent), http://www.sandovalsignpost.com/jan14/html/time_off.html (last accessed April 17, 2018).

41　See Hooker, p. 93.

42 See Jess Price, "Totem Pole," *Albuquerque Journal*, p. 50 (Oct. 16, 1984), https://www.newspapers.com.newspage/157282277/, and "UNM's Totem Pole May be Moved," *Albuquerque Journal*, p. 3 (Oct. 27, 1967), https://www.newspapers.com/newspage/157008055/ (last accessed April 17, 2018). See also UNM *Mirage*, vol. 38, n. 1, p. 8 (Spring 2018), https://issuu.com/unm-alumni-association/stacks/7307decf27be4b46a23b78dbd2a9f832 (last accessed April 17, 2018); Katie Williams, "Century-old totem pole becomes inspiration for using the past to fix the future: Anthropologists go back in time to repair relationship over prominent indigenous object," UNM Newsroom (Sept. 14, 2017), https://news.unm.edu/news/ century-old-totem-pole-becomes-inspiration-for-using-the-past-to-fix-the-future; and Sara Yingling, "UNM officials uncover history behind century-old totem pole," KRQE (Sept. 28, 2017), http://krqe.com/2017/09/28/unm-officials-uncover-history-behind-century-old-totem-pole/ (last accessed April 17, 2018).

43 See UNM School of Architecture and Planning, "About George Pearl Hall," https://saap.unm.edu/about/george-pearl-hall.html, and Katie Burford, "Architect Left Indelible Mark on the State," *Albuquerque Journal* (Aug. 18, 2003), https://www.abqjournal.com/obits/profiles/profiles08-18-03.htm (last accessed April 17, 2018).

44 See Albuquerque Community Foundation, "Donor Stories: George Clayton Pearl," http://albuquerquefoundation.org/donor-stories-george-clayton-pearl.aspx (last accessed April 17, 2018).

45 See UNM Office of the University Secretary, "Honorary Degrees," https://graduation.unm.edu/honorarydeg.html and Hilary Mayall Jetty, "Serving Campus and Community: UNM Honors Frontier Founders, Philanthropists Dorothy and Larry Rainosek," UNM Foundation Donor Story (Oct. 23, 2014), https://www.unmfund.org/donor-story/rainosek/ (last accessed April 17, 2018).

46 See Hooker, pp. 64 (photo) and 307 (Building 8).

47 http://econtent.unm.edu/cdm/ref/collection/ULPhotoImag/id/99 (last accessed April 7, 2018).

48 See Hooker, p. 307 (Building 16).

49 http://econtent.unm.edu/cdm/ref/collection/ULPhotoImag/id/2830 (last accessed April 7, 2018).

50 http://econtent.unm.edu/cdm/ref/collection/ULPhotoImag/id/3350 (last accessed April 7, 2018).

51 See Hooker, pp. 52-53 and 64.

52 http://econtent.unm.edu/cdm/ref/collection/ULPhotoImag/id/3306 (last accessed April 7, 2018).

53 U.S. Dept. of the Interior, National Register of Historic Places, "Carlisle Gymnasium," https://npgallery.nps.gov/pdfhost/docs/ NRHP/Text/88001541.pdf (last accessed April 17, 2018).

54 See "Elizabeth H. Water, Choreographer, 83," *New York Times* (1993), http://www.nytimes.com/1993/07/06obituaries/elizabeth-h-waters-choreographer-83.html (last accessed Oct. 22, 2018).

55 University of New Mexico Regents, Executive Vice President (EVP) for Administration. "April 5, 2012 Finance & Facilities (F&F) Committee Meeting" (2012), http://digitalrepository.unm.edu/regents_ffc/51 (last accessed April 17, 2018), and "Elizabeth Waters Center for Dance" in: Gabrielle Esperdy and Karen Kingsley, eds., *SAH Archipedia*, U. Virginia Press (2012), http://sah-archipedia.org/buildings/NM-01-001-0014-03 (last accessed April 17, 2018).

56 See Hooker, pp. 52-53.

57 http://econtent.unm.edu/cdm/ref/collection/ULPhotoImag/id/3308 (last accessed April 7, 2018).

58 See Hooker, pp. 109 (photographs) and 308 (Building 21); see also UNM Libraries, Center for Regional Studies, Celebrating New Mexico Statehood, "Castetter Hall, 1970s," https://nmstatehood.unm.edu/taxonomy/term/122?page=13 (last accessed April 17, 2018).

59 http://econtent.unm.edu/cdm/ref/collection/ULPhotoImag/id/115 (last accessed April 7, 2018); see also https://sites.google.com/site/unmgame/clickable-map/castetter-hall (last accessed Jan. 26, 2017).

60 http://econtent.unm.edu/cdm/ref/collection/ULPhotoImag/id/3052 (last accessed April 7, 2018).

61 http://econtent.unm.edu/cdm/ref/collection/ULPhotoImag/id/116 (last accessed April 7, 2018).

62 See "Loren David Potter," ObitTree, (Mar. 6, 2016), http://obittree.com/obituary/us/new-mexico/albuquerque/french-funerals--cremations/loren-potter/2430167/ (last accessed April 17, 2018).

63 See UNM School of Engineering, "Our History," http://engineering.unm.edu/about/history.html (last accessed April 17, 2018).

64 http://econtent.unm.edu/cdm/ref/collection/ULPhotoImag/id/2936 (last accessed April 7, 2018).

65 UNM School of Engineering, "Centennial Engineering Center Opens for Fall '08," *UNM Engineering*, vol. 5, n. 2, pp. 2 and 18 (Fall 2008), http://engineering.unm.edu/common/documents/magazine/fall08.pdf (last accessed April 17, 2018).

66 See Kim Delker, "UNM Alumnus Robert J. Stamm dies at 93: Stamm valued for his involvement in many departments," UNM Newsroom (Dec. 17, 2014), https://news.unm.edu/news/unm-alumnus-robert-j-stamm-dies-at-93; "Robert Jenne Stamm, 1921-2014," ObitTree, https://obittree.com/obituary/us/new-mexico/albuquerque/french-funerals--cremations/robert-stamm/2255699/; and, UNM School of Engineering, "Building History," *UNM Engineering*, vol. 6, n. 1, p. 17 (Spring 2009), https://engineering.unm.edu/common/documents/magazine/spring09.pdf (last accessed April 17, 2018).

67 UNM Office of the University Secretary, "Regents' Awards Recipients," https://secretary.unm.edu/recognition-and-awards/regents-awards-recipients.html (last accessed April 17, 2018).

68 UNM Alumni Association, "Zimmerman Award," https://www.unmalumni.com/zimmerman-past.html (last accessed April 18, 2018).

69 UNM Office of the University Secretary, "Honorary Degrees," https://graduation.unm.edu/honorarydeg.html (last accessed Jan. 26, 2017).

70 See Hooker, pp. 107-08 and 308 (Building 22), and Color Plate 4.

71 http://econtent.unm.edu/cdm/ref/collection/ULPhotoImag/id/2824 (last accessed April 7, 2018).

72 https://sites.google.com/site/unmgame/clickable-map/clark-hall (last accessed Jan. 26, 2017).

73 See Hooker, p. 198 (photograph).

74 https://sites.google.com/site/unmgame/clickable-map/clark-hall (last accessed Jan. 26, 2017).

75 See Hooker, p. 313 (Building 117).

76 http://econtent.unm.edu/cdm/ref/collection/ULPhotoImag/id/2965 (last accessed April 7, 2018).

77 See Hooker, pp. 95 (middle photograph) and 312-313 (Building 115).

78 http://econtent.unm.edu/cdm/ref/collection/ULPhotoImag/id/463 (last accessed April 7, 2018); see also https://sites.google.com/site/unmgame/clickable-map/communication-and-journalism-building (last accessed Jan. 26, 2017).

79 See UNM Libraries, "e-Hillerman: The Tony Hillerman Portal," http://ehillerman.unm.edu (last accessed April 17, 2018). See also The Authors Road, "Tony Hillerman: Journalist, Novelist," http://www.authorsroad.com/TonyHillerman.html (last accessed April 17, 2018).

80 Oklahoma Hall of Fame, Gaylord-Pickens Museum, "Hillerman, Tony, 1997," http://oklahomahof.com/archives/h/hillerman-tony-1997 (last accessed April 17, 2018).

81 See Charles C. Poling, "Tony Hillerman: An Open Book," *New Mexico Magazine* (October 2015), http://www.nmmagazine.com/article/?aid=93374#.WIp5ZunRGfQ (last accessed April 16, 2018).

82 UNM Alumni Association, "Alumni Award Recipients," https://www.unmalumni.com/award-recipients.html (last accessed April 17, 2018).

83 See Marilyn Stasio, "Tony Hillerman, Novelist, Dies at 83," *New York Times* (Oct. 27, 2008), http://www.nytimes.com/2008/10/28/books/28hillerman.html (last accessed April 17, 2018).

84 "Palacios," *Albuquerque Journal* (Aug. 20, 2006) http://obits.abqjournal.com/obits/show/166819 (last accessed April 17, 2018).

85 UNM Communication and Marketing Department, "2007-06-18 UNM NEWS MINUTE" (2007), http://digitalrepository.unm.edu/news_minute_2007/43 (last accessed April 26, 2018).

86 See Hooker, p. 314 (Building 155).

87 http://econtent.unm.edu/cdm/ref/collection/ULPhotoImag/id/47 (last accessed April 7, 2018).

88 See Hooker, pp. 187 (photograph), and 311 (Buildings 74, 75, and 77).

89 http://econtent.unm.edu/cdm/ref/collection/ULPhotoImag/id/54 (last accessed April 7, 2018).

90 UNM Resident Life and Student Housing, "Laguna DeVargas Hall," https://housing.unm.edu/residence-halls/laguna-devargas.html (last accessed April 18, 2018).

91 http://econtent.unm.edu/cdm/ref/collection/ULPhotoImag/id/21 (last accessed April 7, 2018).

92 See UNM Dean of Students, "Dean of Students History," https://dos.unm.edu/about/history.html (last accessed April 17, 2018).

93 See Hooker, pp. 20 (photograph) and 309 (Building 58); see also W.T. Comstock, "A Revival of Old Pueblo Architecture," *Architects' and Builders' Magazine*, vol. 41, pp. 282-285 (1909), and Ramon Jurado, "Prehistoric Home for New University," *The Technical World Magazine*, vol. 10, pp. 367-375 (1908).

94 http://econtent.unm.edu/cdm/ref/collection/ULPhotoImag/id/2749 (last accessed April 7, 2018).

95 http://econtent.unm.edu/cdm/ref/collection/ULPhotoImag/id/2753 (last accessed April 7, 2018).

96 http://econtent.unm.edu/cdm/ref/collection/ULPhotoImag/id/2765 (last accessed April 7, 2018). See also "Hokona Hall," https://housing.unm.edu/residence-halls/hokona-hall.html (last accessed July 23, 2018).

97 http://econtent.unm.edu/cdm/ref/collection/ULPhotoImag/id/3194 (last accessed April 7, 2018).

98 See UNM Dean of Students, "Dean of Students History," https://dos.unm.edu/about/history.html, and UNM Alumni Association, "Alumni Award Recipients," https://www.unmalumni.com/award-recipients.html (last accessed April 17, 2018).

99 See Betty Huning Hinton, "UNM's First Dean of Women: Lena C. Clauve" (1989), http://digitalrepository.unm.edu/archives_documents/3; see also UNM "The Fight Song," http://www.unm.edu/welcome/traditions/the-fight-song.html (last accessed April 16, 2018).

100 "Gutierrez," *Albuquerque Journal* (Dec. 13, 2003), http://obits.abqjournal.com/obits/show/140000 (last accessed April 17, 2018).

101 UNM Department of Education, "Previous Teaching Awards," http://ctl.unm.edu/faculty/assets/teacher-of-the-year-award-recipients.pdf (last accessed April 17, 2018).

102 Brigham Young University (BYU) Religious Studies Center, Authors, "McNamara, Patrick H.," https://rsc.byu.edu/authors/mcnamara-patrick-h (last accessed April 17, 2018); see also "Popular N.M. Professor Dies of Brain Tumor at 72," *Deseret News* (Nov. 26, 2001), https://www.deseretnews.com/article/876506/Popular-NM-professor-dies-of-brain-tumor-at-72.html (last accessed April 16, 2018).

103 See Hooker, p. 19 (photograph).

104 http://econtent.unm.edu/cdm/ref/collection/ULPhotoImag/id/2780 (last accessed April 7, 2018).

105 See Hooker, p. 314 (Building 157).

106 UNM Resident Life and Student Housing, "Alvarado Hall," https://housing.unm.edu/residence-halls/alvarado-hall.html (last accessed April 18, 2018).

107 See Hooker, pp. 310-311 (Building 71).

108 See Hooker, p. 310 (Building 61).

109 http://econtent.unm.edu/cdm/ref/collection/ULPhotoImag/id/133 (last accessed April 7, 2018).

110 http://econtent.unm.edu/cdm/ref/collection/ULPhotoImag/id/149 (last accessed April 7, 2018).

111 See Hooker, p. 314 (Building 156).

112 http://econtent.unm.edu/cdm/ref/collection/ULPhotoImag/id/135 (last accessed April 7, 2018).

113 See, for example, New Mexico Office of the State Historian, People, "Juan de Oñate," http://newmexicohistory.org/people/juan-de-onate (last accessed April 17, 2018).

114 See Hooker, pp. 59, 61, 79, 89, and 307 (Building 7).

115 http://econtent.unm.edu/cdm/ref/collection/ULPhotoImag/id/137 (last accessed April 7, 2018).

116 See Hooker, pp. 238-239.

117 See Hooker, p. 37 (sidebar note).

118 See, e.g., University of New Mexico, "*U.N.M. Weekly*, Volume 019, No 27, 3/6/1917" (advertisement for shoe repair at Earl's Grotto), http://digitalrepository.unm.edu/unm_weekly_1917/9 (last accessed April 16, 2018).

119 See Hooker, pp. 100 (photograph) and 309 (Building 57).

120 http://econtent.unm.edu/cdm/ref/collection/ULPhotoImag/id/465 (last accessed April 7, 2018), and UNM Libraries, Center for Regional Studies, Celebrating New Mexico Statehood, "Bratton Hall I, Economics," https://nmstatehood.unm.edu/node/67743 (last accessed April 17, 2018).

121 "Sam G. Bratton," *Wikipedia* (April 16, 2018), https://en.wikipedia.org/wiki/Sam_G._Bratton, and John "J-Cat" Griffith, "Sam Gilbert Bratton," Find A Grave, https://www.findagrave.com/memorial/6886242 (last accessed Oct. 22, 2018).

122 See Hooker, pp. 160-164, and 310 (Buildings 63-70).

123 The Conference Room is located within the College of Education Complex, Building 63, known as the Faculty Office Building (see Hooker, p. 310 (Building 63)), and was demolished several years ago due to recurring structural problems.

124 UNM Office of the University Secretary, "Honorary Degrees," https://graduation.unm.edu/honorarydeg.html, (last accessed April 17, 2018).

125 Lloyd Jojola, "Hispanic was famed educator," *Albuquerque Journal* (June 4, 2005), https://www.abqjournal.com/obits/profiles/357759profiles06-04-05.htm (last accessed April 17, 2018).

126 UNM Board of Regents, "University of New Mexico Board of Regents Minutes for October 11, 1988" (1988), http://digitalrepository.unm.edu/bor_minutes/1030 (last accessed April 16, 2018).

127 See Hooker, p. 310 (Building 70).

128 http://econtent.unm.edu/cdm/ref/collection/ULPhotoImag/id/258 (last accessed April 7, 2018).

129 UNM Newsroom, "College of Education's Manzanita Counseling Center Provides Hands-on Training," (Feb. 4, 2016), http://news.unm.edu/news/unms-manzanita-counseling-center-provides-hands-on-training (last accessed April 17, 2018).

130 See Hooker, pp. 162, 270, and 310 (Building 68); see also UNM Art Education, "Gallery: Masley Art Gallery Mission," http://arted.unm.edu/gallery/, and UNM Art Education, "Alexander Masley," http://arted.unm.edu/alexander-masley/ (last accessed April 17, 2018).

131 See Hooker, p. 310 (Building 66).

132 http://64.106.42.24/cdm/ref/collection/ULPhotoImag/id/236 (last accessed April 7, 2018).

133 UNM Alumni Association, "Alumni Award Recipients," https://www.unmalumni.com/award-recipients.html (last accessed April 17, 2018).

134 See Hooker, p. 310 (Building 65). See also Lloyd Jojola, "UNM Provost Famed for Stance on Racism," *Albuquerque Journal* (Dec. 29, 2006), https://www.abqjournal.com/news/metro/524801metro12-29-06.htm, and Stefan Johnson, "Albuquerque Modernism: Travelstead Hall, Case Study," UNM School of Architecture and Planning, http://albuquerquemodernism.unm.edu/wp/travelstead-hall/ (last accessed Oct. 22, 2018).

135 http://econtent.unm.edu/cdm/ref/collection/ULPhotoImag/id/155 (last accessed April 7, 2018).

136 UNM Alumni Association, "Alumni Award Recipients," https://www.unmalumni.com/award-recipients.html (last accessed April 17, 2018).

137 UNM Office of the University Secretary, "Honorary Degrees," https://graduation.unm.edu/honorarydeg.html (last accessed April 17, 2018).

138 See "Chester Travelstead," *Bowling Green Daily News* (Jan. 4, 2007), http://www.bgdailynews.com/obituaries/chester-travelstead/article_03c67130-20f0-5d38-9650-1eafe99169d7.html (last accessed April 17, 2018).

139 See New Mexico Library Association, "What is the Anita Osuna Carr Collection," *NMLA Newsletter*, vol. 8, n. 4, p. 3 (Oct. 1980), http://nmla.org/docs/newsletters/NMLA_1980_October.pdf (last accessed April 17, 2018).

140 See Hooker, pp. 27, 62, and 303, and UNM Libraries, Center for Regional Studies, Celebrating New Mexico Statehood, "Estufa, 1948," https://nmstatehood.unm.edu/node/67622 (last accessed April 17, 2018). See also UNM Planning and Campus Development, "UNM Building List, by Campus, by Number,"rev. Nov. 14, 2012, https://ppd.unm.edu/assets/documents/campus-maps/UnmBuildingsNum.pdf (last accessed April 17, 2018).

141 http://econtent.unm.edu/cdm/ref/collection/ULPhotoImag/id/349 (last accessed April 7, 2018).

142 See Hooker, pp. 194 (photograph) and 313 (Building 119), Color Plate 13 (top photograph). See also UNM Mechanical Engineering, "History of Mechanical Engineering," https://me.unm.edu/about/history-of-mechanical-engineering.html (last accessed April 17, 2018).

143 http://econtent.unm.edu/cdm/ref/collection/ULPhotoImag/id/312 (last accessed April 7, 2018).

144 UNM Mechanical Engineering, "A History of Leadership," *Our Magazine* (Spring 2007), http://engineering.unm.edu/about/ our-magazine/magazine-archives/spring-2007/a-history-of-leadership.html (last accessed April 17, 2018). See also https://www.findagrave.com/memorial/64039883 (last accessed Oct. 22, 2017).

145 See Hooker, pp. 129 and 310-311 (Buildings 62, 72, and 84).

146 http://econtent.unm.edu/cdm/ref/collection/ULPhotoImag/id/413 (last accessed April 7, 2018).

147 See UNM College of Fine Arts, "Venues," https://finearts.unm.edu/venues/ (last accessed April 17, 2018).

148 See Sari Krosinsky, "Art Museum Celebrates New Expansion, Shows," UNM Newsroom (Nov. 22, 2010), http://news.unm.edu/news/art-museum-celebrates-new-expansion-shows (last accessed April 17, 2018).

149 See Sari Krosinsky, "Art Museum Celebrates New Expansion, Shows," UNM Newsroom (Nov. 22, 2010). http://news.unm.edu/news/art-museum-celebrates-new-expansion-shows (last accessed April 17, 2018).

150 See Ken Johnson, "Clinton Adams, 83, a Painter Who Helped Resurrect Lithography," *New York Times* (June 2, 2002), http://www.nytimes.com/2002/06/02/nyregion/clinton-adams-83-a-painter-who-helped-resurrect-lithography.html, and "Adams," *Albuquerque Journal* (May 19, 2002), http://obits.abqjournal.com/obits/show/109739 (last accessed April 17, 2018).

151 See Tamarind Institute, Artist, "Clinton Adams," http://tamarind.unm.edu/artists/view/3-clinton-adams (last accessed April 17, 2018). See also Smithsonian Institution, Archives of American Art, "Oral History Interview with Clinton Adams," 1995, August 2-3, https://www.aaa.si.edu/collections/interviews/oral-history-interview-clinton-adams-12197 (last accessed April 17, 2018).

152 See Tamarind Institute, Artist, "Clinton Adams," http://tamarind.unm.edu/artists/view/3-clinton-adams (last accessed April 17, 2018). See also Jon Thurber, "Clinton Adams, 83, Led Renaissance in Lithography in U.S.," *Los Angeles Times*, Obituaries (May 30, 2002), http://articles.latimes.com/2002/may/30/local/me-adams30, and New Mexico Dept. of Cultural Affairs, Governor's Awards for Excellence in the Arts, "Clinton Adams, 1985," http://artsawards.newmexicoculture.org/video.php?select=4 (last accessed April 17, 2018).

153 See International Photography Hall of Fame and Museum, "Beaumont Newhall, 1908-1993," http://iphf.org/inductees/beaumont-newhall/, and Charles Hagen, "Beaumont Newhall, a Historian of Photography, is Dead at 84," *New York Times* (1993), http://www.nytimes.com/1993/02/27/arts/beaumont-newhall-a-historian-of-photography-is-dead-at-84.html (last accessed April 17, 2018).

154 See Kathleen Teltsch, "25 Cited as 'Exceptionally Talented'; an Actor is Among Cash Recipients," *New York Times* (1984), http://www.nytimes.com/1984/10/23/us/25-cited-as-exceptionally-talented-an-actor-is-among-cash-recipients.html (last accessed April 17, 2018).

155 See UNM Art Museum, "Beaumont Newhall Study Room," http://unmartmuseum.org/collections/beaumont-newhall-study-room-enyeartmalone-library-archive/, and Sari Krosinsky, "Art Museum Celebrates New Expansion, Shows," UNM Newsroom (Nov. 22, 2010), http://news.unm.edu/news/art-museum-celebrates-new-expansion-shows (last accessed April 17, 2018).

156 See Charles Hagen, "Beaumont Newhall, a Historian of Photography, is Dead at 84," *New York Times* (1993), http://www.nytimes.com/1993/02/27/arts/beaumont-newhall-a-historian-of-photography-is-dead-at-84.html (last accessed April 17, 2018).

157 Sari Krosinsky, "Art Museum Celebrates New Expansion, Shows," UNM Newsroom (Nov. 22, 2010), http://news.unm.edu/news/art-museum-celebrates-new-expansion-shows (last accessed April 17, 2018).

158 UNM Art Museum, "Enyeart/Malone Library and Archive," http://unmartmuseum.org/collections/eanyartmalone-library-and-archive/ (last accessed April 17, 2018).

159 See UNM College of Fine Arts, "Bunting Visual Resources Library," http://www.unm.edu/~bbmsl/ and http://bvrl.unm.edu (last accessed April 17, 2018).

160 See "Bainbridge Bunting," *Wikipedia*, https://en.wikipedia.org/wiki/Bainbridge_Bunting (last accessed Feb. 10, 2017).

161 See Lannan Foundation, http://www.lannan.org/about/ (last accessed April 17, 2018).

162 See UNM College of Fine Arts, "Bunting Visual Resources Library," http://bvrl.unm.edu (last accessed April 17, 2018).

163 See Sari Krosinsky, "Art Museum Celebrates New Expansion, Shows," UNM Newsroom (Nov. 22, 2010), http://news.unm.edu/news/art-museum-celebrates-new-expansion-shows (last accessed April 17, 2018), and Michele M. Penhall, ed., *Stories from the Camera: Reflections on the Photograph*, UNM Press, p. 9 (2016).

164 See Wolfgang Saxon, "Van Deren Coke, 83, Dies; Curator and Photographer," *New York Times* (July 27, 2004), http://www.nytimes.com/2004/07/27/arts/van-deren-coke-83-dies-curator-and-photographer.html?_r=0, and "Coke," *Albuquerque Journal* (July 22, 2004), http://obits.abqjournal.com/obits/show/146067 (last accessed April 17, 2018).

165 http://econtent.unm.edu/cdm/ref/collection/Robb/id/113 (last accessed Feb. 10, 2017).

166 New Mexico Dept. of Cultural Affairs, Governor's Awards for Excellence in the Arts, "The Award Winners," http://artsawards.newmexicoculture.org/search.php?type=name (last accessed April 17, 2018).

167 UNM Office of the University Secretary, "Honorary Degrees," https://graduation.unm.edu/honorarydeg.html (last accessed April 17, 2018).

168 See Hooker, p. 156 (photographs).

169 http://econtent.unm.edu/cdm/ref/collection/ULPhotoImag/id/396 (last accessed April 7, 2018).

170 UNM College of Fine Arts, Venues, "Keller Hall," https://finearts.unm.edu/venues/keller-hall/ (last accessed April 17, 2018).

171 See Bldg. 123, UNM Planning and Campus Development, "UNM Building List, by Campus, by Number," rev. Nov. 14, 2012, https://ppd.unm.edu/assets/documents/campus-maps/UnmBuildingsNum.pdf (last accessed April 17, 2018).

172 Stephen Schwartz, "Obituary: Charles Mattox," *San Francisco Chronicle* (April 24, 1996), http://www.sfgate.com/news/article/OBITUARY-Charles-Mattox-2985373.php (last accessed April 17, 2018).

173 See Hooker, pp. 228-229 and 311 (Building 72).

174 http://econtent.unm.edu/cdm/ref/collection/ULPhotoImag/id/383 (last accessed April 7, 2018).

175 UNM Lobos, "Tom Popejoy," http://www.golobos.com/news/2011/8/15/209069983.aspx (last accessed April 17, 2018).

176 UNM Lobos, "Hall of Honor," http://www.golobos.com/sports/2015/5/12/GEN_2014010147.aspx (last accessed April 17, 2018).

177 UNM Alumni Association, "Alumni Award Recipients," https://www.unmalumni.com/award-recipients.html (last accessed April 17, 2018).

178 UNM Office of the University Secretary, "Honorary Degrees," https://graduation.unm.edu/honorarydeg.html (last accessed April 17, 2018).

179 See UNM College of Fine Arts, Center for Southwest Research, "UNM Robb Archives," http://www.robbtrust.org/unm-robb-archives.html, (last accessed Nov. 20, 2016). See also endnote 165.

180 UNM Alumni Association, "Alumni Award Recipients," https://www.unmalumni.com/award-recipients.html (last accessed April 17, 2018).

181 UNM Office of the University Secretary, "Honorary Degrees," https://graduation.unm.edu/honorarydeg.html (last accessed April 17, 2018).

182 See New Mexico Music Commission, "Robb, John Donald," http://www.newmexicomusic.org/2015/11/16/robb-john-donald/ (last accessed April 17, 2018), and UNM College of Fine Arts, Center for Southwest Research, "About John Donald Robb," http://www.robbtrust.org/jd-robb-the-man--his-music.html (last accessed Oct. 22, 2018).

183 See UNM College of Fine Arts, Venues, "Rodey Theatre," http://finearts.unm.edu/exhibition-spaces/rodey-theatre/ (last accessed April 17, 2018).

184 http://econtent.unm.edu/cdm/ref/collection/ULPhotoImag/id/1757 (last accessed April 7, 2018).

185 UNM, "*U.N.M. Weekly*, Volume 011, No 18, 12/19/1908." 11, 18 (1908), http://digitalrepository.unm.edu/unm_weekly_1908/36 (last accessed April 17, 2018)

186 UNM Libraries, Center for Regional Studies, Celebrating New Mexico Statehood, "Bernard S. Rodey," https://nmstatehood.unm.edu/node/50380 (last accessed April 17, 2018).

187 "Bernard Shandon Rodey," http://www.rodey.com/uploads/files/AboutUs/rodey_bernard_shandon_rodey.pdf (last accessed April 17, 2018).

188 Social Networks and Archival Context, "Rodey, Pierce C. (Pierce Coddington), 1889-1958," http://snaccooperative.org/static/about/about.html (last accessed Oct. 22, 2018).

189 UNM Libraries, Center for Regional Studies, Celebrating New Mexico Statehood, "Pierce C. Rodey Papers, 1923-1939," https://nmstatehood.unm.edu/node/78590 (last accessed April 17, 2018).

190 See UNM College of Fine Arts, Dept. of Art and Art History, "John Sommers Gallery," http://art.unm.edu/john-sommers-gallery/ (last accessed April 17, 2018).

191 UNM College of Fine Arts, Venues, "John Sommers Gallery," https://finearts.unm.edu/venues/john-sommers-gallery/ (last accessed April 17, 2018).

192 National Gallery of Art, Collections, "Sommers, John," http://www.nga.gov/content/ngaweb/Collection/artist-info.3098.html (from a memorial by Harry Nadler, 1988) (last accessed April 17, 2018).

193 Tamarind Institute, http://tamarind.unm.edu/about-us/2-what-is-tamarind-institute (last accessed April 17, 2018), and Bldg. 162, UNM Planning and Campus Development, "UNM Building List, by Campus, by Number," rev. Nov. 14, 2012, https://unm.edu/assets/documents/campus-maps/UnmBuildingsNum.pdf (last accessed April 17, 2018).

194 http://econtent.unm.edu/cdm/ref/collection/Tamarind/id/17 (last accessed April 7, 2018).

195 See image of remodeled facility at Tamarind Institute, "What is Tamarind Institute?" http://tamarind.unm.edu/about-us/2-what-is-tamarind-institute and http://econtent.unm.edu/cdm/ref/collection/route/id/491 (last accessed April 17, 2018).

196 See http://econtent.unm.edu/cdm/ref/collection/route/id/490 (last accessed April 7, 2018).

197 See Social Networks and Archival Context, "Hartung, Robert," http://snaccooperative.org/static/about/about.html (last accessed Oct. 22, 2018).

198 UNM College of Fine Arts, Cinematic Arts, "Interdisciplinary Film and Digital Media," http://ifdm.unm.edu/facilities/ (last accessed April 17, 2018).

199 UNM College of Fine Arts, Cinematic Arts, " Robert Hartung Building," http://cinematicarts.unm.edu/facilities/the-robert-hartung-building/ (last accessed April 17, 2018).

200 See Hooker, pp. 95 (bottom photograph) and 313 (Building 116).

201 http://econtent.unm.edu/cdm/ref/collection/ULPhotoImag/id/551 (last accessed April 7, 2018).

202 See UNM Physical Plant Department, Utilities Division, http://ppd.unm.edu/services/utilities-division.html, and UNM Mechanical Engineering Dept., History and Past News, "The History of Mechanical Engineering at UNM " (noting Albert D. Ford, Department Chairman, 1942-1953), http://www.me.unm.edu/about-hist.shtml (last accessed April 17, 2018).

203 See Hooker, pp. 41-42.

204 See John R. Green with amendments by Daniel Finley, "Physics and Astronomy: 1892-1989," UNM Department of Physics & Astronomy, http://physics.unm.edu/pandaweb/history/ (last accessed April 19, 2018). See also Hooker, p. 13 (bottom photograph); "Hadley Hall I and Hodgin Hall, circa 1890s," http://econtent.unm.edu/cdm/ref/collection/ULPhotoImag/id/433; and, "Hadley Hall I – Interior – Desk with Scientific Instruments, circa 1890s," http://econtent.unm.edu/cdm/ref/collection/ULPhotoImag/id/435 (last accessed April 7, 2018).

205 http://econtent.unm.edu/cdm/ref/collection/ULPhotoImag/id/436 (last accessed April 7, 2018).

206 http://econtent.unm.edu/cdm/ref/collection/ULPhotoImag/id/441 (last accessed April 7, 2018).

207 See Robert Hixson Julyan, *The Place Names of New Mexico*, University of New Mexico Press, Albuquerque, NM, p. 159 (1996).

208 https://nmstatehood.unm.edu/node/67723 (last accessed Feb. 12, 2017).

209 See Hooker, pp. 45, 94 (photograph of Hadley Hall II after explosion) and 312 (Building 106).

210 http://econtent.unm.edu/cdm/ref/collection/ULPhotoImag/id/281 (last accessed April 7, 2018).

211 UNM Libraries, Center for Regional Studies, Celebrating New Mexico Statehood, "Hadley Hall II, 1920," https://nmstatehood.unm.edu/node/67550 (last accessed April 19, 2018).

212 See Hooker, p. 312 (Building 103).

213 http://econtent.unm.edu/cdm/ref/collection/keleher/id/459 (last accessed April 7, 2018).

214 http://econtent.unm.edu/cdm/ref/collection/ULPhotoImag/id/1604 (last accessed April 7, 2018).

215 See, e.g., Danielle Bauer, "Hodgin Hall: Its Place in History," UNM *Mirage*, vol. 31, n. 1, pp. 6-19 (Fall 2011), https://issuu.com/unm-alumni-association/docs/mirage_f11_2 (last accessed April 19, 2018)). See also "Charles E. Hodgin," Find A Grave, https://www.findagrave.com/memorial/49399717 (last accessed Oct. 22, 2018).

216 William E. Davis, "William George Tight - Biography" (2006), http://digitalrepository.unm.edu/president_bios/12 (last accessed April 19, 2018).

217 See Hooker, p. 303.

218 See UNM Alumni Association, "The Place to Visit: Hodgin Hall Walking Tour," https://www.unmalumni.com/uploads/images/hodgin/pdf/hodgin-hall-walking-tour.pdf (last accessed April 19, 2018).

219 See UNM Alumni Association, "The Place to Visit: Hodgin Hall Walking Tour," https://www.unmalumni.com/uploads/images/hodgin/pdf/hodgin-hall-walking-tour.pdf (last accessed April 19, 2018).

220 See UNM Board of Regents, "Regents Photo in 1933" (2005). *Photographs*. 2, http://digitalrepository.unm.edu/regents_photographs/ (last accessed Oct. 16, 2018).

221 UNM Alumni Association, "Zimmerman Award," https://www.unmalumni.com/zimmerman-past.html (last accessed April 19, 2018).

222 UNM Office of the University Secretary, "Honorary Degrees," https://secretary.unm.edu/recognition-and-awards/honorary-degrees.html (last accessed April 17, 2018).

223 See UNM Alumni Association, "The Place to Visit: Hodgin Hall Walking Tour," https://www.unmalumni.com/uploads/images/hodgin/pdf/hodgin-hall-walking-tour.pdf (last accessed April 19, 2018).

224 http://econtent.unm.edu/cdm/ref/collection/ULPhotoImag/id/1727 (last accessed April 7, 2018).

225 See UNM Alumni Association, "The Place to Visit: Hodgin Hall Walking Tour," https://www.unmalumni.com/uploads/images/hodgin/pdf/hodgin-hall-walking-tour.pdf (last accessed April 19, 2018). See, e.g., Danielle Bauer, "Hodgin Hall: Its Place in History," UNM *Mirage*, vol. 31, n. 1, pp. 6-19 (Fall 2011), https://issuu.com/unm-alumni-association/docs/mirage_f11_2 (last accessed April 19, 2018).

226 "University of New Mexico Student Newspaper Editors," https://www.unm.edu/~pubboard/Stu%20Pubs%20Editors.pdf (last accessed April 19, 2018).

227 UNM, "*The Mirage*, 1910," p. 19 (1910), http://digitalrepository.unm.edu/unm_yearbooks/17, (last accessed Oct. 22, 2018).

228 UNM Office of the Registrar, "1905-1906-Catalog" (1906), http://digitalrepository.unm.edu/course_catalogs/ (last accessed Oct. 22, 2018), and see "Lillian Gertrude Huggett," Find A Grave, https://findagrave.com/memorial (last accessed Oct. 22, 2018).

229 UNM, "*The Mirage*, 1910," p. 19 (1910), http://digitalrepository.unm.edu/unm_yearbooks/17 (last accessed Oct. 22, 2018).

230 "New Mexico Football 2005," https://www.nmnathletics.com/fls/26000/old_site/pdf/m-footbl/05-fb-university.pdf?DB_OEM_ID=26000, and "University of New Mexico Football Record Book (1892-Present), 2014-15 University of New Mexico All Sports Record Book," https://admin.xosn.com/pdf9/2760912.pdf (last accessed Oct. 22, 2018).

231 Charles Elkanah Hodgin, "War Service of the University of New Mexico," *University of New Mexico Bulletin*, vol. 32, n. 2 (June 1919), https://archive.org/stream/warserviceofuniv00hodg#page/n3/mode/2up and https://archive.org/details/warserviceofuniv00hodg (last accessed April 19, 2018).

232 UNM Lobos, "Hall of Honor," http://www.golobos.com/sports/2015/5/12/GEN_2014010147.aspx (last accessed April 19, 2018).

233 "Luksich," *Albuquerque Journal* (Aug. 19, 2001), http://obits.abqjournal.com/obits/show/100201 (last accessed April 19, 2018).

234 UNM Alumni Association, "The Place to Visit: Hodgin Hall Walking Tour," https://www.unmalumni.com/uploads/images/hodgin/pdf/hodgin-hall-walking-tour.pdf (last accessed April 19, 2018).

235 "McKay," *Albuquerque Journal* (Jan. 24, 2008), http://obits.abqjournal.com/obits/show/183196 (last accessed April 19, 2018).

236 UNM Alumni Association, "Hodgin Hall: The Heart and Soul of UNM," https://www.unmalumni.com/hodgin-hall.html (last accessed April 19, 2018).

237 UNM Alumni Association, "The Brick Brigade: Be a Part of Alumni History," https://www.unmalumni.com/brick-brigade.html (last accessed April 19, 2018).

238 UNM Alumni Association, "The Place to Visit: Hodgin Hall Walking Tour," p. 11, https://www.unmalumni.com/uploads/images/hodgin/pdf/hodgin-hall-walking-tour.pdf, and Sarah Trujillo, "UNM honors alumna by breaking new and historic ground," UNM *Daily Lobo* (July 21, 2016), http://www.dailylobo.com/article/2016/07/umm-honors-alumna-with-renovation (last accessed April 19, 2018).

239 UNM Alumni Association, "Dr. Karen Abraham Courtyard," https://www.unmalumni.com/dr-karen-abraham-courtyard.html (last accessed April 19, 2018).

240 UNM Alumni Association, "Special Edition! About Place: Hodgin Hall 1892-2011," UNM *Mirage*, vol. 31, n. 1 (Fall 2011), https://issuu.com/unm-alumni-association/docs/mirage_f11_2 (last accessed April 19, 2018).

241 http://econtent.unm.edu/cdm/ref/collection/ULPhotoImag/id/1754 (last accessed April 7, 2018).

242 Rachel Stone, "UNM arborists inventory campus trees," UNM Newsroom (May 8, 2014), http://news.unm.edu/news/unm-arborists-inventory-campus-trees (last accessed April 19, 2018).

243 U.S. Department of the Interior, National Register of Historic Places, Inventory – Nomination Form, "Hodgin Hall," https://npgallery.nps.gov/GetAsset/9cf4660a-3c39-4070-9254-9d96c281b6a9/ (last accessed Sept. 20, 2018); Kenneth B. Bork, "New Frontiers: The Evolution of William G. Tight from Geomorphologist to University President," *Earth Sciences History*, vol. 22, n. 1, pp. 10-35 (2003), https://doi.org/10.17704/eshi.22.1.c5145lgmm6634055 (last accessed Sept. 20, 2018); William E. Davis, "William George Tight - Biography" (2006), http://digitalrepository.unm.edu/president_bios/12 (last accessed April 19, 2018); and *Memorial Volume of Denison University, 1931-1906: Part I. The Development of the College. Part II. Seventh General Catalogue*, p. 191 (1907).

244 UNM Alumni Association, "The Place to Visit: Hodgin Hall Walking Tour," https://www.unmalumni.com/uploads/images/hodgin/pdf/hodgin-hall-walking-tour.pdf, and "Hodgin Hall: Its place in history," https://www.unmalumni.com/uploads/images/hodgin/pdf/Hodgin-Brochure.pdf (last accessed April 19, 2018).

245 http://econtent.unm.edu/cdm/ref/collection/ULPhotoImag/id/1747 (last accessed April 7, 2018).

246 See Hooker, pp. 213 (photograph by Jerry Goffe), and 311 (Building 81).

247 See Hooker, pp. 202-203 and 217.

248 http://econtent.unm.edu/cdm/ref/collection/ULPhotoImag/id/3370 (last accessed April 7, 2018).

249 http://econtent.unm.edu/cdm/ref/collection/ULPhotoImag/id/3459 (last accessed April 7, 2018).

250 Social Networks and Archival Context, "Smith, Sherman Everitt, 1909-," http://snaccooperative.org/search (last accessed Oct. 22, 2018).

251 Rick Nathanson, "Van Dorn Hooker, Jr., UNM architect, dies at 93," *Albuquerque Journal* (June 23, 2015), https://www.abqjournal.com/602671/architect-for-unm-dies-at-age-93.html/c01_jd_23jun_hooker2 (photograph of Van Dorn Hooker and Sherman Smith (right), UNM Archives) (last accessed April 19, 2018).

252 See Hooker, p. 254.

253 See Hooker, pp. 126 (Photographs by Tyler Dingee and Dick Kent) and 309-310 (Building 59).

254 http://econtent.unm.edu/cdm/ref/collection/ULPhotoImag/id/1575 (last accessed April 7, 2018).

255 http://econtent.unm.edu/cdm/ref/collection/ULPhotoImag/id/3643 (last accessed April 7, 2018).

256 http://econtent.unm.edu/cdm/ref/collection/ULPhotoImag/id/3329 (last accessed April 7, 2018).

257 See UNM Lobos, "Roy Johnson," http://www.golobos.com/sports/2015/5/12/GEN_20140101320.aspx and "Roy W. Johnson," *Sports Illustrated Vault* (Mar. 10, 1958), http://www.si.com/vault/1958/03/10/572427/roy-w-johnson (last accessed April 19, 2018).

258 UNM Lobos, "Roy Johnson," http://www.golobos.com/sports/2015/5/12/GEN_20140101320.aspx, (last accessed April 19, 2018).

259 For more information about Roy Johnson, see *Roy Johnson: A Short Biography* by Robert Barney, who in 2002 was also inducted into the UNM Athletics Hall of Honor (see UNM Lobos, "Robert Barney," http://www.golobos.com/sports/2015/5/12/GEN_20140101116.aspx, last accessed April 19, 2018).

260 http://econtent.unm.edu/cdm/ref/collection/ULPhotoImag/id/3474 (last accessed April 7, 2018).

261 http://econtent.unm.edu/cdm/ref/collection/ULPhotoImag/id/587 (last accessed April 7, 2018).

262 See also Hooker, p. 90 (photograph of "Lobo").

263 See "The Spirit of the Wolf," http://lobospirit.weebly.com, and "The Art of New Mexico: The Works of John Tatschl," http://www.drivehq.com/web/tatsch73/NewMexico/inside_template6a.html (includes link to biography) (last accessed April 19, 2018).

264 See UNM Libraries, Center for Regional Studies, Celebrating New Mexico Statehood, "Tatschl," https://nmstatehood.unm.edu/search/node/tatschl, and, e.g., "The Lobo Statue," https://nmstatehood.unm.edu/node/67875, and https://nmstatehood.unm.edu/node/67876, and "Hodgin Hall - Tatschl Lobo Head and Logan Hall," https://nmstatehood.unm.edu/node/66760 (last accessed April 19, 2018). (Note that an additional lobo statue is located in Tight Grove and was sculpted by Michelle Middleton.)

265 UNM Libraries, Public Art at UNM: Writing and Research, "History of Writing," https://libguides.unm.edu/publicart/unm_examples (last accessed April 19, 2018).

266 See The Art of New Mexico: The Works of John Tatschl, "Biography," http://www.drivehq.com/web/tatsch73/NewMexico/bio.html (last accessed April 19, 2018).

267 Mara Kerkez, "UNM's Sprit of the Lobos program roams campus: bronze statues create lasting impression," UNM Newsroom (Feb. 9, 2014), http://news.unm.edu/news/unm-s-spirit-of-the-lobos-program-roams-campus (last accessed April 19, 2018).

268 Len Kravitz, "Doctor Heyward's Retirement Salute," (May 10, 2000), https://www.unm.edu/~lkravitz/ES%20News/vivretirement.html; see also UNM College of Education, "Previous Teaching Award Winners," http://ctl.unm.edu/faculty/assets/teacher-of-the-year-award-recipients.pdf, Len Kravitz, *April 2002 Exercise Science News Brief*, http://www.unm.edu/~lkravitz/ES%20News/april2002news.html, and UNM Alumni Association, Alumni Award Recipients, "Faculty Teaching Award," https://www.unmalumni.com/award-recipients.html (last accessed Oct. 22, 2018).

269 http://econtent.unm.edu/cdm/ref/collection/ULPhotoImag/id/111 (last accessed April 7, 2018).

270 See Joseph Suilmann, "A Tribute to Armond Harold 'Army' Seidler," UNM Newsroom (May 8, 2017), https://news.unm.edu/news/a-tribute-to-armond-harold-army-seidler, (last accessed April 19, 2018).

271 http://econtent.unm.edu/cdm/ref/collection/ULPhotoImag/id/462 (last accessed April 7, 2017).

272 See http://news.unm.edu/news/art-museum-celebrates-new-expansion-shows (last accessed Nov. 21, 2016). See also Hooker, p. 313 (Building 152).

273 UNM Art Museum, "The Raymond Johnson Collection," http://unmartmuseum.org/collections/the-raymond-johnson-collection/, and "Pure Feeling: Raymond Jonson in Albuquerque 1934-1978," http://unmartmuseum.org/online-exhibitions/pure-feeling/ (last accessed April 19, 2018).

274 UNM Office of the University Secretary, "Honorary Degrees," https://graduation.unm.edu/honorarydeg.html (last accessed April 17, 2018).

275 See Hooker, p. 308 (Building 34).

276 http://econtent.unm.edu/cdm/ref/collection/ULPhotoImag/id/499 (last accessed April 7, 2018).

277 See Association for Psychological Science, "In Appreciation: Frank A. Logan (1924-2004)," http://www.psychologicalscience.org/observer/in-appreciation-frank-a-logan-1924-2004# (last accessed April 19, 2018).

278 See Hooker, pp. 78-79, 86 (top photograph) and 307 (Building 9) and UNM Planning and Campus Development, "UNM Building List, by Campus, by Number," rev. Nov. 14, 2012, https://ppd.unm.edu/assets/documents/campus-maps/UnmBuildingsNum.pdf (Bldg. 9) (last accessed April 19, 2018).

279 http://econtent.unm.edu/cdm/ref/collection/ULPhotoImag/id/473 (last accessed April 7, 2018).

280 See "Governor appoints two UNM regents: Koch reappointed to the board," UNM Newsroom (April 3, 2015), http://news.unm.edu/news/governor-appoints-two-as-unm-regents (last accessed April 19, 2018).

281 See Hooker, p. 20 (top photograph).

282 See Hooker, p. 313 (Building 151).

283 See Hooker, pp. 78-79.

284 See Hooker, pp. 86 (bottom picture) and 87.

285 See Hooker, p. 309 (Building 56).

286 http://econtent.unm.edu/cdm/ref/collection/ULPhotoImag/id/3530 (last accessed April 7, 2018).

287 See Hooker, pp. 90-91.

288 See News Staff, "Updated at 5:45 am – UNM Grad Who Died in Spain Lived a Full Life," *Albuquerque Journal* (June 18, 2008), https://www.abqjournal.com/20849/updated-at-545am-unm-grad-who-died-in-spain-lived-full-life.html (last accessed April 19, 2018).

289 See Hooker, pp. 106 (top photo) and 308 (Building 23).

290 http://econtent.unm.edu/cdm/ref/collection/ULPhotoImag/id/3512 (last accessed April 7, 2018).

291 Hooker, p. 99.

292 Hooker, p. 313 (Building 151).

293 http://econtent.unm.edu/cdm/ref/collection/ULPhotoImag/id/509 (last accessed April 7, 2018).

294 Legacy.com, "Henry McDonald Willis," http://www.legacy.com/obituaries/name/henry-willis-obituary?pid=1000000178340186 (last accessed April 19, 2018).

295 See Hooker, pp. 111 (top and bottom photographs) and 308 (Building 24). See also http://universityofnewmexico.myuvn.com/campus-map/ (Number 12) (last accessed Jan. 21, 2017).

296 http://econtent.unm.edu/cdm/ref/collection/ULPhotoImag/id/422 (last accessed April 7, 2018).

297 UNM Meteorite Museum, "Institute of Meteoritics History," http://meteorite.unm.edu/iom-history/ (last accessed April 19, 2018).

298 See Barry S. Kues, "Stuart A. Northrup (1904-1994)," *New Mexico Geology*, vol. 16, n. 1, p. 14 (Feb. 1994), http://geoinfo.nmt.edu/publications/periodicals/nmg/16/n1/nmg_v16_n1_p14.pdf (last accessed April 19, 2018).

299 See UNM Department of Earth & Planetary Sciences, "The Silver Family Geology Museum," http://epswww.unm.edu/online-educational-resoures/geology-museum/ (last accessed April 19, 2018).

300 See Nolan Ashburn, "Memorial to Caswell Silver, 1916-1988," *Geological Society of America, Memorials*, vol. 29 (Dec. 1988), Reprinted from the *AAPG Bulletin*, 1989, vol. 73, n. 5, by permission of the American Association of Petroleum Geologists, ftp://rock.geosociety.org/pub/Memorials/v29/silver.pdf (last accessed April 19, 2018).

301 UNM Office of the University Secretary, "Honorary Degrees," https://secretary.unm.edu/recognition-and-awards/honorary-degrees.html (last accessed April 19, 2018).

302 See Hooker, p. 261.

303 See Hooker, pp. 195-198, 218, and 311 (Building 79), and Color Plate 8.

304 http://econtent.unm.edu/cdm/ref/collection/ULPhotoImag/id/3352 (last accessed April 7, 2018).

305 https://sites.google.com/site/unmgame/clickable-map/ortega-hall (last accessed Jan. 26, 2017).

306 See Hooker, p. 307 (Building 8). See also University of New Mexico Press, "Joaquin Ortega, 1892-1955," *New Mexico Quarterly*, vol. 25, n. 2 (1955), http://digitalrepository.unm.edu/nmq/vol25/iss2/3 (last accessed June 3, 2018).

307 UNM Office of the University Secretary, "Honorary Degrees," https://graduation.unm.edu/honorarydeg.html (last accessed April 17, 2018).

308 See UNM Department of Spanish & Portuguese, "Graduate Programs," https://spanport.unm.edu/academics/graduate-studies/index.html (last accessed April 19, 2018).

309 See "Duncan," *Albuquerque Journal* (June 19, 1998), http://obits.abqjournal.com/obits/show/132290 (last accessed April 19, 2018).

310 http://econtent.unm.edu/cdm/ref/collection/ULPhotoImag/id/515 (last accessed April 7, 2018).

311 See Hooker, pp. 59-60, and 63 (top photograph).

312 William E. Davis, "John Perovich - Biography" (2006), http://digitalrepository.unm.edu/president_bios/9 (last accessed April 19, 2018).

313 UNM Office of the University Secretary, "Regents' Awards Recipients," https://secretary.unm.edu/recognition-and-awards/regents-awards-recipients.html (last accessed April 19, 2018).

314 UNM Alumni Association, Alumni Award Recipients, "Lobo Award," https://www.unmalumni.com/award-recipients.html (last accessed April 19, 2018).

315 UNM Office of the University Secretary, "Honorary Degrees," https://graduation.unm.edu/honorarydeg.html (last accessed April 17, 2018).

316 See Hooker, pp. 47-49 and 312 (Building 104) and UNM Planning and Campus Development, "UNM Building List, by Campus, by Number," rev. Nov. 14, 2012, https://ppd.unm.edu/assets/documents/campus-maps/UNMBuildingsNum.pdf (Bldg.104) (last accessed April 17, 2018).

317 http://econtent.unm.edu/cdm/ref/collection/ULPhotoImag/id/529 (last accessed Oct. 16, 2018).

318 "Sara Raynolds Hall," *Wikipedia*, https://en.wikipedia.org/wiki/Sara_Raynolds_Hall (last accessed April 19, 2018).

319 See Hooker, pp. 206 and 308 (Building 35).

320 http://econtent.unm.edu/cdm/ref/collection/ULPhotoImag/id/524 (last accessed April 7, 2018).

321 UNM Office of the University Secretary, "Regents' Awards Recipients," https://secretary.unm.edu/recognition-and-awards/regents-awards-recipients.html (last accessed April 19, 2018).

322 See John R. Green, "Physics and Astronomy, 1892-1989," with recent amendments by Daniel Finley, http://physics.unm.edu/pandaweb/history/, "Physics & Astronomy Faculty," http://physics.unm.edu/pandaweb/history/faculty.php/, and Mary DeWitt, "Obituary of Victor H. Regener," *Physics Today* (Jan. 30, 2006), http://physicstoday.scitation.org/do/10.1063/PT.4.2273/full/ (last accessed April 19, 2018).

323 http://econtent.unm.edu/cdm/ref/collection/Manuscripts/id/9893 (last accessed April 7, 2018). See also Hooker, pp. 198 and 307 (Building 10) and Color Plates 2 and 7.

324 See, e.g., Dan Bullis, *New Mexico Historical Biographies*, Rio Grande Books, Albuquerque, NM (2011). See also Richard E. Greenleaf, "Francis Vinton Scholes (1897-1979): A Personal Memoir," *Hispanic American Historical Review*, vol. 60, no. 1, pp. 90-94 (1980) and UNM Office of the University Secretary, "Honorary Degrees," https://graduation.unm.edu/honorarydeg.html (last accessed April 17, 2018).

325 See University of New Mexico Board of Regents, "University of New Mexico Board of Regents Minutes for March 09, 1968" (1968), http://digitalrepository.unm.edu/bor_minutes/701 (last accessed April 19, 2018).

326 http://econtent.unm.edu/cdm/ref/collection/ULPhotoImag/id/3587 (last accessed April 7, 2018).

327 See https://sites.google.com/site/unmgame/clickable-map/dane-smith-hall-1 (last accessed Jan. 26, 2017).

328 See Bldg. 73, UNM Planning and Campus Development, "UNM Building List, by Campus, by Number," rev. Nov. 14, 2012, https://ppd.unm.edu/assets/documents/campus-maps/UnmBuildingsNum.pdf (last accessed April 19, 2018).

329 See Hooker, pp. 193 (top photograph) and 311 (Building 73).

330 See UNM Student Health and Counseling (SHAC), https://shac.unm.edu, and UNM University College, "Contact," http://ucollege.unm.edu/contact.html (last accessed April 20, 2018).

331 UNM Board of Regents, "University of New Mexico Board of Regents Minutes for April 12, 1988" (1988), http://digitalrepository.unm.edu/bor_minutes/56 (last accessed April 20, 2018).

332 See V.B. Price, "UNM Honors College: Bigger Isn't Better," *New Mexico Mercury* (May 12, 2013), http://newmexicomercury.com/blog/comments/unms_honors_college_bigger_isnt_better (last accessed April 20, 2018).

333 UNM Board of Regents, "University of New Mexico Board of Regents Minutes for February 10, 1972" (1972), http://digitalrepository.unm.edu/bor_minutes/326 (last accessed April 20, 2018).

334 http://econtent.unm.edu/cdm/ref/collection/ULPhotoImag/id/3613 (last accessed April 7, 2018). See also "University College Advisement Center changes name," UNM Newsroom (April 6, 2018), https://news.unm.edu/news/university-college-advisement-center-changes-name (last accessed April 20, 2018).

335 UNM Dean of Students History, https://dos.unm.edu/about/history.html (last accessed April 20, 2018).

336 UNM Alumni Association, "Rodey Award," https://www.unmalumni.com/rodey-past.html (last accessed April 20, 2018).

337 See Hooker, p. 310 (Building 60).

338 UNM Alumni Association, Alumni Award Recipients, "Lobo Award," https://www.unmalumni.com/award-recipients.html (last accessed April 20, 2018).

339 See Hooker, p. 313 (Building 118).

340 http://econtent.unm.edu/cdm/ref/collection/ULPhotoImag/id/297 (last accessed April 7, 2018).

341 UNM Board of Regents, "University of New Mexico Board of Regents Minutes for February 10, 1972" (1972), http://digitalrepository.unm.edu/bor_minutes/326 (last accessed April 20, 2018).

342 UNM School of Engineering, A History of Leadership, "Ralph Tapy," http://engineering.unm.edu/about/our-magazine/magazine-archives/spring-2007/a-history-of-leadership.html (last accessed April 20, 2018).

343 See Hooker, pp. 219 (photograph) and 311 (Building 82).

344 http://econtent.unm.edu/cdm/ref/collection/ULPhotoImag/id/558 (last accessed April 7, 2018).

345 UNM Office of the University Secretary, "Honorary Degrees," https://secretary.unm.edu/recognition-and-awards/honorary-degrees.html, and University of California, Berkeley, Dept. of Geography, "Living New Deal," https://livingnewdeal.org/projects/university-new-mexico-zimmerman-library-albuquerque-nm/ (last accessed April 20, 2018).

346 See Hooker, pp. 52 (bottom photograph), 87, 135, and 309 (Building 53) and Plate 1.

347 http://econtent.unm.edu/cdm/ref/collection/ULPhotoImag/id/3086 (last accessed April 7, 2018).

348 UNM Libraries, Center for Regional Studies, Celebrating New Mexico Statehood, "Zimmerman, James F.," https://nmstatehood.unm.edu/node/68172, and William E. Davis, "James Fulton Zimmerman - Biography" (2006), http://digitalrepository.unm.edu/president_bios/7 (last accessed April 20, 2018).

349 See Mike Bush, "UNM's Zimmerman Library marking 75th Anniversary," *Albuquerque Journal* (Oct. 15, 2013), https://www.abqjournal.com/281881/library-a-diamond.html, and National Park Service, National Register of Historic Places, "Zimmerman Library," https://www.nps.gov/nr/feature/places/pdfs/16000549.pdf (last accessed Oct. 15, 2018). See also Richard Flint and Shirley Cushing Flint, "James Fulton Zimmerman," N.M. Office of the State Historian, http://newmexicohistory.org/people/james-fulton-zimmerman (last accessed April 20, 2018).

350 http://econtent.unm.edu/cdm/ref/collection/ULPhotoImag/id/2655 (last accessed April 7, 2018).

351 http://econtent.unm.edu/cdm/ref/collection/ULPhotoImag/id/3059 (last accessed April 7, 2018).

352 http://econtent.unm.edu/cdm/ref/collection/ULPhotoImag/id/562 (last accessed April 7, 2018).

353 See, e.g., U.S. Congress, Biographical Directory, "Anderson, Clinton Presba (1895-1975)," http://bioguide.congress.gov/scripts/biodisplay.pl?index=a000186 (last accessed Oct. 22, 2018).

354 New Mexico Museum of Space History, International Space Hall of Fame, "Clinton P. Anderson," http://www.nmspacemuseum.org/halloffame/detail.php?id=36 (last accessed Oct. 22, 2018).

355 See Social Networks and Archival Context, "Bell, Thomas S. (Thomas Sidney), 1883-1960," http://snaccooperative.org/search (last accessed Oct. 22, 2018).

356 UNM Office of the University Secretary, "Honorary Degrees," https://secretary.unm.edu/recognition-and-awards/honorary-degrees.html (last accessed April 20, 2018).

357 UNM General Library, "A Virtual Tour of the Alice Clark Room," http://www.unm.edu/~wzahner/alice.html (last accessed Oct. 22, 2018).

358 See David Kammer, "Buildings Designed by John Gaw Meem, 1925-1959," N.M. Office of the State Historian, http://newmexicohistory.org/people/buildings-designed-by-john-gaw-meem-1925-1959 (last accessed April 20, 2018).

359 UNM Office of the University Secretary, "Honorary Degrees," https://secretary.unm.edu/recognition-and-awards/honorary-degrees.html (last accessed April 20, 2018).

360 UNM Libraries, "John Gaw Meem: New Mexico Architect," https://libguides.unm.edu/meem (last accessed April 20, 2018).

361 Wolfgang Saxon, "John Gaw Meem, architect who led in 'Santa Fe' style," *New York Times* (1983), http://www.nytimes.com/1983/08/07/obituaries/john-gaw-meem-architect-who-led-in-santa-fe-style.html (last accessed April 20, 2018).

362 UNM Writing the Southwest, "Frank Waters," https://www.unm.edu/~wrtgsw/waters.html and Carolyn Gonzales, "University of New Mexico (UNM) Library remembers Frank Waters at centennial" (originally published in the *Taos News Online* issue July 19, 2002), http://www.frankwaters.org/fw_reading_room.htm (last accessed April 20, 2018).

363 UNM Office of the University Secretary, "Honorary Degrees," https://secretary.unm.edu/recognition-and-awards/honorary-degrees.html (last accessed April 19, 2018).

364 See Wolfgang Saxon, "Frank Waters, Novelist, Dies; Chronicler of Southwest was 92," *New York Times* (1995), http://www.nytimes.com/1995/06/06/obituaries/frank-waters-novelist-dies-chronicler-of-southwest-was-92.html (last accessed April 19, 2018).

365 http://econtent.unm.edu/cdm/ref/collection/ULPhotoImag/id/563 (last accessed April 7, 2018).

366 UNM Foundation, "Willard Room and Lecture Series," https://www.unmfund.org/fund/willard-room-lecture-series/ and UNM Foundation, "Dedicated Librarian Billie Willard Remembered," *Developments at the University Libraries* (Spring 2010), https://library.unm.edu/about/development/newsletter/developments-spring-2010.pdf (last accessed April 19, 2018).

Section Two—North Campus

Belén Marbles (Photograph by A. Clarke).

THE LAW SCHOOL[1]

Bratton Hall II (Bratton Hall)

Fig. 1. Bratton Hall II – Law School – Exterior Entry Doors, Trees, and Bicycle Racks, circa 1970s (Photograph by Kate Nash, Center for Southwest Research, UNM Libraries). [2]

Fig. 2. Bratton Hall II – Law School – Exterior Close-up on Doors, 1998 (Photograph by Kate Nash, Center for Southwest Research, UNM Libraries). [3]

When Dean Thomas Christopher came to UNM as Dean of the Law School in 1965, he objected to a proposed addition to Bratton Hall I[4] on the main campus. The Dean received approval for a new building, and since it was for a graduate program, University Architect Van Dorn Hooker suggested the present site on the North Campus. The building was completed on February 1, 1971, and dedicated on April 17 of that year. Byron "Whizzer" White, Associate Justice of the U.S. Supreme Court was honored guest and speaker. Representatives of the Navajo Nation conducted a ceremony blessing the building, which was followed by a symposium entitled "Identity for Modern Man." The name Bratton Hall was transferred to the new Law School building from the first so-named building on the main campus.

Judge Sam Gilbert Bratton Plaque[5]

Fig. 3. Bratton Hall I – Plaque (Center for Southwest Research, UNM Libraries). [6]

A large bronze plaque designed by Professor John Tatschl, which originally hung in Bratton Hall I, now hangs in the main entrance hall of Bratton Hall II. The plaque reads:

> Bratton Hall is named for Sam Gilbert Bratton, Prime Mover in the Establishment of the School of Law. Judge of the 5th Judicial District Court of New Mexico 1919-23; Associate Justice of the Supreme Court of New Mexico, 1923-24; United States Senator, 1925-33; President of the Regents of the University, 1939-51; Judge of the United States Court of Appeals for the 10th Circuit, 1933-63.

Sam Bratton, born in 1884 in Kosse in Limestone County, Texas, finished high school there, and started teaching. After studying law, he was admitted to the Texas Bar in 1909. Moving to Clovis, New Mexico, in 1915, he practiced law there until 1919, when he was appointed to the District Court of the 5th Judicial District of New Mexico. When the District was divided, he was appointed to the 9th Judicial District. He was elected to the U.S. Senate in 1924. In 1933, he resigned to become a judge of the U.S. Circuit Court of Appeals for the 10th Circuit, serving until 1961. In 1954, UNM awarded Bratton an honorary Doctorate of Law and Letters.[7] Bratton died in 1963. His son, Judge Howard C. Bratton, who died in 2002, followed in his father's footsteps as a federal judge in Las Cruces, New Mexico, and as a UNM regent.[8]

William E. Bondurant Lecture Hall

A lecture hall in the Law School is named for William E. Bondurant, Jr., who was a member of the firm Hinkle, Bondurant, Cox & Eaton in New Mexico and Chair of the New Mexico Board of Bar Examiners. Bondurant was born in 1913 and moved with his family to New Mexico in 1922. After graduating from the New Mexico Military Institute, he obtained his law degree from the University of Colorado and practiced law in Roswell until he retired. U.S. District Court Judge Howard C. Bratton wrote, "Bill's approach to the law was always scholarly in part because of his devotion to the law and in part because of his substantial ability, he was truly a lawyer's lawyer…" Bondurant made a significant gift to the UNM Law School in 1975 to fund scholarships. The gift was considered at the time one of the largest gifts ever made to a law school. The scholarships, named for his parents William E. and Hazel J. Bondurant, were to be awarded to students based on need and scholarship ability, and if possible, to New Mexico residents.[9]

Bruce King Reading Room and Archive

The Governor Bruce King Reading Room and Archive is named for the former New Mexico governor, who was also a UNM alumnus and strong supporter of higher education. The room, located on the second level of the Law Library, contains memorabilia of Bruce and his wife Alice King. The room features a very long and beautiful conference table.

Bruce King was born in Stanley, New Mexico, on April 6, 1924. During World War II, he served in the U.S. Army Field Artillery in the Asiatic Theater. Upon his return, he attended UNM. Beginning his political career as a two-term member of the Santa Fe County Commission (1954-58), he was elected to the New Mexico House of Representatives in 1959 and served five terms, three of those as Speaker of the House. King defeated Pete Domenici in the governor's race in 1970 and served three non-consecutive terms as governor of New Mexico: 1971-74, 1979-82, and 1991-94.

King was chair of many commissions, associations, federations, and organizations in his many years of public service and he helped the University in many ways while he was in office. In 1979, the UNM Alumni Association presented King with the Erna Fergusson Award. UNM awarded Regents Recognition Medals to Alice King in 1982 and Bruce King in 2000. King retired to his ranch near Stanley and died there on November 11, 2009.[10]

The Edward, Beatrice and John Rickert Memorial Garden

The Edward, Beatrice & John Rickert Memorial Garden is located on the southeast side of the Law School on a site that was chosen because of the association of the Rickert family with the Law School and Health Sciences Center. John R. Rickert was born on March 17, 1950, in Lubbock, Texas. He graduated from Highland High School in Albuquerque. He had received his B.A. from UNM and M.A. from the University of Texas. Rickert also attended John Hopkins University. In 1986, while on a Fulbright Scholarship in Tübingen University in Germany, Rickert died. At the time of his death, he was writing his dissertation for his Ph.D. in philosophy.

Edward J. Rickert, John's father, was born on June 13, 1913, in Houston, Texas, and attended law school there before dropping out due to the Great Depression. He served in the U.S. Navy in World War II on the USS Pittsburgh in the taking of Okinawa and Iwo Jima. After the war, he worked for many years with the Atchison, Topeka and Santa Fe Railroad and then with Amtrak. For much of that time, he headed the New Mexico Chapter of the Brotherhood of Railway and Airline Clerks (BRAC). He died in 1991.

Beatrice "Bea" Pierros Rickert, John's mother, was born on September 17, 1910, in Houston, Texas, and attended the Lady of the Lake College in San Antonio, before dropping out during the Depression. An accomplished musician, she played the violin as a child member of the Houston Symphony. She was also a pianist and had her own radio show in Houston for a time. For many years, she was associated with the Sherwood Conservatory of Music in Chicago. Beatrice Rickert moved her family to New Mexico in 1940 for health reasons, living first in Clovis, then in Carlsbad, and finally moving to Albuquerque in the 1960s. While working for the Federal Aviation Administration, she was injured in a fall and retired. She received rehabilitation at the UNM Health Sciences Center for may years and was able to walk again and care for her husband, Edward J. Rickert, until his death. Beatrice Rickert died on October 2, 1999.

The garden in the Rickerts' memory was provided by John Rickert's siblings: Kay Marr, Beatrice "Bea" R. Bevell, and Dr. Edward J. Rickert. Kay Marr received a B.A. and J.D. from UNM and served as Deputy Attorney General and Cabinet Secretary of the New Mexico Department of Finance and Administration. Bea Bevell graduated from the University of Albuquerque and attended UNM. Bea Bevell served until her retirement as assistant to the Director of Disabled Student Services, Student Support Services, and the Upward Bound Program. She also served on the State Health Policy Commission. Bea Bevell died on January 4, 2014. The UNM Alumni Memorial Chapel Garden – Beatrice Bevell Tree Fund was established in her honor. Dr. Edward J. Rickert of Atlanta, Georgia, received three degrees from UNM, including a Ph.D. in psychology in 1968. Dr. Rickert also received a M.P.H. from the University of Alabama Medical School, where he taught for thirty years until retiring.[11]

Utton Transboundary Resources Center

The Utton Transboundary Resources Center is named for the late Professor Albert E. Utton, the first native New Mexican to join the faculty of the School of Law. Born in Aztec, New Mexico, Utton's first degree was with honors in geology at UNM in 1953. In addition to being elected to Phi Beta Kappa, Utton was elected student body president. A Rhodes Scholar, Utton obtained his law degree from Oxford University with honors in 1956 and did postgraduate work at the University of London and Yale University. He joined the Inner Temple of the English Bar and the New Mexico Bar.

After serving in England as Assistant Judge Advocate in the United States Air Force, Utton returned to New Mexico and joined the UNM Law School faculty in 1962, teaching hundreds of students and at one point acting as Interim Dean of the Law School.

Utton was known as a "gifted mediator and negotiator" and an internationally recognized expert in transboundary resource law and policy, particularly water law. He was the Editor of the *National Resources Journal* and the *New Mexico Law Review*. He authored many articles and books. In the 1980s, he founded and directed the International Transboundary Resources Center, now the Utton Transboundary Resources Center. In 1994, he gave the annual UNM Research Lecture, which he titled "Water in the Arid Southwest: An International Region Under Stress." His many honors in addition to being chosen to deliver the University's annual Research Lecture included receiving the Law School Distinguished Achievement Award and the Aztec Eagle Award, Mexico's highest award to a non-citizen for distinguished service to Mexico. The Utton Center in 2015 published an extensive biography by Michele Minnis entitled *Al Utton-Aztec Eagle: International Waters, Research, Diplomacy, and Friendship*.

Laurie Mellas Ramirez wrote in *Quantum*:

> The Utton Transboundary Resources Center at the UNM School of Law was created in 2000 to help those with shared interests manage the use of water supplies and avoid litigation. …Utton, a Rhodes Scholar who gained an international reputation by using multidisciplinary scholarship to address complex resource issues, primarily along the Rio Grande/Rio Bravo and United States border. … Using impartial 'preventive diplomacy,' a facilitative tactic Utton honed, the center helps resolve various issues related to transboundary resources – natural resources intersected by political boundaries.

Al Utton died on September 29, 1998.[12]

Henry P. Weihofen Faculty Library

Henry Weihofen was born in Chicago in 1904 and received both a J.D. and J.S.D. from the University of Chicago School of Law. He taught at the University of Colorado until 1941, when he moved to Washington, D.C., to serve on the War Labor Board and the Department of Justice Court of Claims. After World War II, Weihofen moved to Albuquerque to teach at UNM. In 1955, he gave the annual UNM Research Lecture.

Weihofen was known not only as "Henry the Hawk" for his engagement with unprepared students, but also as a leader in the field of legal forensic psychiatry. In 1955, he received the Isaac Ray Award for his contributions to the field of law and psychiatry. Weihofen authored several books on legal subjects and many articles for legal journals. In New Mexico, he was active in several organizations including the ACLU, the Democratic Party, and the New Mexico Conference on Social Welfare. After retiring, he authored "History of the Law School, 1947-1987," and established the Henry Weihofen Endowed Professorship, later known as the Henry Weihofen Chair. Weihofen received numerous awards and citations for his lifetime of work. He died in October 1993 at the age of 89. The Henry F. Weihofen Faculty Library is named in his honor.[13]

The Frederick Hart Wing

Fig. 4. Fred Hart Wing (Photograph by Suzanne Mortier, UNM Landscape Architect, 2013).

The Frederick Hart Wing, located on the south side of the original Law School building and completed in 2002, is named for Emeritus Professor Frederick "Fred" Michael Hart.

Hart was born in Flushing, New York, and received his B.S. in 1951 and his J.D. in 1955 from Georgetown University. He received a Master of Law and Letters from New York University, in 1956, and did postgraduate work at Frankfurt University in Germany. After teaching at Albany Law School, Union College, and Boston College, he came to UNM in 1966, and served as Dean of the Law School from 1971 to 1979 and 1985 to 1986. Hart was instrumental in efforts to diversify the student body and faculty. He is best known for his efforts in establishing the American Indian Law Center and other programs designed to provide Native American students with access to law schools. Hart noted, "When we started the program there were only twenty American Indian lawyers nationwide and now there are more than 2,000." He also established the school's Clinical Law Program, which served as a model for similar programs at other law schools. Hart has written many articles and legal textbooks and is well known for his contribution to the Uniform Commercial Code. He received the UNM Alumni Association's Rodey Award in 2016.[14]

The John Morgan-Johnson Tsosie Patio

Fig. 5. John Morgan and Johnson Tsosie Patio (Photograph by Suzanne Mortier, UNM Landscape Architect, 2013).

Fig. 6. John Morgan and Johnson Tsosie Marker (Photograph by Ann Clarke).

John Morgan and Johnson Tsosie were members of the Class of 1979. On the east wall of Bratton Hall at the entrance to the library is a plaque associated with a small walled patio with three concrete planter boxes, which once held three trees. Only one tree remains. The plaque reads:

> Given in memory of
> John Morgan and Johnson Tsosie,
> the Class of 1979.

Other donations by family and friends resulted in the establishment of the Morgan Memorial Library Fund.

Robert Desiderio Seminar Room

The Robert Desiderio Seminar Room is named for the long-time professor known to his friends as "Desi." Graduating from St. Joseph's College (Pennsylvania), he received his law degree from Boston College in 1966. He joined the UNM Law School faculty in 1967 and became a full professor in 1974. In 1978, he served as a special counsel to the Northern Marianas Commonwealth Legislature. Desiderio served as Dean of the Law School from 1979 to 1985 and 1997 to 2002. He was appointed interim Vice President for Academic Affairs at UNM from 1985-1986. He retired in 2002 as Professor Emeritus. [15]

The James Quinn Memorial Tree

James Quinn was a member of the Class of 2010 at the UNM School of Law when he and his wife were killed in a bicycle accident on September 15, 2007. James Quinn was born on November 22, 1979, in Philadelphia, Pennsylvania. Very interested in the environment, Quinn received an Associate in Applied Science degree with highest honors in photographic imaging from the Community College of Philadelphia in 2000. He completed a B.S. *summa cum laude* in conservation science at the College of Santa Fe in 2003 and an M.S. in water resources from UNM in 2007, before enrolling in the Law School. He was a member of the Environmental Law Society. In his memory, the student body secured funds for a crabapple tree and plaque. The plaque is attached to a bench beside a square plot containing the tree on the east side of Bratton Hall. In addition, the students established the James Quinn Memorial Scholarship. [16]

The Mary Coon Walters Classroom

The Mary Coon Walters Classroom is named for the first woman to serve on the New Mexico Supreme Court. Friends gave money to name the room in Justice Walters honor. Justice Walters was born in Baraga, Michigan, on January 29, 1922, , to Marvin L. and Nancy Coon. During World War II, Justice Walters, at age 20, joined the Women Airforce Service Pilots (WASP) and served as a C-45 transport pilot from 1943 to 1944. She served in the United States Air Force in the early 1950s. Justice Walters enrolled under the G.I. Bill in UNM Law School and was the only female in her graduating class of 1962. She began her law practice in 1963. In 1971, Governor Bruce King appointed Walters as the first woman on a District Court (2nd District). She was elected to the New Mexico Court of Appeals (4th and 10th Circuits) from 1978 to 1984. In 1984, she was appointed to the N.M. Supreme Court. She was inducted into the New Mexico Women's Hall of Fame in 1986. Justice Walters died on April 4, 2001, at age 79. [17]

Other Donor Named Rooms in UNM School of Law

- Court Room 3410 is named for the law firm of Mondrall, Sperling, Roehl, Harris and Sisk, PA, of Albuquerque.
- Classroom 3416 is named for James A. Branch, Jr., and Estaban A. Aguilar of Albuquerque.

- Seminar Room 2532 is named for the law firm of Keleher and McCleod of Albuquerque.
- Court Room 2525 is named for the law firm of Rodey, Dickason, Sloan, Akin and Robb of Albuquerque.

THE NEW MEXICO LAW CENTER

A small building was erected in 1974 just south of Bratton Hall and originally named the Dale Bellamah Law Center for the homebuilder Dale Bellamah. It has since been renamed the New Mexico Law Center. Construction funds came from various sources, including UNM. Bellamah also made a contribution toward the cost of the building. The occupants have changed through the years. The building was intended to house the New Mexico Bar Association and related organizations. Today, the building houses the Institute of Public Law, which includes the Judicial Education Center, the Corinne Wolf Center for Child and Family Justice, and the Legal Practice and Training Center.

Dale Bellamah constructed low-cost residences in large planned communities after World War II and soon became the world's 6th largest homebuilder. He did much of his building in Albuquerque and Santa Fe. Princess Jeanne Park, which in 1954 offered affordable housing in a quality environment, was featured in a 1994 Smithsonian exhibit. [18] A bronze plaque in the entry to the New Mexico Law Center reads:

> Dale H. Bellamah, 1914-1972, These Chambers are Provided to Perpetuate the Spirit and Objectives of the Law. May the Ideals of the Young Scholars be Inspired by the Free Communication with the Wise and Experienced Members of the Profession.

The Pamela B. Minzer Law Center

Fig. 7. Pamela B. Minzer Law Center, Court of Appeals (Albuquerque) (Source unknown).

In 2009, the State Court of Appeals named its building located to the west of the UNM Law School for Justice Pamela B. Minzer. Justice Minzer was the first woman to become Chief Justice of the New Mexico Supreme Court. She received a B.A. from Miami University and her law degree from Harvard in 1968. She taught at UNM Law School for twelve years. In 1984, she was appointed to the N.M. Court of Appeals. In 1994, she became the second woman to be appointed to the N.M. Supreme Court and was Chief Justice from 1998 until 2001. Minzer died on August 31, 2007, at 63. Chief Justice Edward Chavez noted at Justice Minzer's passing:

Justice Minzner enjoyed unconditional respect and admiration from the legal community because she was hard working, articulate and an excellent writer. Yet her best qualities were her human qualities. With an ever present smile, she treated everyone with dignity, respect and genuine thoughtfulness.[19]

THE MEDICAL SCHOOL

Reginald Heber Fitz Hall (Basic Medical Sciences Building)

Fig. 8. Basic Medical Sciences – Horizontal View, 1998 (Photograph by Kate Nash, Center for Southwest Research, UNM Libraries).

Fig. 9. Reginald Heber Fitz Hall, 2014 (Photograph by Sara Mora, UNM Health Sciences College).[20]

The Basic Medical Sciences Building (BMSB) was the first permanent building constructed for the School of Medicine. It was designed to house the basic sciences taught to first- and second-year students. Courses included physiology, microbiology, pharmacology, anatomy, and pathology. The building also housed several administrative offices and named spaces.

On August 1, 2014, the BMSB was renamed the Reginald Heber Fitz Hall in honor of the School of Medicine's first dean, who died on May 28, 2013. Fitz received his B.A. and M.D. from Harvard and completed his residency at the University of Colorado, where he taught before coming to New Mexico. Fitz was known as a visionary for creating an environment that blended basic and clinical education.[21]

Frederick Harvey, MD, Library Room

Dr. Frederick Huckel Harvey, a general practitioner with an interest in pathology, joined the UNM medical faculty as a professor of pathology in the 1970s. Harvey left UNM to pursue a Ph.D. in neuropathology at the University of Washington and returned to become the first forensic neuropathologist in New Mexico. Harvey's great, great grandfather was Fred Harvey, founder of the Fred Harvey hotels. While at UNM, Dr. Harvey funded a departmental library in the Basic Medical Sciences Building and a teaching resource center. Harvey died in 1982. That same year, the Frederick H. Harvey Endowed Chair of Pathology and the Harvey Family Professorship in Pathology were created.[22]

The Sidney Soloman Conference Room

Sidney Soloman, born in Worcester, Massachusetts, on February 22, 1923, attended Worcester State College for a short time in the early 1940s until enlisting in the Marine Corps during World War II. He received a B.S. from the University of Massachusetts in 1949 and his Ph.D. in physiology from the University of Chicago in 1952. From 1952 through 1963, he taught at the Medical College of Virginia in the Department of Physiology. During his last year there, Soloman received a Guggenheim Fellowship and studied in Germany. While in Germany, he is thought to have worked with Karl Ullrich (1925-2010), who was a well-known renal physiologist.[23]

Soloman was one of the earliest faculty members recruited by Dean Reginald Fitz, the founding Dean of the School of Medicine,[24] to teach at the University of New Mexico. Soloman came to UNM on June 28, 1963, first serving as a professor and then as Chair of the Department of Physiology. Soloman assisted Fitz in recruiting other faculty while continuing his research in a World War II wooden barracks building that had been remodeled into his laboratory.[25]

During his time at UNM, Soloman served with the National Science Foundation first as Program Director of Metabolic Biology and a year as Acting Director of the Division of Physiology, Cellular and Molecular Biology. Soloman retired in 1989 and died in Albuquerque in 1993.

Interior Garden Memorial to Joseph P. Leonard

After attending Texas Tech University, Joseph P. Leonard came to UNM, where he received his M.D. in 1973 from the School of Medicine. Leonard interned at the Kaiser Foundation Hospital in San Francisco, California. While at UNM, he was a member of Alpha Omega Alpha and received the Merck Manual Award, which recognizes outstanding graduating students. Leonard died at a young age. A plaque located in the patio between Fitz Hall and the Biomedical Research Facility reads:

In Memory of Joseph Patrick Leonard MD,
by Friends and Members of the Class of 1973.

UNM CANCER CENTER[26] AND CANCER RESEARCH AND TREATMENT CENTER

Fig. 10. Cancer Research and Treatment Center – Front Entrance, 1998 (Photograph by Kate Nash, Center for Southwest Research, UNM Libraries).[27]

Fig. 11. Cancer Research Center, 1974 (Center for Southwest Research, UNM Libraries).[28]

The Cancer Research and Treatment Center, built in 1974 and located north of UNM Hospital, was the first facility constructed for cancer research and treatment at the UNM Health Sciences Center. The Cancer Research and Treatment Center was planned primarily around the use of radiation therapies. The building still functions as the Cancer Research Facility.

After a decade of planning and construction, a new building for the Cancer Research and Treatment Center was erected on the west side of University Boulevard. This building was subsequently incorporated into the first phase of a new state-of-the-art UNM Cancer Center (also called the UNM Comprehensive Cancer Center), which was opened in 2009. The UNM Cancer Center includes healing gardens, private alcoves, a reflective pool and a meditation chapel to provide an environment of hope and healing.[29]

Carl Anderson and Marie Jo Anderson Charitable Foundation Healing Garden and Pool

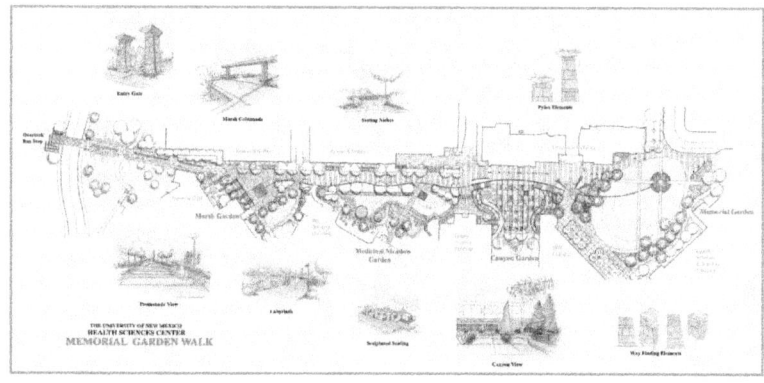

Fig. 12. Healing Garden Rendering (Photograph by Suzanne Mortier, UNM Landscape Architect, 2013).

The Carl C. Anderson and Marie Jo Anderson Charitable Foundation made a considerable contribution to the new UNM Cancer Center. The Healing Garden and Pool on the site and the Radiation Oncology/Radio Surgery Suite are named for Mr. and Mrs. Anderson, both deceased. Their daughter, Jennifer Jo Bird, chair of the Foundation Board of Trustees, is a graduate of UNM.[30]

The Philip and Olga Eaton Sculpture Garden of Healing

Fig. 13. *Philip and Olga Eaton Sculpture Garden of Healing (Photograph by Suzanne Mortier, UNM Landscape Architect, 2013).*

Philip Eaton was born in Grand Rapids, Michigan, and received his M.D. from the University of Chicago. Olga, born in Pagosa Springs, Colorado, received her M.D. from the University of Colorado. They met and came to UNM in 1968. Olga began working as a Student Health Center physician and Philip established the Division of Endocrinology in the Medical School.

The Eatons spent their entire professional lives at the University. Olga became Director of the Student Health Center, a position she held until she retired in 2003. In the early 1980s, Philip collaborated with William Spencer, the former director of systems development at Sandia National Laboratories, in developing the first implantable insulin pump for diabetics. In 2015, the School of Medicine recognized Philip Eaton as a "Living Legend."[31] Philip became the first Associate Dean for Research in the Medical School and Vice President for the Health Sciences. He retired in 2005. During his tenure as Vice President, the campus was expanded to accommodate new space for research, patient care, education, neuroscience, forensic medicine, and the Cancer Center.

As part of the transformation of the campus, the Eatons initiated the Sculpture Garden of Healing as a reassuring interface between the Health Sciences Center and the public that the Center serves. A larger landscape architecture initiative envisioning all of the exterior space on the Health Sciences campus as an area of welcoming art.[32] An excerpt from the *Walking Guide* notes:

> The Phil and Olga Eaton Sculpture Garden of Healing fuses traditional and contemporary sculptures to create an atmosphere conducive to healing and learning. One goal of the garden is to improve and enhance the well-being of our community by integrating sculpture, with its healing and spiritual qualities, into the heart of the UNM Health Sciences Center.

The Eaton Sculpture Garden of Healing will also include the School of Medicine Faculty Memorial, designed by Christine Williams while an art and architecture student. The Faculty Memorial is also known as Corazones de Nuevo México. Groundbreaking for the Faculty Memorial was October 11, 2013.[33]

Several pieces of sculpture are located in the garden on the east side of the Basic Medical Sciences Building. These pieces were acquired over time. Some were purchased by the University, though most were donated by individuals. Examples include:

- *Cloud/Rift*, by John Christensen. Funded by New Mexico Art in Public Places.
- *Jericho*, by Ernest Shaw, MD. Donated by Michael Rosenblum and Family.

- *Our Lady of Sorrows,* by Paul Harris. Donated by Peggy and Douglas Kirkland.
- *Parade,* by Beverly Maginnis. Funded by New Mexico Art in Public Places.
- *Genesis,* by Arthur Williams. Purchased by UNM.
- Blair Coker Memorial Garden and Bench. Donated by Jackie and Don Schlegel. (See also "Blair's Garden".)
- *Votive XXXXII,* by Ernest Shaw, MD. Donated by Ernest Shaw and Michael Rosenblum and Family.
- *Ruins,* by Ernest Shaw, MD. Donated by Michael Rosenblum and Family.

Paul Harris, the creator of *Our Lady of Sorrows,* wrote the following description:

> *Our Lady of Sorrows* was given to the University in 2001, in loving memory of Billie Cannedy Earnest by her sister and brother-in-law Peggy and Douglas Kirkland. Billie Earnest had strong connections with UNM –both donors received their degrees here and her son – Bob Earnest worked for the University for more than 28 years before retiring in the spring of 2003.

In the 1940s during his tenure as an art student at UNM, Paul Harris decided his calling was to become a sculptor. Harris has dedicated his life to the pursuit of discovering and exposing his own sense of uniqueness in form and vision, which is manifested in his work. *Our Lady of Sorrows* is made of bronze and was cast at New Mexico's premier Shidoni Foundry. Harris currently lives in Bolinas, California.

UNM Helix Garden Memorial

The UNM Health Sciences Center has begun efforts to develop a trellised walkway starting near Novitski Hall. The intent is to memorialize those who have donated their bodies for research. [34]

Billy McKibben Recognition Plaque

On the wall of the entrance lobby of the Cancer Research and Treatment Center, a plaque reads:

> In Recognition of the Outstanding Support, Service and Advocacy of The Honorable Billie McKibben, New Mexico State Senator, to the University of New Mexico Cancer Research and Treatment Center, April 1998.

Billy Jess McKibben was born June 2, 1936, in Eunice, N.M., the son of an oil field worker. He died of natural causes in Big Spring, Texas, on August 4, 2017. McKibben attended New Mexico Military Institute and graduated from New Mexico State University. He served 10 years in the U.S. Air Force, including as a pilot in the Vietnam War. McKibben became a real estate developer and served in the State Senate for two decades where he was known for his efforts to curb state government spending and for his ability to make people laugh as "Chainsaw." McKibben was Senate GOP Leader from 1992 to 1996. As a cancer survivor, he generously supported the UNM

Cancer Center. Also in the lobby is a display of the Oso Sandor Society, which lists donors of more than $1,000 to the Cancer Research and Treatment Center.[35]

Steve Schiff Center for Skin Cancer Research

Steven Schiff, born March 18, 1947, in Chicago, Illinois, served as Representative from the First Congressional District of New Mexico from 1989 to 1998. Schiff received a B.A. in political science from the University of Illinois in Chicago in 1968 and a J.D. from the University of New Mexico in 1972. Schiff enlisted in the New Mexico National Guard in 1969. He achieved the rank of colonel in the U.S. Air Force Reserves in 1994 and undertook missions in Bosnia and Iraq during the NATO operations in the Balkans.

After a time as Assistant District Attorney (1972-1977) and as Assistant Albuquerque City Attorney and Counsel for the Albuquerque Police Department (1979-1981), Schiff was elected Bernalillo County District Attorney in 1980 and reelected in 1984. That same year, he successfully ran for the open congressional seat in the First Congressional District of New Mexico. Schiff served five terms.

While in Congress, Schiff served on multiple committees, including the Committee on Science, Space, and Technology, the Judiciary Committee, and the Ethics Committee, and on numerous subcommittees. After an extended battle with skin cancer, Schiff died in Albuquerque on March 25, 1998.[36] The Steve Schiff Center for Skin Cancer Research is named in his memory.

CARRIE TINGLEY HOSPITAL

Fig. 14. Carrie Tingley Hospital (Source unknown).

The Carrie Tingley Hospital for Crippled Children was founded in Hot Springs (now named Truth or Consequences), New Mexico in 1937. The location was inspired by the treatment President Franklin D. Roosevelt received at Warm Springs, Georgia. The organizers planned that the New Mexico hot springs could be used in the same manner. The hospital was named for Carrie Wooster Tingley, the wife of Governor Clyde Tingley.[37] Carrie Tingley had a great love for children though she had none of her own. With the help of Governor Tingley and private donations, she obtained federal funds for the construction of the children's hospital. She visited often and every Christmas she saw to it that all the patients received gifts.

Carrie Tingley travelled to the desert in 1911 from her home in Bowling Green, Ohio, seeking a cure for tuberculosis, as many did in those days. While en route by train to Phoenix, Arizona, with her mother, Carrie had an acute attack and remained in Albuquerque for treatment. Clyde and Carrie were sweethearts, so when she settled in New Mexico, he followed and they soon married. Pat Kailer, in an article in the *Albuquerque Journal*, described her thus:

> Carrie Tingley was a somewhat flamboyant looking woman with dyed red hair and a penchant for purple, big hats and lots of jewelry. She liked pretty things and had a house full of silver and crystal and art objects. She loved the movies and went to them almost every afternoon.

Another reporter wrote:

> She really preferred staying behind the scenes and she was definitely independent. She didn't care what other people thought. If she liked something and wanted to do it, that's what she did.

Carrie Tingley died in 1964 leaving the hospital as a wonderful and lasting memorial in her name. The present building on University Boulevard was constructed as an osteopathic hospital. The State of New Mexico purchased the property when it came on the market and the Carrie Tingley Hospital was moved to Albuquerque in 1981 and became part of UNM Health Science Center. The original Carrie Tingley Hospital is now the N.M. State Veterans Home.

CASA ESPERANZA (HOUSE OF HOPE)

Fig. 15. Casa Esperanza (Source unknown).

Although Casa Esperanza is not a University building, it offers a home to people who come to Albuquerque for treatment at the University Medical Center. Built with private funds, the building sits on land leased from UNM and is in close proximity to the health facilities.

DOMENICI CENTER FOR HEALTH SCIENCES EDUCATION

Fig. 16. Domenici Center for Health Sciences Education (Source unknown).

The Center for Health Sciences Education, which consists of three buildings, is named for the late U.S. Senator from New Mexico, Pete Vichi Domenici.[38] The Center is also referred to as the HSC Interdisciplinary Education Center. Pietro "Pete" Vichi Domenici was born in Albuquerque on May 7, 1932, to Cherabino Domenici and Alda Vichi, both immigrants from northern Italy. As a boy, Domenici worked in his father's wholesale grocery business and graduated from St. Mary's High School. He attended UNM where he was a star baseball player. In 1954, he received his B.A. in education. He taught junior high science and math for a year before attending the University of Denver School of Law. He received his J.D. in 1958 and began practicing law. Domenici also pitched for a short time with the Albuquerque Dukes baseball team. Domenici was inducted into the UNM Athletics Hall of Honor in 1987.[39]

Domenici began his political career in 1966 when he won election to the Albuquerque City Commission and was elevated to Chair, the equivalent of mayor, the next year. After election to the U.S. Senate in 1972, he served six terms, the longest of any U.S. Senator from New Mexico. Domenici was known for his bi-partisanship and served on several important Senate committees including the Budget, Appropriations, Energy and Resources, and Indian Affairs. For his public service, he received many honors and awards, including the Fergusson Award in 1977, the Zimmerman Award in 1982, and an honorary Doctorate of Law and Letters from UNM in 1983.[40]

Through the years he obtained funding for numerous state and university projects and for Sandia and Los Alamos scientific laboratories. For his many contributions to New Mexico, the press began to refer to him as "Saint Pete." Domenici decided not to run for reelection in 2008 and died on September 13, 2017, in Albuquerque at age 85.[41]

The Fred H. Hanold, MD, Memorial Student Study Room

An 8-person study room (Room 2122) in the West Building of the Domenici Center is named for Professor Fred Heath Hanold.[42] Hanold was born in Bloomfield, New Jersey, on April 23, 1915, and attended New York University, where he received his undergraduate degrees and his M.D., the latter in 1940. Hanold started his residency at Bellevue Hospital that same year, but was called into service in World War II as part of the U.S. Navy Medical Corps.

Hanold finished his training in 1949 and saw an advertisement for a salaried position with private practice opportunities. In 1950, he moved his family to Albuquerque to take the position with the Santa Fe Railway Company Hospital, where he worked until 1954. He also established a private practice, which he ran until 1974. Hanold returned to the Hospital and worked there until his retirement in 1980. From 1952 to 1972, he was Chief of the Bernalillo County Cardiac Clinic as well as Chief of Medicine and Chief of Staff at Memorial Hospital, St. Joseph's Hospital, Bernalillo County Hospital, and Presbyterian Hospital. During this time, Hanold was also an attending physician at the Veteran's Hospital and a clinical professor of medicine at the UNM School of Medicine.

Hanold founded the New Mexico Chapter of the American College of Physicians and served as Governor of the Chapter from 1975 to 1979. In 1989, he received the Ralph O. Claypool, Sr., Memorial Award for devotion to a career in internal medicine and to the care of patients. After his retirement, Hanold pursued his interest in the history of medicine in New Mexico and for many years served as chair of the History of Medicine Committee in the Medical Society of New Mexico. Hanold died on April 17, 2006.[43]

The Leonard M. Napolitano, PhD, Anatomical Education Center

Fig. 17. Leonard M. Napolitano, Ph.D., Anatomical Education Foundation Center (Photograph by Suzanne Mortier, UNM Landscape Architect, 2013).

The northeast building within the Domenici Center for Health Sciences Education houses the Napolitano Anatomical Education Center, named for Leonard Michael Napolitano.

Napolitano was born in Oakland, California, on January 8, 1930, to Filippo and Angela Napolitano.[44] Napolitano received his B.S. from Santa Clara University in 1951 before moving to St. Louis University, where he received his M.S. in 1954 and his Ph.D. in 1956. While at Santa Clara University, he played quarterback on the varsity football team, which in the 1950 Orange Bowl upset the University of Kentucky Wildcats. From 1956 to 1958, he was an instructor in anatomy at Cornell Medical College. From 1958 to 1964, he was an instructor at the University of Pittsburgh. In 1964, he came to UNM as an associate professor of anatomy and one of seven founding faculty members of the new School of Medicine.

Napolitano became a full professor and in 1972 was appointed Interim Dean and then Dean of the School of Medicine. He retired in 1994. Napolitano was the longest serving medical school dean in the United States. He received the UNM Regents Meritorious Service Medal in 1993 and in 2009 was the recipient of the School of Medicine's first "Living Legend Award".[45] Napolitano died on January 7, 2013. The naming request to the UNM Naming Committee stated:

> During Dr. Napolitano's 22 years as Dean of the SOM, there was a tremendous amount of growth in all areas of education, research and clinical/service. Dr. Napolitano had the vision to build the medical school from the ground up, from a 7-Up bottling plant and an old mortuary to 15 buildings on 45 acres. There were many new departments and programs established, facilities constructed, and centers started during Dr. Napolitano's years as Dean. Dr. Napolitano was dedicated to a quality educational experience for all medical students and that led him to recruit top faculty. The result he was trying to achieve was a medical center with the potential to touch the life of every New Mexican. In 1991, Dr. Napolitano received the Bernard S. Rodey Award from the UNM Alumni Association in recognition of his leadership accomplishments.

PETE AND NANCY DOMENICI HALL (THE MIND INSTITUTE)

Fig. 18. Pete and Nancy Domenici Hall and MIND Institute (Photograph by Suzanne Mortier, UNM Landscape Architect, 2013).

The Pete and Nancy Domenici Hall is a cluster of relatively new buildings located on the North Campus north of the Law School and west of the North Campus golf course. Domenici Hall, not to be confused with the Domenici Center for Health Sciences Education, was expanded to include the MIND (Mental Illness and Neuroscience Discovery) Institute, the UNM Mind Imaging Center, and UNM BRaIN (Biomedical Research and Integrative Neuro-imaging) Center.[46]

Pete had married Nancy Burk, a physical therapist, in 1958, the same year he received his J.D. Due to the mental illness of one of their children, Pete and Nancy Domenici became interested in research being done on the human brain. For this effort, Senator Domenici obtained funding to establish the non-profit MIND Institute, which opened in 1998.[47] The MIND Institute and BRaIN Center, as well as the Mind Research Network (MRN) and Brain & Behavioral Health Institute, are involved in mapping the brain for a better understanding of how it works.

The Ronald McDonald House

Fig. 19. Ronald McDonald House (Source unknown).

Ray Kroc was the founder of the worldwide chain of McDonald's fast food restaurants. In 1954, he was a distributor of a milkshake mixer. Kroc became interested in a company owned by Dick and Mac McDonald in California. Impressed by how many people the McDonald brothers could serve very quickly, Kroc proposed setting up a chain of their restaurants. They agreed, so Kroc opened the first one in Des Plaines, Illinois, in 1955. From then on the fantastic development of the company is history.

Early in the expansion of McDonald's, a clown figure was created named Ronald McDonald to give fun and cheer to the patrons. In 1974, Fred Hill of the Philadelphia Eagles teamed up with McDonald's to create the first Ronald McDonald House in Philadelphia. Since then, many such houses have been built to provide the families of critically ill children a "home away from home" while the children are undergoing treatment for their illnesses. Though not a University building, the Ronald McDonald House on the UNM campus was built in 1981 by a group of people who received permission from the UNM Board of Regents to build it on land leased from the University on the North Campus.[48]

MEDICAL SCHOOL MEMORIAL TREES

The Fred A. Collatz III, MD, Memorial Tree

Fig. 20. Fred A. Collatz III, MD Memorial Elm Tree (Photograph by Suzanne Mortier, UNM Landscape Architect, 2013).

Fred A. Collatz, III, graduated from Highland High School in Albuquerque, where he participated in many sports. He graduated from UNM with a bachelor's degree *cum laude* and was elected to Phi Beta Kappa. He graduated from the UNM School of Medicine in 1983. Collatz completed his residency and cardiology fellowship at the University of Kentucky and practiced in Manchester, Kentucky. He founded Christian Cardiology in 1996. He bought a helicopter and learned to fly with the goal of reaching patients in remote areas of eastern Kentucky.

On December 4, 2000, Collatz died at age 45 when a helicopter he was piloting crashed in the hills of Kentucky. An elm tree was planted at UNM in his memory.[49]

The Jeanne Smith Jordan Memorial Tree

Fig. 21. Jeanne Smith Jordan Plaque (Photograph by Suzanne Mortier, UNM Landscape Architect, 2013).

On March 22, 1991, Jeanne Smith Jordan, a second-year medical student, died after a long illness. The first tree planted in her memory, a saucer magnolia, died, and a Hawthorne tree was planted in 2009. The plaque states:

Serve with Compassion

Michael J. McCaughey Memorial Tree

The London Plane tree planted in memory of Michael J. McCaughey is located near the plaza of the School of Medicine. McCaughey was born in 1954, graduated from UNM in 1978, and died in May 1985 at age 30 in an accident in Albuquerque.

NOVITSKI HALL

Fig. 22. Novitski Hall – Dental Hygiene School, 1978 (Photograph by Jerry Goffe, Center for Southwest Research, UNM Libraries).[50]

Novitski Hall is named for Monica Novitski, the former Professor and Director of the Dental Hygiene Program. The building contains the Division of Dental Hygiene, founded in 1961, the Division of Dental Service, founded in 1999, and the Dental Clinic.

Margaret Novitski, secretary of the Office of the University Architect for many years, wrote this about her sister:

> The dedication of Novitski Hall was the high point event in a career that began in 1935 in Dr. Novitski's hometown of Green Bay, Wisconsin when she was employed by a dentist. To enhance her skills, she entered Marquette University and received a certificate in Dental Hygiene. During World War II she served in the Army Air Force as a dental hygienist. After the war, she again enrolled at Marquette and received a Doctor of Dental Surgery in 1951, the only woman in her class. After graduation, she moved to New Mexico and served as a periodontist in Los Alamos and then started her office in Albuquerque. She and other dentists became concerned about the shortage of trained hygienists and assistants in New Mexico and began the process, which culminated in the establishment of dental programs at UNM.

The dental hygiene program was housed in World War II wood-framed buildings, when, on September 27, 1973, the Board of Regents authorized the planning of a Dental Programs building. Novitski and the deans of the Colleges of Nursing and Pharmacy had been lobbying for the building and the completion of Novitski Hall made it possible to remove the last of the World War II "temporary" buildings from the UNM campuses. As quoted from the book *Only in New Mexico*:

> The year 1978 ended on a high note on December 29, when the last two remaining wooden barracks, relics of World War II, were bulldozed. A total of thirty-eight barracks had been brought to the campus immediately after the war to take care of the influx of veterans enrolling under the GI Bill. The demolition was covered by the city and campus news media as the significant event it was.

THE COLLEGE OF NURSING

The Diane Lynn Adamo Tree

Fig. 23. The Adamo Tree (Source unknown).

In memory of Diane Lynn Adamo, a plaque and a Scotch pine tree were placed in front of the main entrance of the College of Nursing. Adamo, a native of Pennsylvania, graduated from the College of Nursing in 1984 and one month later was killed in a car accident at the age of 23. Adamo's family established the Diane Adamo Memorial Scholarship to aid nursing students planning to enter the field of pediatrics. To date, the scholarship has aided almost one hundred students with tuition and the cost of books.

THE UNIVERSITY OF NEW MEXICO HOSPITAL (UNMH)

Fig. 24. UNM Hospital - Aerial View, 1966 (Center for Southwest Research, UNM Libraries) [51]

Fig. 25. University of New Mexico Hospital today (Photograph by Suzanne Mortier, UNM Landscape Architect, 2013).

The first part of the UNM Hospital, constructed in 1952, was known as the Bernalillo County Indian Hospital (BC-1). It was built partially with federal funds, which required a bed quota for Native American patients. As more additions were made, it became the Bernalillo County Medical Center (BCMC). When the University took control of the facility and began to use it as a teaching hospital, the name changed to the University of New Mexico Hospital. Many areas within the University Hospital are named in memory of particular people.

The Jonathan Abrams, MD, Art Gallery

Fig. 26. Abrams Gallery (Photograph by Suzanne Mortier, UNM Landscape Architect, 2013).

The School of Medicine's art gallery is named for Professor of Cardiology Jonathan Abrams. Abrams was an art connoisseur who believed that art has the ability to soothe the troubled soul. The Gallery contains more than 2,000 pieces of art, many of which are hung in the rooms and corridors of the University Hospital. The Gallery itself is located on the fifth floor of the central area of the hospital in a corridor, as there is no dedicated room for the gallery.

Jonathan Abrams graduated from the University of California at Berkeley in 1960 with honors and was elected a member of Phi Beta Kappa. After obtaining his M.D. from the University of California Medical School in San Francisco in 1964, he completed his internship and residency at Boston City Hospital and the West Roxbury Veterans Administration Hospital and a cardiology fellowship at Georgetown University Hospital in Washington, D.C. From 1968 to 1970, he served as staff cardiologist at Sandia Base Hospital and then worked at the Veterans Administration Hospital in Albuquerque. In 1973, he became Chief of the Cardiology Division of the UNM School of Medicine. Abrams was made a Professor of Medicine in 1979 and was subsequently declared a Distinguished Professor. He retired in 2008.

Abrams was a Fellow of the American College of Cardiologists, the American Heart Association, and the American College of Physicians. He served as Secretary of the New Mexico Chapter of the American College of

Physicians and as President of the New Mexico Division of the American Heart Association. Abrams authored or co-authored eleven books and many articles and has given numerous lectures and interviews concerning cardiovascular and heart disease. In 2007, Abrams was rated one of Albuquerque's "Top Docs" by *Albuquerque Magazine*. He was known for his compassion.

Abrams served on the UNM Faculty Senate and Committee on Art in Public Places and on the City of Albuquerque Arts Board. In 2000, Jonathan Abrams received the Governor's Award for Excellence in the Arts. From 2004 to 2009, Jonathan Abrams was President of the Capitol Art Foundation, which oversees the collection of works by New Mexico artists at the State Capitol Building in Santa Fe. Fay Abrams received her master's degree in art education from UNM and founded Mariposa Gallery in Albuquerque. The Abrams, in addition to establishing the UNM School of Medicine Art Gallery in 1991, established a bequest to the UNM Art Museum known as the Jonathan Abrams and Fay Pfaelzer Abrams Art Collection. Jonathan Abrams died on July 18, 2014, in Albuquerque.[52]

Barbara and Bill Richardson Pavilion

Fig. 27. Barbara and Bill Richardson Pavilion (Photograph by Suzanne Mortier, UNM Landscape Architect, 2013).

A relatively recent addition to the UNM Hospital is the Richardson Pavilion named for former New Mexico Governor Bill Richardson and his wife Barbara. The Pavilion, which opened in 2007, added significant capacity to the UNM Hospital's Level 1 Trauma Center, the only such facility in New Mexico. The Pavilion also includes the UNM Children's Hospital, New Mexico's only dedicated children's hospital and an Intensive Care Unit.[53] UNM Children's Hospital provides neonatal care for children in New Mexico that would not otherwise be available. In addition to a newborn intensive care unit, the Children's Hospital includes a maternity center, pediatric emergency department, pediatric cancer infusion center, and child life center.

William Blaine Richardson, III, was born in Pasadena, California, to William Blaine Richardson, Jr., and Maria Luisa López-Collada Márquez. His father worked as a banker in Mexico City for decades and Richardson grew up in Mexico until age thirteen, when his parents sent him to Middlesex Preparatory School in Massachusetts. Richardson received his B.A. in French and political science from Tufts University in 1970, where he was a pitcher on the baseball team. He also pitched in an amateur league and briefly considered playing professional baseball. In 1971, Richardson received his M.A. in international affairs from Tuft's Fletcher School of Law and Diplomacy. Shortly thereafter, he married Barbara Flavin.

Richardson worked at various jobs in Congress, including on the staff of the Senate Foreign Relations Committee, until moving to Santa Fe in 1978. In 1982, he was elected to the U.S. House of Representatives in the newly created 3rd District. He served in that position for fourteen years. From 1983 to 1985, he chaired the

Congressional Hispanic Caucus, and from 1993 to 1994, he chaired the House Natural Resources Committee Subcommittee on Native American Affairs. He received Mexico's Aztec Eagle Award. In 1997, President Bill Clinton appointed him Ambassador to the United Nations. The following year, Richardson became the Secretary of Energy, serving in that capacity from 1998 to 2000. In 1998, UNM awarded him an honorary Doctorate of Law and Letters.[54] Richardson was elected Governor of New Mexico in 2002 and reelected in 2006. He received several Nobel Prize nominations for his work.[55]

Barbara Richardson was raised in Concord, Massachusetts, and received an Associate of Arts degree from Colby Junior College and a B.A. from Wheaton College, graduating *magna cum laude*. She and Bill Richardson lived in Washington, D.C., during his terms as a congressman and Secretary of Energy, and later in New York City while Bill was the U.S. Ambassador to the United Nations.

Barbara Richardson has actively supported children's education and welfare, serving as Honorary Chair of the New Mexico Immunization Coalition, which helps increase the number of children receiving immunization shots. She was also instrumental in working to establish the Governor's Domestic Violence Board, later serving as its chair. In addition, she has served as a member of the Georgia O'Keeffe Museum's Educational Committee, board member of the Big Brothers Big Sisters of Santa Fe, and program coordinator for the Muscular Dystrophy Association of Washington, D.C.[56]

Adult Emergency Department Exam Room 1 – Will Ferguson and Associates

The Adult Emergency Department Exam Room 1 includes recognition of Will Ferguson & Associates. Will Ferguson, who is the managing partner of his firm, was born in New York City on October 13, 1948. Ferguson attended the University of Exeter in Devon, England, and went on to obtain his B.A. from Wofford College in Spartanburg, South Carolina, in 1971 and his J.D. from UNM in 1974. His wife Sarah, who received her J.D. from Yale, is of counsel to the firm.

After serving in the U.S. Air Force from 1971 to 1976, Ferguson opened his own office in Albuquerque in 1983 and limited his practice to representing plaintiffs in personal injury cases. He was civic minded and as a sports car enthusiast, he joined with other community members to open Sandia Motorsports Park for auto racing. He also founded Bank 1st in Albuquerque, now Main Bank, and co-owned and operated Taos Motors, which was in the process of closing as of this writing.[57] Ferguson continues to be a principal in Motiva Performance Engineering, a high-tech automotive performance shop. He has been a strong supporter of the UNM Children's Hospital.[58]

Geoffrey S.M. Hedrick Imaging Suite

A suite of facilities named for Geoffrey S.M. Hedrick includes two radiology rooms, one ultrasound unit, one Magnetic Resonance Imaging (MRI) machine, one 16-slice Computed Tomography (CT) scan, and one 64-dual slice CT scan. In 1988, Hedrick founded Innovative Solution & Support, LLC, an international avionics supplier to military, business, and commercial operations. He serves as the Chief Executive Officer and Chairman of the Board. Before establishing his company, he was President and CEO of Smiths Industries North American Aerospace Companies. Hedrick holds a number of patents in the electronics, optoelectric, electromagnetic, aerospace and contamination-control fields. A biographer stated:

> Throughout his life Mr. Hedrick has shown a dedication to the advancement of technology and, through life-changing events, has developed a true appreciation for the advancement of medical technology and a desire to make UNM Hospital the cutting-edge medical facility in the state of New Mexico.

Hedrick, in appreciation for the care he received while a patient at UNM Hospital, donated $2.5 million to UNM to purchase the Dual Tube 64 Computed Tomography (CT) Scan instrument.[59]

First Floor Main Lobby – Gerald and Barbara Landgraf

The First Floor Main Lobby of the Richardson Pavilion recognizes Gerald and Barbara Landgraf for their generous support of UNM Children's Hospital and College of Nursing. Gerald Landgraf was instrumental in creating a managed care business in New Mexico and developing a partnership with the UNM Hospital. The Landgrafs also established the Dorothy Landgraf Memorial Scholarship in Nursing in honor of Jerry Landgraf's mother, who was a nurse as were Jerry's five sisters. Jerry Landgraf began his long career in healthcare with Blue Cross Blue Shield of Iowa and Florida and developed health maintenance organizations (HMO) in Michigan, Puerto Rico, and New Mexico. In 1984, he co-founded and was president of Health Care Horizons until it was acquired by Molina Healthcare of New Mexico. Health Care Horizons was the parent company of Cimarron Health Plan, which provided a variety of services primarily in support of low-income populations in New Mexico and at the UNM Hospital. Landgraf has served as past chairman and director of the American Medical Care and Review Association and a board member of the American Health Insurance Plans (a national association). He has also served on the board of the Anderson Abruzzo International Balloon Museum Foundation and as treasurer of NDI New Mexico, which promotes dance education programs for young people. Landgraf graduated from Iowa State University and received an M.B.A. from the University of North Florida.[60]

Newborn Intensive Care Unit – The Thomas Silva Family Lounge

Thomas Silva Family Lounge, located in the a Newborn Intensive Care Unit of the Barbara and Bill Richardson Pavilion, is named in honor of Thomas Silva, who was born prematurely with many physical problems that kept him in UNM Hospital for long periods of time. The Lounge provides a soothing environment for family members awaiting treatment of newborn children at the Hospital. The dedication recognized the contributions and support by Thomas Silva's friend State Representative Henry "Kiki" Saavedra and grandfather Representative Daniel Silva during their tenure in the State Legislature.[61]

Dr. Edward "Ed" William Sengel, III, Consulting Room, Pediatric Special Services

Danielle Sengel dedicated the consulting room in Pediatric Special Services to the memory of her husband Dr. Edward "Ed" William Sengel, III, who died on December 21, 2000. Sengel received degrees from the University of Washington, Boston University, and the University of Southern California. He served in the United States Army for 20 years, retiring as lieutenant colonel. The UNM Advancement Employer of the Year Award was named in his memory and the College of Education's Dr. Edward Sengel III Memorial Endowed Scholarship was established to honor an outstanding doctoral student in the college. [62]

Carrie Tingley Rehabilitation Unit

The Carrie Tingley Hospital Foundation, on March 2, 2001, announced its $1.6 million pledge to fund the new Carrie Tingley Hospital Inpatient Unit and one pediatric operating room at the Richardson Pavilion, which have been completed. For more information about Carrie Tingley, see the section on Carrie Tingley Hospital.

Pediatric Intensive Care Unit – Patient Rooms – Lyle and Gale McDaniels

Lyle McDaniels and his wife Gale are 1982 graduates of UNM. Lyle is CEO and Gale McDaniels is Secretary/Treasurer of United Building Products, a company they started in 1989 that now employs 25 people. The company carries a wide range of products used by the construction community. The McDaniels are recognized in the Pediatric Intensive Care Unit Patient Rooms.

Pediatric Surgery Center – Staff Lounge – Charles Kassell

Charles Kassell was born in New York City on September 17, 1908, and moved to New Mexico in the early 1950s. Kassell worked for many years on *New Mexico Magazine*, travelling throughout the state. He spent the last thirteen years of his life in the La Vita Llena retirement community and died at the age of 96 on March 15, 2005. The staff lounge in the Pediatric Surgery Center at UNM Hospital is named in his memory.

Jeff Apodaca Multi-Media Center

The Multi-Media Center, which opened in September 2007 on the sixth floor of the Richardson Pavilion, is named for Jeff Apodaca, the son of former Governor Jerry Apodaca and his wife Clara. Jeff was diagnosed with a rare form of cancer at the age of 17 while he was a student at Santa Fe High School. His doctors told him he would never play football again as he would need to concentrate on fighting for his life. Jeff received treatment at the UNM Cancer Center and the M.D. Anderson Memorial Hospital in Houston. Overcoming all odds, he proved his doctors wrong and continued to play football for four years in college, first at Southern Methodist

University and then at UNM. He graduated from UNM in 1986 with a B.A. in broadcast management.[63] He began his career in media at CBS, which led to being Vice President of Univision Television in Los Angeles and Executive Vice President of Entravision Communications. He is a member of the board of the Albuquerque Chamber of Commerce and in 2015, the UNM Regents appointed him to the board of InnovateABQ, the non-profit research park. In 2018, he was a candidate for governor of New Mexico.[64] In remembering the care he received at UNM, Apodaca wrote:

> This is why I started the Jeff Apodaca Celebration of Life Fund to help those kids see their potential. It was the time I spent at the Children's Hospital and the Cancer Center that has given me the chance to celebrate more than 29 years of living and seeing what my future was all about. Thanks to hundreds of friends and supporters, we have been able to raise more than $1,000,000 and develop the Jeff Apodaca Celebration of Life Scholarships, the Jeff Apodaca Multi-Media Canter, and the educational and entertainment programs at the University of New Mexico Children's Hospital.

Pete's Playground

Fig. 28. Pete's Playground
(Photograph by Suzanne Mortier, UNM Landscape Architect, 2013).

Peter James Blueher was born in 1986 with a congenital birth defect, which led to his death in 1989. He spent almost all of his short life in the UNM Hospital. When he died, his parents, Thomas and Francesca Blueher, wanted to create a playground for small children who were receiving treatment at the hospital. They received many contributions toward creating one in Pete's memory.[65] The original playground sat on the roof of the old part of the hospital, but when the Richardson Pavilion was built, Pete's Playground was placed in the Child Life Unit on the northwest corner of the sixth floor. Pete's Playground includes both an outdoor and indoor play area. The blue awnings make it visible from the ground. The original site of the playground is being revived by Healthy Neighborhoods Albuquerque as an aquaponics garden to supply fresh produce for food service operations and provide training opportunities.[66]

Another contributor to Pete's Playground was the Alice G. Hanson Family Foundation, established by Alice Hanson before she died in 1998 and designed to provide a lasting gift to UNM Hospital. Hanson volunteered her time helping patients in local hospitals. She also created endowed scholarships for music students. Her foundation gave a grand piano to Pete's Playground.

The J. Mario Molina, MD, Advised Family Foundation also contributed to Pete's Playground. Joseph Mario Molina is president and chief executive of Molina Healthcare, Inc., a company founded by his father, C. David Molina, M.D., in 1980 to address the special needs of low income patients. J. Mario Molina received his M.D. from the University of Southern California. He completed his internship and residency at Johns Hopkins University Hospital.

Among other contributors to Pete's Playground are Vicente Solman Romero, the A & R Valo Trust, and the Service League.

The Tree of Life Project – Meditation Room

Fig. 29. Tree of Life Door, University Hospital (Photograph by Suzanne Mortier, UNM Landscape Architect, 2013).

In a large hospital like UNM Hospital, it is important to have a space for meditation, reflection or prayer. The Meditation Room on the first floor of the Children's Hospital in the Barbara and Bill Richardson Pavilion offers such a space. The room contains a stained glass mural 25-feet long and 8-feet high on the west wall depicting the mountains and other natural features of north central New Mexico. The room also features a fountain that represents the beginning of the river of life. Visitors enter the room through the Tree of Life door, which is a stained glass double door featuring a tree having 500 leaves, each of which can hold up to 30 characters. Donors purchased leaves or branches of leaves in memory of loved ones or to honor someone. The project was started by the family of Jerry and Ed White and their daughter Shannon in memory of Shannon's premature daughter, Mackenzie, and the wonderful care and compassion they received at UNM Hospital. The Whites are famous door makers in the Southwest. The one leaf falling from the cottonwood tree is named in memory of Mackenzie. Below the windows are dedication plaques recognizing the White family and other major donors. Denise Taylor of Taylor Made Glass, LLC, in New Mexico, designed both the Tree of Life doors and the stained glass window in the Meditation Room.[67]

The A. Earl and Agnes Walker Library

The library in the Department of Surgery is named for Professor A. Earl Walker and his wife Agnes. Earl Walker was born in 1907 in Winnipeg, Manitoba, Canada, and received his M.D. from the University of Alberta in 1930. After an internship at Toronto Western Hospital, he became a resident in neurosurgery at the University of Chicago. He later received specialty training at the University of Iowa and Yale University and at academic medical centers in Belgium and the Netherlands. He worked at the University of Chicago until 1947, when he was appointed head of the Division of Neurological Surgery at Johns Hopkins Medical School and Hospital, where he remained until his retirement in 1972. Walker came to the University of New Mexico soon after and became a professor of teaching and research in the Department of Neurology in the School of Medicine. He died in March 1995, a year after fully retiring from UNM.

Walker specialized in the study of the brain and did basic clinical and laboratory research in the field of epilepsy. He chose surgery as the best way to correct problems of the central nervous system. During his career Walker wrote many books and articles in his field of expertise and was honored by the professional communities in this country and abroad. He was President of the American Association of Neurological Surgery, the American Association of Neurology, and the American Electroencephalographic Society. He was made an honorary member of related societies in ten countries, including Britain and Russia.[68]

Additional Contributions To The Richardson Pavilion

THE SERVICE LEAGUE
- Emergency Department Lobby and Waiting Area
- Emergency Department Meditation Room and Chapel
- Critical Care Center Family Lounge/ Waiting Area
- Post Partum Unit
- NBICU Family Center (in support area)
- NBICU Pre Discharge Family Sleep Room
- Tingley Rehabilitation Unit Playroom
- Child Life Area Playroom
- Child Life Area Patient Library
- Pete's Playground

CARRIE TINGLEY REHABILITATION UNIT (CTRU)
- CTRU Patient Rooms
- CTRU Rehabilitation Suite CTRU Nurses Station
- CTRU Pediatric Surgery Center OR Suite

WALMART
- CTRU Kitchen/Dining/Therapy Room
- Pediatric Surgery Waiting Room
- Pre Op Playroom
- Child Life Unit Teen Lounge and Classroom

RONALD McDONALD HOUSE CHARITIES
- Ronald McDonald Room

CREDIT UNION ASSOCIATION OF NEW MEXICO
- Pediatric Emergency Department

BLACK FAMILY TRUST
- Child Life Unit Nurses Station

PGA SUN COUNTRY GOLF
- Nurses Station

ANDERSON FOUNDATION
- Nurses Station
- Dialysis Unit Nurses Station

ROTARY INTERNATIONAL
- Pediatric Oncology Patient Rooms

CHILDREN'S CANCER FUND
- Playroom

Lions Club Eye Clinic

In 2008, the UNM Board of Regents Finance and Facilities Committee approved the naming of the UNM Hospital's Eye Clinic for the Lions Club.

Endnotes: Section Two—North Campus

1. See UNM School of Law, "60 for 60: Shaping Law in New Mexico Since 1950," pp. 10-13, 71, 78-79 (2010), http://lawschool.unm.edu/alumni/60for60/book-sample.pdf (last accessed April 23, 2018).

2. http://econtent.unm.edu/cdm/ref/collection/ULPhotoImag/id/2550 (last accessed April 23, 2018); see also Hooker, pp. 314-15 (Building 218).

3. http://econtent.unm.edu/cdm/ref/collection/ULPhotoImag/id/2538 (last accessed April 8, 2018).

4. See Hooker, p. 309 (Building 57).

5. See U.S. Congress, Biographical Directory, "Bratton, Sam Gilbert (1888-1963)," http://bioguide.congress.gov/scripts/biodisplay.pl?index=b000774 (last accessed April 23, 2018).

6. http://econtent.unm.edu/cdm/ref/collection/ULPhotoImag/id/466 (last accessed April 8, 2018).

7. UNM Office of the University Secretary, "Honorary Degrees," https://secretary.unm.edu/recognition-and-awards/honorary-degrees.html (last accessed April 23, 2018).

8. See Paul Logan, "Bratton called a model judge," *Albuquerque Journal* (May 7, 2002), https://www.abqjournal.com/obits/profiles/676529news05-07-02.htm (last accessed April 23, 2018).

9. See Frederick M. Hart, Clarence E. Hinkle & Howard C. Bratton, "Dedication of W. E. Bondurant, Jr.," New Mexico Law Review vol. 5, n. 171 (1975), http://digitalrepository.unm.edu/nmlr/vol5/iss2/2; see also UNM School of Law, "60 for 60: Shaping Law in New Mexico Since 1950," pp. 100-101 (2010), http://lawschool.unm.edu/alumni/60for60/index.html (last accessed April 23, 2018).

10. See Bruce King (as told to Charles Poling), *Cowboy in the Roundhouse: A Political Life,* Sunstone Press, Santa Fe (1998). See also Bruce Weber, "Bruce King, 3-term Governor, dies at 85," *New York Times* (Nov. 14, 2009), https://www.nytimes.com/2009/11/14/us/14king.html; Associated Press, "Bruce King, 85: Cattleman, 3-term NM governor," *Washington Post* (Nov. 15, 2009),http://www.washingtonpost.com/wp-dyn/content/article/2009/11/14/AR2009111402666.html (last accessed April 25, 2018); "UNM School of Law Library: King Room," http://lawschool.unm.edu/assets/documents/king_room.pdf; "Governor Bruce King papers, 2nd Term," New Mexico State Records Center, Santa Fe, NM (1979-82), http://164.64.110.131/webcat/request/Action?SystemName=New+Mexico+State+Archives& UserName=NMA+Public&Password=&CMD_(DetailRequest)[0]=&ProcessID=6000_1980(0)&KeyValues=KEY_50980; and, "Bruce King," N.M. Office of the State Historian, http://newmexicohistory.org/people/bruce-king (last accessed April 25, 2018).

11. See Bevell, Beatrice (Bea) Rickert," *Albuquerque Journal* (Jan. 8, 2014), http://obits.abqjournal.com/obits/show/239875, and "Rickert," (Beatrice P.), *Albuquerque Journal* (Oct. 17, 1999), http://obits.abqjournal.com/obits/show/130067 (last accessed April 24, 2018).

12. See UNM School of Law, "Utton Transboundary Resources Center," http://uttoncenter.unm.edu; see also UNM Law School, "60 for 60: Shaping Law in New Mexico Since 1950," pp. 54-55 (2010), http://lawschool.unm.edu/alumni/60for60/index.html; Scott Sandlin, "'Brilliant impresario' expert in natural resources law," *Albuquerque Journal* (Sept. 24, 2015), https://www.abqjournal.com/648672/brilliant-impresario-expert-in-natural-resources-law.html; and, New Mexico Water Resources Research Institute, "In fond memory of Albert E. Utton 1931-1998," Michael Browde, Robert Desiderio, and John Utton, contributors, https://nmwrri.nmsu.edu/in-fond-memory-of-albert-e-utton-1931-1998/ (last accessed April 23, 2018). See also Michele Minnis, *Al Utton-Aztec Eagle*, UNM Utton Transboundary Resources Center, Albuquerque, NM (2015).

13. See UNM Law School, "60 for 60: Shaping Law in New Mexico Since 1950," pp. 16-17 (2010), http://lawschool.unm.edu/alumni/60for60/index.html (last accessed Sept. 11, 2018).

14 See UNM School of Law, Faculty, "Professor Frederick M. Hart," http://lawschool.unm.edu/faculty/hart/index.html; see also Tamara Williams, "UNM Law Emeritus Fred Hart and alumnus Henry Rivera receive prestigious awards from UNM Alumni Association," UNM Law School (Jan. 12, 2016), http://lawschool.unm.edu/news/2016/01/hart.html; UNM Newsroom, "UNM Alumni Association announces 2016 winter award honorees" (Jan. 11, 2016), https://news.unm.edu/news/unm-alumni-association-announces-2016-winter-award-honorees; and, UNM Law School, "60 for 60: Shaping Law in New Mexico Since 1950," pp. 72-73 (2010), http://lawschool.unm.edu/alumni/60for60/index.html (last accessed April 23, 2018).

15 See UNM Law School, Faculty, "Professor Robert J. Desiderio," http://lawschool.unm.edu/faculty/desiderio/index.html, and UNM Law School, "60 for 60: Shaping Law in New Mexico Since 1950," p. 74 (2010), http://lawschool.unm.edu/alumni/60for60/index.html (last accessed April 23, 2018).

16 See "James M. Quinn," Ghost Bike List, Ghost Bikes.org, http://ghostbikes.org/albuquerque/james-m-quinn, and "James M. Quinn," *Ghost Bikes, Duke City Wheelman* (2008), http://www.dukecitywheelmen.org/category/ghostbikes/page/2/ (last accessed April 24, 2018).

17 See "Mary Coon Walters New Mexico Judge," *The Washington Post* (April 12, 2001), https://www.washingtonpost.com/archive/local/2001/04/12/mary-coon-walters-new-mexico-j/34297e95-bde2-4604-b94e-2d4452e04ad9/?utm_term=.c490606d189b; see also UNM Law School, "60 for 60: Shaping Law in New Mexico Since 1950," pp. 48-49 (2010), http://lawschool.unm.edu/alumni/60for60/index.html (last accessed April 23, 2018).

18 See UNM Law School, Institute for Public Law, http://lawschool.unm.edu/ipl/index.html (last accessed April 23, 2018); see also Cameron Townsend, "Princess Jeanne Park: Case Study," UNM School of Architecture and Planning, Albuquerque Modernism Project, http://albuquerquemodernism.unm.edu/wp/princess-jeanne-park-albuquerque-nm/, and Albuquerque Historical Society, Factoids, "F254 and F258," http://albuqhistsoc.org/factoids/fAnswfactoid.htm (last accessed April 23, 2018).

19 See photographs and description at http://www.courthouses.co/us-states/n/new-mexico/new-mexico-court-of-appeals-albuquerque/; see also UNM Law School, "60 for 60: Shaping Law in New Mexico Since 1950," pp. 94-95 (2010), http://lawschool.unm.edu/alumni/60for60/index.html (last accessed April 23, 2018). See also Deborah Baker, "State Supreme Court Justice Pamela Minzer Dead at 63," *Albuquerque Journal* (Aug. 31, 2007), https://www.abqjournal.com/news/apminzner08-31-07.htm (last accessed April 24, 2018).

20 http://econtent.unm.edu/cdm/ref/collection/ULPhotoImag/id/2526 (last accessed April 8, 2018).

21 See UNM Health Sciences Center, *NewsBeat*, "Reginald Heber Fitz Hall," http://hscnews.unm.edu file?fid=53e25dc5ee750e4130017226, and "Reginald Heber Fitz Hall Dedication," http://hscnews.unm.edu/file?fid=53e25dbdfe058b7e31045cf4 (last accessed April 24, 2018).

22 See UNM School of Medicine, Department of Pathology, "Harvey Endowed Chair and Professorship," https://pathology.unm.edu/make-a-gift/harvey-endowed-professorships.html (last accessed April 24, 2018).

23 Social Networks and Archival Context, "Solomon, Sidney, 1923-1992," http://snaccooperative.org/ark:/99166/w6943v2c (last accessed April 8, 2018), and Heini Murer and Gerhard Burckhardt, "Professor Karl Julius Ullrich--In Memoriam," *Kidney International*, vol. 78, pp. 827-828 (2010), http://www.kidney-international.org/article/S0085-2538(15)54667-X/pdf (last accessed April 24, 2018).

24 See UNM School of Medicine, "Founding Department Chairs," https://som.unm.edu/about/founding-chairs.html (last accessed April 24, 2018).

25 See, e.g., UNM School of Medicine, Faculty Memorial, "Sidney Solomon, PhD," https://som.unm.edu/faculty/memorial/remembrances/solomon-sidney.html (last accessed April 24, 2018).

26 See UNM Health Sciences Center, "UNM Comprehensive Cancer Center" (photograph), https://hsc.unm.edu/health/locations/cancer-center.html (last accessed April 24, 2018).

27 http://econtent.unm.edu/cdm/ref/collection/ULPhotoImag/id/2505 (last accessed April 8, 2018).

28 http://econtent.unm.edu/cdm/ref/collection/ULPhotoImag/id/486 (last accessed April 8, 2018).

29 See UNM Comprehensive Cancer Center, "UNM Cancer Center Opens Doors to New State-of-the-Art Comprehensive Cancer Treatment Facility" (Aug. 24, 2009), http://cancer.unm.edu/2009/08/24/unm-cancer-center-opens-doors-to-new-state-of-the-art-comprehensive-cancer-treatment-facility/ (last accessed April 24, 2018).

30 See UNM Board of Regents, "Minutes of Special Board of Regents Meeting, June 10, 2008," http://regents.unm.edu/meetings/minutes/2008/bor_minutes_2008-06-10.pdf (last accessed Sept. 15, 2018). See also UNM Cancer Center, *El Oso De Salud* (Summer 2011).

31 See UNM Health Sciences Center, "School of Medicine Living Legends: R. Philip Eaton, MD" (from HSC *NewsBeat*, Nov. 16, 2015), https://som.unm.edu/faculty/living-legends/eaton.html (last accessed April 24, 2018) and http://hscnews.unm.edu/news/unm-school-of-medicine-honors-living-legend111615 (last accessed Sept. 15, 2018).

32 See "UNM Health Sciences Center," Library and Infomatics Center, "From the Desk of the Director," *Adobe Medicus*, vol. 29 no. 6 (Nov./Dec. 2006), http://digitalrepository.unm.edu/adobe-medicus/18 (last accessed Jan. 21, 2019).

33 See UNM School of Medicine, "The Design of the School of Medicine Faculty Memorial," https://som.unm.edu/faculty/memorial/design/index.html (last accessed April 24, 2018).

34 See "UNM Helix Garden, New Mexico Chapter of the American Society of Landscape Architects, *Quarterly News*, (2015), http://www.nmasla.org/quarterly-news-2015-issue-4/ (last accessed April 25, 2018).

35 See *Hobbs News Sun*, "State Senator Billy McKibben died" (Aug. 9, 2017), http://www.hobbsnews.com/2017/08/09/state-senator-billy-mckibben-died/ (last accessed April 24, 2018); see also Daniel J. Chaćcon, "Senator used quick wit, humor in legislative battles," *Santa Fe New Mexican* (Aug. 22, 2017), http://www.santafenewmexican.com/news/local_news/senator-used-quick-wit-humor-in-legislative-battles/article_f530e139-e799-5ed3-b45c-c0bffc3db275.html (last accessed Aug. 24, 2018).

36 See Associated Press, "Steven H. Schiff, 51, New Mexico Congressman," *New York Times* (Mar. 26, 1998), http://www.nytimes.com/1998/03/26/us/steven-h-schiff-51-new-mexico-congressman.html (last accessed April 24, 2018); see also Social Networks and Archival Context, "Schiff, Steven, 1947-1998," http://snaccooperative.org/search (last accessed Oct. 31, 2018).

37 See Zana Alcadi with Ruth Vise, "Borderlands: Carrie Tingley Hospital and the Couple Behind It," El Paso Community College Libraries, http://epcc.libguides.com/tingley (reprinted from *EPCC Borderlands*, vol. 31, pp. 10-12 (2015-2016), http://epcc.libguides.com/ld.php?content_id=37556515)); Suzanne Stamatov, "There was a time and it was Tingley's," New Mexico Office of the State Historian, http://newmexicohistory.org/people/clyde-tingley (last accessed April 24, 2018).

38 See UNM Health Sciences Library & Informatics Center, "Domenici Center for Health Sciences Education," https://hslic.unm.edu/about-hslic/domenici/index.html (last accessed April 24, 2018).

39 See UNM Lobos, Hall of Honor, "Pete Domenici," http://www.golobos.com/sports/2015/5/12/GEN_20140101148.aspx (last accessed April 24, 2018).

40 See UNM Office of the University Secretary, "Honorary Degrees," https://secretary.unm.edu/recognition-and-awards/honorary-degrees.html; UNM Alumni Association, "Zimmerman Award," https://www.unmalumni.com/zimmerman-past.html; and, "Fergusson Award," https://www.unmalumni.com/fergusson-past.html (last accessed April 24, 2018).

41 See Keith Schneider, "Pete Domenici, Long a Powerful Senate Voice on Fiscal Policy, Dies at 85," *New York Times* (Sept. 13, 2017), https://www.nytimes.com/2017/09/13/us/politics/pete-domenici-dead.html (last accessed April 24, 2018).

42 See UNM Health Sciences Library & Informatics Center, "Domenici Center for Health Sciences Education, 2011," https://hslic.unm.edu/about-hslic/docs/DomeniciCenter_2011.pdf (last accessed April 24, 2018).

43 See Social Networks and Archival Context, "Hanold, Fred H., 1915-2006," http://snaccooperative.org/ark:/99166/w6b125zn (last accessed April 24, 2018).

44 See UNM Health Sciences Library & Informatics Center, "Domenici Center for Health Sciences Education," https://hslic.unm.edu/about-hslic/domenici/index.html; "Domenici Center for Health Sciences Education, 2011, p. 2," https://hslic.unm.edu/about-hslic/docs/DomeniciCenter_2011.pdf; and, UNM School of Medicine, Faculty Memorial, "Leonard Napolitano, 1930-2013," https://som.unm.edu/faculty/memorial/remembrances/napolitano-leonard.html (last accessed April 24, 2018).

45 See UNM Office of the University Secretary, "Regents Awards Recipients," https://secretary.unm.edu/recognition-and-awards/regents-awards-recipients.html, and UNM Health Sciences, School of Medicine "School of Medicine Living Legends," https://som.unm.edu/faculty/living-legends/index.html (last accessed September 15, 2018).

46 See UNM Health Sciences Center *NewsBeat*, "UNM Health Sciences Center recognizes Pete and Nancy Domenici's commitment to mental health" (Aug. 20, 2003), http://hscnews.unm.edu/news/unm-health-sciences-center-recognizes-pete-and-nancy-domenici-s-commitment-to-mental-health; The Mind Research Network, "BRaIN and The University of New Mexico," https://www.mrn.org/about/brain-and-the-university-of-new-mexico; UNM Health Sciences Center, Brain & Behavioral Health Institute, "Locations," https://brain.health.unm.edu/findus.php#dhall; and, Jenny Savage, "Domenici Hall Architecture Recognized," UNM Health Sciences Center, *NewsBeat* (Jan. 19, 2006), http://hscnews.unm.edu/news/domenici-hall-architecture-recognized (last accessed April 24, 2018).

47 See "MIND Institute expands to 'MIND Research Network,'" UNM Health Sciences Center, *NewsBeat* (Sept. 26, 2007), http://hscnews.unm.edu/news/mind-institute-expands-to-mind-research-network (last accessed April 24, 2018).

48 See Ronald McDonald House Charities, New Mexico, "Ronald McDonald House," http://www.rmhc-nm.org/what-we-do/ronald-mcdonald-house/, and McDonalds Corporation, "The Ray Kroc Story," https://www.mcdonalds.com/us/en-us/about-us/our-history.html (last accessed Sept. 15, 2018).

49 "Fed A. Collatz III," *Albuquerque Journal* (Dec. 16, 2000), http://obits.abqjournal.com/obits/print_obit/121800. See also Ashley Elkins, "q8731 BC-SOUT-HelicopterCrash 1stLd-Writethru 12-06 0747," *Daily Journal* (Dec. 7, 2000), http://www.djournal.com/news/q-bc-sou-helicoptercrash-stld-writethru/article_486e355b-d9b6-54d2-9310-802a6362a877.html (last accessed Sept. 15, 2018).

50 See http://econtent.unm.edu/cdm/ref/collection/ULPhotoImag/id/510 (last accessed April 8, 2018); see also UNM School of Medicine, Department of Dental Medicine, "A History of the UNM Department of Dental Medicine," https://dentalmedicine.unm.edu/about/history.html (last accessed Sept. 15, 2018).

51 See http://econtent.unm.edu/cdm/ref/collection/ULPhotoImag/id/548 (last accessed April 8, 2018).

52 See "Jonathan Abrams," *Boston Globe* (first published in the *Santa Fe New Mexican,* July 27, 2014), http://www.legacy.com/obituaries/bostonglobe/obituary.aspx?pid=171807617; UNM Foundation, Donor Story, "To UNM, with love: The bequest of two friends brings art to the people," https://www.unmfund.org/donor-story/to-unm-with-love-the-bequest-of-two-friends-brings-art-to-the-people/; UNM School of Medicine, Faculty Memorial, "Jonathan Abrams, MD," https://som.unm.edu/faculty/memorial/remembrances/abrams-jonathan.html (last accessed April 24, 2018); and, Cindy Foster, "A legacy of art and medicine," HSC *NewsBeat* (July 22, 2014), http://hscnews.unm.edu/news/a-legacy-of-art-and-medicine072314 (last accessed Sept. 15, 2018). See also UNM Art Museum, "This Art is Not Mine: The Jonathan Abrams and Fay Pfaelzer Abrams Art Collection" (2015), http://artmuseum.unm.edu/past-exhibitions/this-art-is-not-mine-the-jonathan-abrams-and-fay-pfaelzer-abrams-art-collection/ (last accessed April 25, 2018).

53 See "Barbara & Bill Richardson Pavillion Opens," UNM Health Sciences Center, HSC *NewsBeat* (June 10, 2007), http://hscnews.unm.edu/news/barbara-bill-richardson-pavilion-opens (last accessed April 24, 2018). See also Associated Press & *Albuquerque Journal,* "New UNM Hospital plans move forward, early childhood programs net mixed results in New Mexico," KUNM News (Aug. 16, 2017), http://kunm.org/post/new-unm-hospital-plans-move-forward-early-childhood-programs-net-mixed-results-new-mexico (including photograph of the Richardson Pavilion with article describing plans for a new adult care hospital expected to be completed in 2022), and UNM Health Sciences, "UNM Children's Hospital," https://hsc.unm.edu/health/locations/childrens-hospital.html (last accessed Sept. 15, 2018).

54 See UNM Office of the University Secretary, "Honorary Degrees," https://secretary.unm.edu/recognition-and-awards/honorary-degrees.html (last accessed April 24, 2018).

55 See "Bill Richardson, Biography," https://www.billrichardson.com/about-bill/biography (last accessed April 24, 2018).

56 See Kimberly Slick Slover, "A First Lady for the People: Barbara Flavin Richardson," *Colby-Sawyer Alumni Magazine*, pp. 12-13, 17 (Spring/Summer 2005), http://colby-sawyer.edu/assets/pdf/Barbara-Richardson.pdf (last accessed April 24, 2018).

57 See Will Ferguson & Associates, Our Attorneys, "Will Ferguson," https://www.fergusonlaw.com/our-attorneys/will-ferguson/, and J.R. Logan, "Update: Taos Motors clears lot, shuts doors over weekend," *The Taos News* (Sept. 15, 2018) (last accessed Sept. 15, 2018).

58 See Barbara Lemaire, "Will Ferguson bats for UNM Children's Hospital," UNM Health Sciences Center, HSC *NewsBeat* (Aug. 16, 2006), http://hscnews.unm.edu/news/will-ferguson-bats-for-unm-children-s-hospital (last accessed April 24, 2018).

59 See UNM Health Sciences Center, HSC *NewsBeat*, "Grateful patient donates $2.5 million for scanner," http://hscnews.unm.edu/news/?q=hedrick&year=&s=-date, and UNM Foundation, "Avionics Entrepreneur Funds CT Machine for UNM Trauma Center," *Report of Giving 2006-2007*, p. 7 (Oct. 15, 2007), https://www.unmfund.org/wp-content/uploads/2013/08/unmf-rog-2006-2007.pdf (last accessed April 24, 2018). See also Innovation Solutions & Support, Leadership, "Geoffrey S.M. Hedrick," http://innovative-ss.com/about-iss/leadership/ (last accessed Sept. 15, 2018).

60 See Michelle G. Ruiz, "Long-lived support: Couple's planned gift to UNM Hospital, College of Nursing to benefit all New Mexicans," *Developments at the UNM Foundation* (Spring 2016), https://www.unmfund.org/wp-content/uploads/2014/10/DEV_SP2016_FINAL_WEB.pdf; see also NDI New Mexico, "Gerald Landgraf, Treasurer," https://www.ndi-nm.org/ndi_board/gerald-landgraf-treasurer/ (last accessed Sept. 15, 2018).

61 See Jenny Savage, "Thomas Silva Family Lounge Named," UNM Health Sciences Center, HSC *NewsBeat* (Jan. 11, 2006), http://hscnews.unm.edu/news/thomas-silva-family-lounge-named (last accessed Sept. 15, 2018).

62 See "Sengel," *Albuquerque Journal* (Dec. 31, 2000), http://obits.abqjournal.com/obits/show/118458 (last accessed April 24, 2018). See also UNM College of Education, Scholarship Listings, "Dr. Edward Sengel, III Memorial Endowed Scholarship Fund," https://coe.unm.edu/current-students/scholarships/scholarship-listings.html (last accessed April 24, 2018).

63 See United Press International, "Fifteen months after hearing that not only his gridiron ..." (Mar. 25, 1981), https://www.upi.com/Archives/1981/03/25/Fifteen-months-after-hearing-that-not-only-his-gridiron/3488354344400/ (last accessed April 24, 2018).

64 See Andrew Oxford, "Jeff Apodaca to run for governor," Santa Fe New Mexican (May 2, 2017), http://www.santafenewmexican.com/news/local_news/jeff-apodaca-to-run-for-governor/article_a73bde46-2f49-11e7-91bc-e7cbccaca41d.html; "Jeff Apodaca," Ballotpedia, https://ballotpedia.org/Jeff_Apodaca (last accessed Sept. 15, 2018); and, Innovate ABQ, https://innovateabq.com/team/ (last accessed Sept. 15, 2018).

65 See UNM Health Sciences Center, "Child Life," https://hsc.unm.edu/health/patient-care/pediatrics/child-life.html (last accessed Sept. 15, 2018).

66 See Micheal Haederle, "Health Neighborhoods Albuquerque receives grant funding," UNM Health Sciences, Newsroom (April 7, 2017), http://hscnews.unm.edu/news/healthy-neighborhoods-albuquerque-receives-grant-funding (last accessed Sept. 15, 2018).

67 See UNM Health Sciences, "Spiritual Care," https://hsc.unm.edu/health/patients-visitors/spiritual-care.html (last accessed Sept. 15, 2018). See also Taylor Made Glass, "Our Work," http://denisetaylorstudios.com/ourwork.html (last accessed April 24, 2018).

68 See Wolfgang Saxon, "A. Earl Walker, 87, a Professor and Researcher in Neurosurgery," *New York Times* (Jan. 7, 1995), https://www.nytimes.com/1995/01/07/obituaries/a-earl-walker-87-a-professor-and-researcher-in-neurosurgery.html (last accessed April 24, 2018).

69 See UNM Board of Regents, Finance and Facilities Committee, "Meeting Summary" (Dec. 4, 2008), http://regents.unm.edu/committees/finance-and-facilities/minutes/2008/finance_facilities_minutes_2008-12-04.pdf (last accessed April 23, 2018).

Mitchell Hall in Winter (Center for Southwest Research, UNM Libraries).

Section Three—South Campus

UNM Championship Golf Course (Source unknown).

AMBROSE ALDAY BATTING COMPLEX

A batting cage complex on the South Campus is named for the sixteen-year-old son of the head baseball coach, Richard F. Alday. Before he died, Ambrose Alday used to practice his hitting. Named in his memory by the other coaches and players, the cages have since been removed and placed in storage.

"THE PIT" (DREAMSTYLE BASKETBALL ARENA)

Fig. 1. University Arena – The Pit – Exterior – Northeast Corner, North Side, 1998 (Photograph by Kate Nash, Center for Southwest Research, UNM Libraries).[1]

Fig. 2. "The Pit" Basketball Arena, 2013 (Photograph by Suzanne Mortier, UNM Landscape Architect, 2013).

A book could be written about "The Pit" as the basketball arena is called: its history, the great players, the games, the coaches, and what it has meant to the University and the UNM Athletic Department. The idea for a large arena for basketball originated with President Tom Popejoy, basketball coach Bob King, and athletic director Pete McDavid. Popejoy wanted the arena to seat up to 15,000 people, with the seating area dug into the ground to save construction costs. That design is reflected in the moniker "The Pit." King wanted the seats to be placed as close to the playing floor as possible in order to allow the crowd maximum involvement in the game. The Pit was designed only for basketball.

Architect Joe Boehning designed the building based on these criteria. The project cost was under $2 million, including the construction of parking lots, architect fees, and general inflation, making it a very economical building. The Pit was partially completed in December 1966, allowing it to be used for the basketball season that year. It was an instant success with fans. Rick Wright of the *Albuquerque Journal* wrote, "…the Pit, after all, is more than a building…it is truly a showcase of college basketball." As a building, the Pit won many awards for good design from the American Institute of Architects and other organizations and received accolades proclaiming it to be one of the best places in the country for watching basketball.

Since the initial construction of The Pit in 1960 and its opening in 1966, the University has made many additions and alterations and the name has changed several times. For example, on May 11, 2017, the Board of Regents approved renaming the University Arena "Dreamstyle Arena" and the University Stadium "Dreamstyle Stadium" in response to a naming rights agreement with Larry Chavez.

Chavez, a lifelong Lobos fan and owner of Dreamstyle Remodeling, Inc., of Albuquerque, made a large donation to the UNM Athletic Department that will also benefit the UNM Anderson School of Management,

UNM Hospital and Popejoy Hall. In March 2017, Chavez, a UNM alumnus (B.B.A. '69), was inducted into the UNM Anderson School Hall of Fame. Chavez said "I, and some neighborhood kids, watched the first UNM football game at University Stadium in September of 1960 through the fence. I went home that night and dreamed of being a Lobo." Chavez' first job was selling sodas at University Stadium when he was 15.[2]

Larry Chavez and Joyce Hitchner Sports Bar

As part of the University's agreement, the Larry Chavez and Joyce Hitchner Sports Bar will be built in the club level of the Pit.[3] Joyce Hitchner is Co-founder of Dreamstyle.

Bob King Court

Bob King came to UNM in 1962 after three years as an assistant coach at the University of Iowa and is known as the "Architect of Lobo Basketball."[4] As a high school coach, he had a record of 205 wins and 75 losses in twelve years. In his first year the Lobos had their first winning season in many years. King left UNM in 1972 with a win-loss record of 175-89. His teams won two Western Athletic Conference titles, went to the NCAA tournament in 1968, and the National Invitational Tournaments in 1964, 1965 and 1967. He never had a losing season in his 10 years as UNM Basketball Coach. He and Pete McDavid were also successful in getting the Pit built, which doubled the amount of seating compared to Johnson Gym's 7,000 seats.

King left the University to become athletic director at Indiana State University where he went 61-24, returning to New Mexico to retire. In 1992, UNM named the Pit's basketball court in honor of Bob King. King died on December 10, 2004, at age 81. Mike Roberts, UNM's long-time sportscaster, stated that he was impressed with King's honesty, never having a hint of scandal during his ten years at UNM, and with his devotion to his adoptive state.[5] King was inducted into the UNM Athletics Hall of Fame in 1987.[6]

Pete McDavid Room

The Pete McDavid Room is a room on the concourse level of The Pit, and includes a photographic mural on the wall that depicted basketball players in action. Joe Laval created the mural.

Paul "Pete" McDavid was born in Sullivan, Illinois, played football for the University of New Mexico in the 1930s and upon graduation, coached at Santa Fe High School. His "Demons" won the state football championship in 1942. McDavid next coached at Albuquerque High School, where his teams won the state football championship in 1947 and the state track titles in 1949 and 1950, after which he came to UNM as athletic director. McDavid remained in that position for 23 years until retiring in 1973. He led the UNM athletic program through good times and bad with both outstanding coaches as well as those who were not so great. Two of his greatest accomplishments were hiring Bob King as basketball coach and helping to lead the planning and construction of The Pit. McDavid is credited with establishing UNM athletic facilities on the South Campus, founding the Western Athletic Conference in 1962, and co-founding the New Mexico High School Coaches and Officials Association.[7] McDavid was inducted into the New Mexico Sports Hall of Fame in 1977.[8] McDavid died in Albuquerque in 1983.

JOHN BAKER MEMORIAL WARMUP LOUNGE

Fig. 3. Left, Track at UNM South Campus (Photograph by Suzanne Mortier, UNM Landscape Architect, 2013. Fig. 4. Center, John Baker Memorial Warm Up Lounge (Source unknown). Fig. 5. Right, John Baker Plaque (Photograph by Suzanne Mortier, UNM Landscape Architect, 2013).

On the east side of University Stadium are facilities for track and field events and practice, including running track and field spaces for events such as discus and javelin throwing, pole vaulting and jumping. At the north end is a shelter named for John W. Baker that was erected by his family and friends.

John W. Baker, born in Albuquerque, attended Manzano High School before enrolling at UNM in 1962. As a high school junior, he won his first State mile championship, and in his senior year, he won gold medals in the mile and mile relay races. In his first varsity race at UNM, he broke the school record for the mile run. By 1968, he was ranked eighth in the world for his time on the indoor mile. After graduation, he taught physical education in the Albuquerque Public School system. While training for the 1972 Olympics, he was diagnosed with terminal cancer. He was widely respected for his bravery. He died in November 26, 1970, at age 26.[9] John Baker was posthumously inducted into the UNM Athletics Hall of Honor in 1992.[10]

The Duke City Dashers Track Club installed a bronze plaque in front of the Warmup Lounge in honor of John Baker. The plaque reads:

> The John Baker Memorial Warm-up Lounge
> In Memory of John Baker, Athlete-Teacher-Coach.
> "The time of my departure has come,
> I have fought the good fight; I have finished the race."

SOUTH CAMPUS

THE UNM CHAMPIONSHIP GOLF COURSE

Fig. 6. UNM Championship Golf Course (Source unknown).

In 1963, Dick McGuire sent a memorandum to President Popejoy recommending the construction of, "…an eighteen hole championship golf course…" The University had land on the South Campus west of University Boulevard over to the freeway that could be used for the project. Popejoy agreed and Robert Lawrence, a golf course architect from Tucson, Arizona, was employed to lay out an eighteen-hole course with a three-hole beginner's course and a driving range.

President Popejoy fired the opening drive on December 8, 1966. The grounds include a lake with ducks and geese, well-kept greens, many trees and magnificent views of the city and the Rio Grande Valley. The name "South Campus Golf Course" was changed to the "Championship Golf Course" when in 1972 the NCAA held the National Championship Tournament on the UNM golf course. The golf course has been ranked in the top 25 public courses in the country.

A design competition was held to select an architect for the clubhouse and the jury selected John Reed for the project. The clubhouse contains a pro shop, locker rooms, offices and a food service. The project received an Honor Award for Design from the New Mexico Society of Architects.

The Patty Howard Golf Complex

Fig. 7. Patty Howard Golf Complex (Source unknown).

The UNM Alumni Lettermen's Association awarded Patty Howard Olliges the Athletics Hall of Fame Distinguished Service Award in 2005 for her contribution toward the construction of the Howard Golf Complex.[11] She said, "I just want to give back to the University that gave me so much." The building includes a meeting room with video capability and offices for the coaches of both the men's and women's golf teams. Most recently, Howard was responsible for enhancing the landscaping around the building.

Patty Howard, born in Houston on October 9, 1938, and a graduate of Highland High School in Albuquerque, came to the University in the late 1950s and joined the Kappa Kappa Gamma Fraternity, a women's sorority. At that time, no formal women's golf team existed, so she practiced with the men's team, which was coached by UNM Athletics Hall of Fame recipient Dick McGuire. Howard credits McGuire with "shaping her swing" and teaching her the golf game. She was the first woman golf player and played in the 1957 William H. Tucker Intercollegiate Golf Tournament at UNM.

Howard was selected as Athletic Varsity Queen, Sweetheart of Sigma Chi, and UNM Fiesta Queen. She graduated in 1961 and taught school in Albuquerque until she married, after which she and her husband opened an automobile agency in Las Vegas, Nevada, where she died on October 12, 2012.

RUDY DAVALOS BASKETBALL CENTER

Fig. 8. Rudy Davalos Basketball Center (Source unknown).

Rudy Davalos, born in San Antonio, Texas, received a degree in education from Southwest Texas State University in 1960 and his master's degree from Georgetown College in Kentucky in 1962. Davalos coached at Georgetown College in 1961, the University of Kentucky in 1962, and Auburn University from 1963 to 1970. He then coached at the University of the South in Sewanee, Tennessee. After that, he took a job with the San Antonio Spurs, a National Basketball Association team, until he became Athletic Director for the University of Texas at San Antonio in 1975. Davalos returned to the Spurs in 1984 as Director of Community Relations. In 1987, he became the Athletic Director at the University of Houston, fielded a Heisman Trophy Winner, and oversaw many facility improvements.

During his career, Davalos received many honors including induction into the NAIA Basketball Hall of Fame and the Southwest Texas State University Hall of Fame and has been recognized repeatedly throughout his career for his efforts on behalf of young people. In 1974, the Catholic Youth Organization honored Davalos with its Man in Youth Award.

Davalos came to UNM in December 1992 and was Director of Athletics from 1992 to 2006. During his time at UNM, Davalos saw an increase in donations to the athletic department, raised academic standards for student-athletes, and was instrumental in remodeling and expanding many facilities. UNM teams participated in post-season NCAA competitions 115 times. In 2004, the UNM Ski Team won the NCAA national championship. In 2005, the UNM soccer team was a national runner-up. In 2002, *Sports Illustrated* named him one of the "101 Most Influential Minorities in Sports." When Davalos retired, the Board of Regents named the new basketball practice building in his honor. In 2006, he was inducted into the UNM Athletics Hall of Fame.[12]

THE L.F. "TOW" DIEHM ATHLETIC FACILITY

Fig. 9. L.F. "Tow" Diehm Athletic Facility – Close-up of Front Doors, 1998 (Photograph by Kate Nash, Center for Southwest Research, UNM Libraries).[13]

The L.F. "Tow" Diehm Athletic Facility on the south end of University Stadium was built in three stages and was completed in 2006. The facility contains state-of-the-art training equipment and workout space for athletes participating in all UNM sponsored sports.

Diehm, better known as Tow, was born in Paola, Kansas, and received the nickname while at UNM because of his light brown hair, or "tow head." Diehm played football in high school and his coach, Carney Smith, had a great influence on his decision to become an athletic trainer. During World War II, Diehm entered the service and spent two years in a hospital after being wounded in battle. After his recovery, he worked as a trainer with Smith who was at that time a coach at a high school in California. Diehm entered the college ranks by working at Kansas State Teachers College, after which he became an assistant trainer at Michigan State University in 1955. In 1957, Pete McDavid hired Diehm to become the athletics trainer at UNM where he stayed for the rest of his life, treating thousands of student athletes. In 1988, Diehm was promoted to Associate Athletics Director.[14]

Diehm helped found the National Athletic Trainers Foundation, serving on its board and becoming the national chairman in 1962. In 1975, he was inducted into the Citizens Savings Athletic Foundation Hall of Fame. Diehm also received recognition from the Albuquerque Chamber of Commerce and was made a member of UNM's Lettermen's Club. In 1981, Diehm was awarded the UNM Regents Meritorious Service Medal. After his retirement in 1983, he became a lobbyist in the state legislature. Ed Johnson, writing in the *Albuquerque Journal*, quoted Diehm as saying, "In this business you are dealing with young people's lives. It's not just athletics. It's education. Sometimes the kind of example you set, young people think they can live with the rest of their lives." Sometimes the examples are good. Like the one set by a Coach Smith on a young tow-headed kid from Kansas.

Tow Diehm, known as the "Father of Athletic Training" in New Mexico, was inducted into the UNM Athletics Hall of Fame in 1987.[15] Diehm died on May 1, 1998, at the age of 73.

The L.F. "Tow" and Pearl J. Diehm Sports Medicine Endowment scholarship was established in the UNM College of Education to support qualifying graduate students. Pearl J. Diehm died August 9, 2009. She served on the board of the Albuquerque/New Mexico Sports Hall of Fame.

BRIAN URLACHER INDOOR PRACTICE FACILITY

Fig. 10. Brian Urlacher Indoor Practice Facility
(Photograph by Suzanne Mortier, UNM Landscape Architect, 2013).

The Brian Urlacher Indoor Practice Facility is an air supported structure enclosing a field. It is used by various sports for practice during inclement weather. The indoor field was named for Brian Urlacher in ceremonies held on June 24, 2009. Urlacher was born May 25, 1978, in Pasco, Washington, and grew up in Lovington, New Mexico. An outstanding football player on the Lobo team from 1996 to 1999, he went on to play middle linebacker for 13 years with the Chicago Bears in the National Football League since being drafted number nine in 2000. His number 54 jersey is one of the most recognizable in the entire NFL. According to his Pro-Football Hall of Fame biography, Urlacher was named Associated Press Defensive Rookie of the Year and in 2005, he was named NFL Defensive Player of the Year. Urlacher played in the Pro Bowl eight times and the XLI Super Bowl. He has received many other honors including Mountain West Conference Player of the Year in 1999, finalist for the Jim Thorpe Award, and Second Team All Pro by *Football News*. He finished 12th in balloting for the Heisman Trophy.[16] In 2018, Urlacher was inducted into the Pro-Football Hall of Fame.

Urlacher has never forgotten Lovington High School or the University of New Mexico. He has donated funds to the Brian Urlacher Training Center in Lovington and the UNM Indoor Practice Facility. The *Albuquerque Journal* quoted Urlacher as crediting UNM with giving him the chance to play football. He said, "This school did a lot for me and I felt an obligation to give back and support my school."

THE LINDA ESTES TENNIS COMPLEX

Fig. 11. Linda Estes Tennis Complex
(Photograph by Suzanne Mortier, UNM Landscape Architect, 2013).

Linda Estes was born, on November 29, 1939, in Calico Park, Arkansas. Moving to Albuquerque at an early age, she graduated from Highland High School and entered the University of New Mexico in 1957. While at UNM, she completed three degrees including a B.A. in recreation in 1961, an M.A. in recreation in 1963, and an M.S. in public administration in 1979. She taught physical education at Eldorado High School before coming to UNM permanently in 1969.

Estes became Director of Women's Athletics in 1973, when women's athletics transferred to the Athletics Department. As Director of Women's Athletics, she was responsible for all eleven women's intercollegiate athletic programs. In 1989, she also supervised the men's athletic programs except football and basketball. By 1992, supervision of the department's academic services was added to her list of duties. She also coached tennis. The Linda Estes Tennis Complex is named in her honor.

Estes was one of the first women to become active in the National Collegiate Athletic Association (NCAA) and served on the NCAA executive committee as well as chairing the NCAA Skiing Committee. In 1989, she represented the NCAA at the World University Games in Sofia, Bulgaria, and again in 1993 at the games in Poland. Rudy Davalos, Director of Athletics, wrote: "Thanks to Linda's relentless determination, the University of New Mexico has been a front runner in women's intercollegiate athletics for many years." To this comment, she replied, "I will forever be grateful for the opportunity I've had to work at UNM. I entered UNM as a freshman in 1957 and have affiliated with the institution as a student or as an employee ever since. UNM is like a mother to me." Estes retired in 2000 and moved to Hawaii, where she still lives and plays tennis. Estes was inducted into the UNM Athletics Hall of Fame in 2002 and the New Mexico Sports Hall of Fame in 2007.[17]

Randy Briggs Tennis Domes

Fig. 12. Randy Briggs Tennis Domes interior (Photograph by Suzanne Mortier, UNM Landscape Architect, 2013).

Fig. 13. Randy Briggs Tennis Domes (Photograph by Suzanne Mortier, UNM Landscape Architect, 2013).

In 1992, Dr. Randy Briggs, an avid tennis player, donated funds for two air-supported structures, which hold three tennis courts each. Briggs, who graduated from Carlsbad High School, holds a Doctor of Optometry degree from the University of Houston and did post-graduate study there in Ocular Therapeutics.

Briggs is considered a pioneer in contact lens development and holds several patents related to design and manufacturing of soft contact lenses. Briggs practiced in Albuquerque from 1970 to 1984 and founded the Sunsoft Corporation in 1981 with two employees. The company grew to 400 employees and became the world's foremost and largest manufacturer of specialty soft contact lenses. The company has been listed by the *New Mexico Business Journal* as one of the top 100 companies in the State. Briggs was designated Optometrist of the Year in 1977 and 1991 by the New Mexico Optometric Association. He established the Dr. Charles R. Briggs Endowment for Corneal and Contact Lens Training and Research Scholarship at the University of Houston.

In 2000, Briggs sold the company and established the Briggs Properties Company, which acquires, owns, and manages commercial properties in New Mexico and Colorado. He is the founder and director of F.A.S.T., a non-profit organization dedicated to educating teachers in promoting reading skills in New Mexico students. Briggs has been a regent of Western New Mexico University and a board member of the Taos Art Museum and the Manzano Day School. Along with the tennis domes, he has contributed to the Tow Diehm Athletic Facility, raised funds for the UNM Chorus, and served on the executive committee of the New Mexico Bowl.

Ted Russell Tennis Arena

Fig. 14. Ted Russell Tennis Arena (Source unknown).

The Ted Russell Tennis Arena, consisting of several lighted outdoor tennis courts and a seating area, was named for Ted Russell, a Highland High School and UNM tennis star with "a blazing, well placed serve." Russell led the Lobos team to their first Western Athletic Conference Championship in 1968. Many consider him the best New Mexico tennis player of his generation. He loved restoring automobiles. Ted Russell was killed in an automobile accident in Phoenix, Arizona, at the age of 30.[18]

COLLEEN MALOOF ATHLETIC ADMINISTRATION BUILDING

Fig. 15. Colleen Maloof Athletic Administration Building (Source unknown).

On February 7, 2007, Paul Krebs presented the following to the UNM Naming Committee:

I respectfully propose that we name our current athletics administration building after former UNM Regent, Coleen Maloof. Mrs. Maloof served the University of New Mexico at its highest level of Regent from 1977-88. Prior to that, the Maloof family was extremely supportive of UNM Athletics both financially and with their time and influence. Coleen's late husband, George, was the president of the Lobo Club from 1962-65. The Lobo Club is the fundraising arm of the UNM Athletics department.

One of the biggest influences that Coleen had on Intercollegiate Athletics at UNM during her time as a Regent was the advancement of women's athletics. She was the voice during a time when supporting women's athletics was not necessarily popular. She paved the way for many of the successes women at UNM have had on the fields of play, as well as in the classroom. The April 22, 1981 *Daily Lobo* reported that Coleen received the first annual Inspiration Award for her service to women's athletics.

Krebs went on to say that the naming of the athletic administration building after Maloof is, he believed, the only such building in the country named for a woman. The Board of Regents approved the naming recommendation at their meeting on April 10, 1987.[19]

JAMES CRAIG ROBERTSON SOCCER FIELD

Fig. 16. South Campus Running Track and Soccer Field, 1998 (Photograph by Kate Nash, Center for Southwest Research, UNM Libraries).[20]

James Craig Robertson, a nuclear engineering educator and researcher who was born in Kinlichleven, Scotland, on May 29, 1936, received his B.S. with honors from Glasgow University in 1957 and his Ph.D. in 1961. A licensed reactor operator, he taught radiation safety at Dundee College of Technology.

Robertson and his family moved to the United States in 1976 and he became a citizen in 1982. After working as a visiting professor at the University of Michigan from 1976 to 1978, he came to UNM to teach in the Department of Chemical and Nuclear Engineering. Robertson's wife, Moira, wrote, "When we came to Albuquerque, he founded a team for our sons and coached. It was only a matter of time until he got involved with the University's club soccer team, coaching it and taking it on one occasion to a series of matches in Mexico." Through Robertson's efforts, soccer became a University sport. After his death in March 1986, his sons were instrumental in getting approval for the UNM soccer field to be named in his memory.

UNIVERSITY SCIENCE AND TECHNOLOGY PARK

Dikewood Building

Fig. 17. Dikewood Building, University Science and Technology Park (Source unknown).

The University of New Mexico Science and Technology Park was first approved by the Board of Regents for development in the early 1960s. A group of interested people including Robert Nordhaus, Sheldon Dike, and John Daly, representing Albuquerque Industrial Development Corporation, presented a plan prepared by architect Max Flatow of the firm of Flatow, Moore, Bryan and Fairburn to the Board of Regents. Soon utilities and streets were installed and a building for the Dikewood Corporation was constructed.

The Dikewood Corporation was named for the owners Sheldon Dike and Walter B. Wood. The company was started in 1956 as a "think tank" and was a scientific consulting firm that produced knowledge for government and industry in scientific fields. Dike, born in 1916, wrote of the company in 1965, "Dikewood is a group of consulting scientists engaged in theoretical research, analytical studies, digital systems, programming and computational services for industry and military."

A second building was constructed for the EGG Corporation, which used the building for only a few years before it was leased to the Social Security Administration. Around 1990, development at the park increased with the addition of several buildings.

Research Park Streets

Chuck Wellborn suggested the names of New Mexico scientists who were outstanding in their fields for the street names in the research park. Some of his research is included in the descriptions below.

Basehart Street

Harry W. Basehart, professor emeritus and former chairman of the Department of Anthropology from 1972 to 1974, was editor of the *Southwestern Journal of Anthropology*. Born in Zanesville, Ohio, he attended the University of Chicago until 1942, when he joined the Army and served as an intelligence officer for four and a half years. Basehart received his doctorate from Harvard University and taught briefly at Harvard and Goucher College before coming to UNM in 1954. Primarily an ethnologist, Basehart began his fieldwork among the Jicarilla, Chiricahua, and Mescalero Apaches in the mid-1950s. His research focused on land use, aboriginal economy and early land organization and has been used in efforts to resolve Indian land disputes. He wrote extensively about Apache cultural history and ethnology and was editor of the *Journal of Anthropological Research*. Basehart retired from UNM in 1975 as professor emeritus and died in 1988.[21] In addition to Basehart Street, the Frank J. Broilo, Harry W. and Margaret Basehart Memorial Endowed Scholarship was named in his memory.[22]

Bradbury Drive

One of the main streets in the park is named for physicist Norris Edwin Bradbury, second director of the Los Alamos Scientific Laboratory (LASL), which was established in 1943 and renamed the Los Alamos National Laboratory (LANL) in 1981. Bradbury served as director of the Lab for 25 years. In addition to Bradbury Drive at UNM, the LANL's Bradbury Science Museum is named in his honor.

Bradbury was born in Pomona, California, in 1909. After graduating Phi Beta Kappa from Pomona College, Bradbury received his Ph.D. in physics and mathematics from the University of California at Berkeley in 1932 and was on the Massachusetts Institute of Technology (MIT) Department of Physics faculty from 1932-34 as a Nuclear Research Fellow. He served in the United States Naval Reserve from 1941 to 1945 and taught physics at Stanford University until he succeeded Robert Oppenheimer as Director of LANL in 1945. He received many awards and honorary degrees including an honorary Doctorate of Law and Letters by UNM in 1953. The Atomic Energy Commission in 1970 presented Bradbury with the Enrico Fermi Award, its highest award. Bradbury retired in 1970 and died in 1997 at age 88.[23]

Avenida César Cháves

The City of Albuquerque renamed Stadium Boulevard, which cuts through the center of South Campus, in honor of César Estrada Cháves. Cháves was the leader of the labor effort to improve the lives of low-paid field workers in California and elsewhere in the United States and formed America's first successful union of farm workers.

Chávez was born on March 31, 1927, in Yuma, Arizona, the son of Juana and Librado Chávez. His paternal grandparents had migrated from Mexico in 1880. In 1937, during the Depression, his family moved to California to work in the fields, settling in San Jose. César Chávez later served two years in the U.S. Navy and married Helen Fabela. Many books and articles have been written about César Chávez. In addition to Avenida César Chávez, several schools in New Mexico are named for him. César Chávez died on April 23, 1993, in Arizona at age 66.[24]

Goddard Street

Goddard Street is named for Robert Hutchins Goddard, known as the Father of American Rocketry.[25] Goddard conducted early experiments with rockets in southeastern New Mexico, in Massachusetts, and on the eastern shore of Virginia.

Goddard was born in Worcester, Massachusetts, on October 5, 1882, and graduated from Worcester Polytechnic Institute (WPI) in 1908. Goddard received his master's degree in 1910 and his Ph.D. in 1911, both from Clark University. He subsequently became a research fellow at Princeton for two years, where in 1913, he developed a mathematical theory of rocket propulsion. He joined the faculty of Clark University in 1914 and became a full professor in 1919.

Goddard, almost alone, designed, built, tested, and flew the world's first liquid fueled rocket on March 16, 1926. During the 1930s, he worked near Roswell, New Mexico, with assistance from the Smithsonian Institution and, with the encouragement of Charles Lindbergh, additional assistance from the Guggenheim Foundation. While in New Mexico, he developed more sophisticated boosters and payloads, which laid the foundation for the Moon launches. Goddard's work also led to the making of "bazookas," the hand held grenade launchers used in World War II.

During his life, he received little professional recognition, though he had "first obtained public notoriety in 1907 when he fired a powder rocket in the basement of the physics building at WPI. School officials then took an immediate interest in Goddard's work and, to their credit, did not expel him." At the time of his death, Goddard held more than 200 scientific patents. After his death on August 10, 1945, Goddard became known worldwide as one of three scientific pioneers of rocketry who led the way to space exploration and ballistic missiles. In 1959, Congress approved a gold medal in his honor. In 1961, NASA named Goddard Space Flight Center in Maryland in his name.[26]

Langham Street

Langham Street begins where Basehart Street turns south. The layout was done at the insistence of the City of Albuquerque. Wright Haskell Langham was born in Winnsboro, Texas, on May 21, 1911, and attended Panhandle Agricultural and Mechanical College. He received his M.S. in chemistry from Oklahoma A&M College in 1935. Langham studied organic chemistry at Iowa State College and completed his Ph.D. in biochemistry at the University of Colorado in 1943. The health hazards of the new element called plutonium were not well understood at the time. Langham joined the Manhattan Project at the University of Chicago Metallurgical Laboratory

(Met Lab), where he developed what is known as the "Langham" model for relating body burden of plutonium to the short-term excretion rate of plutonium from a biological sample.[27]

Langham came to Los Alamos Scientific Laboratory in 1945 and played a key role in planning, conducting and interpreting much of the early work on plutonium toxicity. His research specialties were analytical chemistry of special materials, radiation health problems, and metabolism of radioactive isotopes. Langham died in a plane crash in 1972.

Shields Street

Lora Maneum Shields was born in Choctaw, Oklahoma, on March 13, 1912. She received her B.S. in 1940 from UNM, and both an M.S. in 1942 and a Ph.D. in 1947 in botany from the University of Iowa. She was the first Native American to receive a doctorate in botany. Teaching at New Mexico Highlands University from 1947 to 1978, Shields also served as Chair of the Biology Department from 1951 to 1978. Shield's research included studies of nitrogen sources and content in leaves and algae, nuclear effects on plants, serum lipids, birth anomalies in the Navajo uranium district and other effects of uranium exposure in Navajo country.[28]

From 1960 to 1984 Shields represented the New Mexico Academy of Science (NMAS) to the American Association of Academies of Science (AAAS), now known as the National Association of Academies of Science (NAAS). She served as President of the Southwest/ Rocky Mountain (SWARM) Division of AAAS in 1964. She received the NMAS Distinguished Service Award for outstanding contributions to science in 1965. In 1976, she was became the first New Mexican to become President of the NAAS. In 1984, Shields served as President of the NMAS. She edited the *New Mexico Journal of Science* for many years. After her retirement from New Mexico Highlands University in 1980, she began teaching at the Navajo Community College in Shiprock.[29] Shields died in 1996. In addition to Shields Street within the UNM Research Park, the Lora Shields Science Center at New Mexico Highlands University is named in her honor.

Springer Street

Frank Springer was born in Wapello, Iowa, on June 17, 1848, and graduated from the State University of Iowa in 1867 after studying paleontology. He then studied law in a lawyer's office in Iowa and was admitted to the Iowa Bar in 1869. In 1873, he moved to New Mexico as attorney for the Maxwell Land Grant and the Santa Fe Railroad. Moving to Las Vegas in 1883, he lived there until his death in 1926.

Springer, who amassed a fortune, was very generous in supporting the School of American Research, the Finck Linguistic Library, and other deserving ventures as well as many artists. Springer also served as a New Mexico State Senator, the first President of the New Mexico Academy of Science, and President of the first Board of Regents at Highlands University. He became one of the world's foremost authorities in paleontology, specializing in fossil crinoides. From 1867 to 1877, he published sixteen papers and 20 years later with Charles Wachsmuth published a multi-volume treatise entitled *North American Fossil Crinoides Camarata*. George Washington University conferred on Springer the degree of Doctor of Science, and in 1924, he received a Ph.D.

from the University of Bonn. Frank Springer donated his collection of crinoids to the Smithsonian Museum of Natural History in 1911 and provided an endowment for their maintenance. The Springer Collection is the largest repository of fossil crinoids in the world.[30] In 1922, a bronze bust of Springer by sculptor Scarpitta was given to the New Mexico Art Museum in Santa Fe.[31]

UNIVERSITY STADIUM ("DREAMSTYLE STADIUM")

Fig. 18. Left, University Stadium – Stadium Seating and Press Boxes, 1998 (Photograph by Kate Nash, Center for Southwest Research, UNM Libraries).[32] Fig. 19. Center, University Stadium Press Box (Photograph by Suzanne Mortier, UNM Landscape Architect, 2013). Fig. 20. Right, UNM Stadium (Source unknown).

On August 23, 1960, President Popejoy reported to the Regents that names suggested for the new football stadium included University Stadium, Lobo Stadium, Varsity Stadium and New Mexico Stadium. Regent MacGillivray said the New Mexico Boosters Club had suggested Popejoy Stadium. Popejoy said that although he appreciated the gesture, he felt that no structure should be named for a person actively on the University staff. The board agreed to tentatively call it University Stadium and await a suggestion from the Building Committee, which never came. Sherman Smith asked Popejoy when he retired if he would like the stadium named for him, but Popejoy said he would rather have the new symphony hall in the Fine Arts Center as his namesake. For more information about the renaming of University Stadium in 2017 to Dreamstyle Stadium, see discussion above under "The Pit".

Branch Field

Branch Field at Dreamstyle Stadium is named in honor of Turner and Margaret Branch of the Branch Law Firm, who in August 2012 donated funds to replace the grass playing field with a synthetic artificial playing surface.[33] At the time, the Turners' donation was the second largest gift ever made to the University's athletics program. Prior to the opening of the University's football stadium on the South Campus in 1960, games were played on the Central Campus at University Field (1892-1937) and Zimmerman Field (1938-1959).[34]

The Branch law firm, which specializes in personal injury cases, is one of the largest in the southwest, with offices in Albuquerque, Houston, and Washington, D.C. Both Turner and Margaret Branch graduated from UNM and have been long time supporters of its athletic programs. Turner W. Branch was born August 22, 1938, in Houston, Texas. He received his B.A. in political science in 1960 from UNM, where he was Student Body President. In 1965, he received his J.D. from Baylor University. He was section editor of the law review and received the T.R. McDonald Award as the outstanding law student. Turner Branch served with the Marines from 1960-63 as a 1st lieutenant before entering private practice. He also served as a New Mexico State Representative from 1968-74, where he was a member of the Judiciary Committee. Among the many accolades he received, Turner Branch was elected as one of only 500 Fellows worldwide in the International Academy of Trial Attorneys.[35] Turner Branch died in August 2016 in Phoenix at age 77.[36]

Margaret Moses Branch was born in Salzburg, Austria, in 1953. Margaret Branch received her B.S. from UNM with honors in 1975 and her J.D. in 1978 from UNM Law School. In 1977, she was elected President of the Graduate Students Association. In her practice, she specializes in toxic tort and mass tort litigation and has been involved in exceptionally complex cases. She has long been interested in women's health issues and among other activities has served as President of the Women's Bar Association of New Mexico. She is a noted speaker and lecturer.[37]

Franco-Scott Memorial Patio

Myron Fifield wrote in *El Servico Real* in December 1972:

> An outstanding honor has been accorded to the memory of two faithful groundskeepers, the late A.C. "Scotty" Scott and Henry Franco. For at least two years a committee headed by John Dolzadelli and Floyd B. Williams, Jr., has been planning a memorial patio for them. It is located at the southwest corner of the west embankment of University Stadium north of the Athletic Building. It was dedicated on November 3, 1972 with friends and relatives meeting in the Athletic Building for coffee and doughnuts prior to the brief ceremony.

The memorial has a 20-foot by 20-foot concrete slab with a red brick border. When built, it had two benches on it and two dedicatory bronze plaques. The plaques read:

> In Memory of A.C. "Scotty" Scott,
> The Grounds Keeper for
> UNM Athletic Facilities, 1947-1958
>
> In Memory of Henry C. Franco,
> The Grounds Keeper for
> UNM Athletic Facilities, 1958-1970.

Today, thousands of people walk over the memorial on their way to events in University Stadium. Most people would not notice the memorial, as the benches are gone and the single remaining plaque has become badly tarnished.

Arthur C. Scott was born in Arkansas in 1885, one of thirteen children. Shortly after his birth, his family moved to Kansas where he was raised. Scott worked as a gardener for the Indian Service in Oklahoma, the Haskell Institute in North Dakota, and the Albuquerque Veterans Administration. In 1948, he came to UNM to become the Lead Groundskeeper of the athletic and physical education fields.

Henry Franco was born in Los Lunas, New Mexico, and attended Albuquerque schools. He was a veteran of both World War II and the Korean War. After working for UNM for thirteen years, mainly on the South Campus, he died suddenly in 1969. Fifield wrote of Franco, "All of us will miss this very friendly, gregarious fellow employee. Sorry you had to go, Franco. You sure gave us a lot of happy memories while you were with us."

Endnotes: Section Three—South Campus

1. http://econtent.unm.edu/cdm/ref/collection/ULPhotoImag/id/2682 (last accessed April 9, 2018).

2. See Frank Mercogliano, "Larry Chavez makes largest philanthropic agreement in UNM Athletics history: Dreamstyle Stadium, Dreamstyle Arena" (May 3, 2017), http://golobos.com/news/2017/5/3/general-venues-renamed-dreamstyle-stadium-dream-style-arena.aspx, and UNM Board of Regents, "June 13, 2017 Meeting Agenda" (including May 13, 2017 Minutes), http://regents.unm.edu/meetings/documents/2017/bor-ebook-2017-06-13.pdf (last accessed April 23, 2018).

3. See Frank Mercogliano, "Larry Chavez makes largest philanthropic agreement in UNM Athletics history: Dreamstyle Stadium, Dreamstyle Arena" (May 3, 2017), http://golobos.com/news/2017/5/3/general-venues-renamed-dreamstyle-stadium-dream-style-arena.aspx (last accessed April 23, 2018).

4. See UNM Lobos, "Bob King," http://www.golobos.com/sports/2015/5/12/GEN_20140101221.aspx (last accessed April 23, 2018).

5. See UNM Lobos, "UNM mourns passing of Bob King; services next Wednesday at the Pit," (Dec. 10, 2004), http://www.golobos.com/news/2004/12/10/209056710.aspx (last accessed April 23, 2018).

6. See UNM Lobos, "Hall of Honor," http://www.golobos.com/sports/2015/5/12/GEN_2014010147.aspx (last accessed April 23, 2018).

7. See UNM Lobos, "Pete McDavid," http://www.golobos.com/sports/2015/5/12/GEN_20140101263.aspx (last accessed April 23, 2018).

8. See New Mexico Sports Hall of Fame, 1977 Sports Hall of Fame Inductee, "Pete McDavid," http://nmshof.com/pete-mcdavid/ (last accessed April 23, 2018).

9. See UNM Lobos, "John Baker," http://www.golobos.com/sports/2015/5/12/GEN_20140101253.aspx (last accessed April 23, 2018).

10. See UNM Lobos, "Hall of Honor," http://www.golobos.com/sports/2015/5/12/GEN_2014010147.aspx (last accessed April 23, 2018).

11. See UNM Lobos, "Patty Howard Olliges," http://www.golobos.com/sports/2015/5/12/GEN_20140101113.aspx (last accessed April 23, 2018).

12. See UNM Lobos, "Rudy Davalos," http://www.golobos.com/sports/2015/5/12/GEN_20140101216.aspx (last accessed April 23, 2018).

13. http://econtent.unm.edu/cdm/ref/collection/ULPhotoImag/id/2686 (last accessed April 9, 2018).

14. See UNM Lobos, "Tow Diehm," http://www.golobos.com/sports/2015/5/12/GEN_20140101173.aspx (last accessed April 23, 2018).

15. See UNM Lobos, "Hall of Honor," http://www.golobos.com/sports/2015/5/12/GEN_2014010147.aspx (last accessed April 23, 2018).

16. See UNM Lobos, "Bobby Urlacher (Football)," http://www.golobos.com/sports/2015/5/12/GEN_20140101199.aspx (last accessed April 23, 2018).

17. See UNM Lobos, "Linda Estes," http://www.golobos.com/sports/2015/5/12/GEN_20140101285.aspx and http://www.golobos.com/news/2011/8/18/209071115.aspx (last accessed April 23, 2018); see also UNM Board of Regents, Finance and Facilities Committee, "Meeting Summary" (Dec. 4, 2008), http://regents.unm.edu/committees/finance-and-facilities/minutes/2008/finance_facilities_minutes_2008-12-04.pdf (last accessed April 23, 2018).

18. See United States Tennis Association, Southwest, "Ted Russell Memorial Award (Junior Male Player of the Year)," http://www.nnmta.usta.com/About_Us/annual_memorial_awards/ (last accessed April 23, 2018).

19. See UNM Board of Regents, "Minutes" (April 10, 2007), http://regents.unm.edu/meetings/minutes/2007/bor_minutes_2007-04-10.pdf (last accessed April 23, 2018).

20 http://econtent.unm.edu/cdm/ref/collection/ULPhotoImag/id/2615 (last accessed April 9, 2018).

21 See Philip Bock, "The successors: Harry Basehart, Stanley Newman, James Spuhler & Philip Bock," *Journal of Anthropological Research*, vol. 65, n. 1 (Spring 2009), http://www.journals.uchicago.edu/doi/abs/10.3998/jar.0521004.0065.102?journalCode=jar (last accessed April 23, 2018).

22 UNM Foundation, "Frank J. Broilo, Harry W. and Margaret Basehart Memorial Endowed Scholarship," https://www.unmfund.org/fund/frank-j-broilo-harry-w-and-margaret-basehart-memorial-endowed-scholarship/ (last accessed April 23, 2018).

23 Wolfgang Saxon, "Norris E. Bradbury, 88, Chief of Los Alamos Atomic Center," *New York Times* (Aug. 22, 1997), http://www.nytimes.com/1997/08/22/us/norris-e-bradbury-88-chief-of-los-alamos-atomic-center.html; see also Los Alamos National Laboratory, Bradbury Science Museum, "Norris Bradbury: our second director played an important part in the success of the Los Alamos National Laboratory," http://www.lanl.gov/museum/exhibitions/lobby/norris.php, American Institute of Physics (AIP), "Los Alamos National Laboratory," https://history.aip.org/phn/21612002.html, and AIP, "Massachusetts Institute of Technology, Department of Physics," https://history.aip.org/phn/21511001.html (including link to 1976 oral interview with Bradbury) (last accessed April 23, 2018).

24 See, e.g., Robert Lindsey, "Cesar Chavez, 66, Organizer of Union for Migrants, Dies," *New York Times* (April 24, 1993), http://www.nytimes.com/learning/general/onthisday/bday/0331.html (last accessed April 23, 2018).

25 See Robert Hutchings, "Dr. Robert H. Goddard, American Rocketry Pioneer," NASA Goddard Space Flight Center (Aug. 3, 2017), https://www.nasa.gov/centers/goddard/about/history/dr_goddard.html (last accessed April 23, 2018).

26 See Steve Graham, "Robert H. Goddard (1882-1945)," NASA Earth Observatory, Features (Oct. 16, 2000), https://earthobservatory.nasa.gov/Features/Goddard/ (last accessed April 12, 2018).

27 See Atomic Heritage Foundation, Profiles, "Wright Langham," https://www.atomicheritage.org/profile/wright-langham (last accessed April 23, 2018).

28 For more information about Dr. Shields, see Tiffany K. Wayne, *American Women in Science since 1990*, vol. 1, pp. 57 and 857 (2011).

29 See New Mexico Academy of Science, "A Brief History of NMAS and AAAS Affiliation," http://www.nmas.org/history.html (last accessed April 23, 2018).

30 See Smithsonian National Museum of Natural History, Department of Paleobiology, "Springer Collection: Springer Echinoderm Collection," http://paleobiology.si.edu/springer/paleoSpringer.html (last accessed April 23, 2018).

31 For more information on Frank Springer, see, for example, David L. Caffey, *Frank Springer and New Mexico: From the Colfax County War to the Emergence of Modern Santa Fe*, Texas A&M Press and the Texas Book Consortium (2006).

32 http://econtent.unm.edu/cdm/ref/collection/ULPhotoImag/id/2684 (last accessed April 9, 2018).

33 See Karen Wentworth, "Margaret and Turner Branch donate $1.5 million to Lobo Athletics to name field at University Stadium," UNM Newsroom (July 31, 2012), http://news.unm.edu/news/margaret-and-turner-branch-donate-1-5-million-to-lobo-athletics-to-name-the-football-field-at-university-stadium (last accessed April 23, 2018).

34 UNM Lobos, "Branch Field at Dreamstyle Stadium," http://www.golobos.com/sports/2015/5/12/GEN_2014010114.aspx (last accessed April 23, 2018).

35 Branch Law Firm, "Turner W. Branch, In Memory of: N.M. State Bar Memoriam," https://www.branchlawfirm.com/turner-w-branch.html (last accessed April 23, 2018).

36 See Maggie Shepard and Rick Wright, "ABQ attorney Turner Branch dies at age 77," *Albuquerque Journal* (Aug. 5, 2018), https://www.abqjournal.com/820483/branch-attorney-businessman-dies.html (last accessed April 23, 2018).

37 Branch Law Firm, "Margaret Moses Branch, Partner," https://www.branchlawfirm.com/margaret-moses-branch.html (last accessed April 23, 2018).

University Stadium Press Box (Photograph by Suzanne Mortier, UNM Landscape Architect, 2013).

Section Four—Other Spaces

The Duck Pond – Looking North from South Bridge (Center for Southwest Research, UNM Libraries).

ALUMNI MEMORIAL CLOCK

Fig. 1. Alumni Clock, circa 1990s (Center for Southwest Research, UNM Libraries).

Fig. 2. Alumni Memorial Clock – Two Faces (Photograph by Suzanne Mortier, UNM Landscape Architect, 2013).

A large black clock sits on the south side of the Duck Pond beside the concrete walk in front of Mitchell Hall. In the flower garden at the base of the clock is a bronze plaque that reads:

> Dedicated September 20, 1990 to Commemorate
> the University of New Mexico Centennial,
> Reflecting the Past, Looking to the Future,
> Donated by the Following Alumni Association Past Presidents.

Listed below the dedication are names of past Alumni Association presidents beginning with Roy Stamm, Class of 1898 and President in 1907, and ending with Robert Matteucci, Class of 1957 and President from 1989-90.

THE CARMEN L. ALVAREZ ELM TREE

Carmen L. Alverez was born in Las Vegas, New Mexico, to Margarita Martinez C. de Baca and Antonio Martinez on November 21, 1931. She was the granddaughter of New Mexico's second governor Ezequiel C. de Baca. She lived in Havana, Cuba, during the takeover by Fidel Castro, whereupon she moved to San Antonio, Texas, before moving to Albuquerque. Alvarez played an active role in politics and represented New Mexico at the Democratic Convention in 1985. She died on April 22, 2009.[1] An elm tree was planted at UNM in her memory.

BLAIR'S GARDEN

On the North Campus attached to the northeast corner of the Family Practice Center is a small garden named in memory of Blair Leigh Coker, an employee of the Family Practice Center. Her parents Professor Donald P.

Schlegel and Jacqueline Schlegel created the garden, a pleasant spot that includes flowering plants and sheltered seating for the weary. There is a memorial plaque that reads:

> In Memory of Blair Leigh Coker,
> December 16, 1960-March 9, 2004.
> Did We Ever Tell You You're Our Hero?

Blair Leigh Coker was born in Chicago, Illinois, on December 16, 1960, and she died in Albuquerque on March 9, 2004. For 33 years, she fought debilitating multiple sclerosis, never letting the disease slow her down. After working for many years for the U.S. Department of Agriculture Soil Conservation Service, she transferred to the School of Medicine, where she worked in the Family and Community Medicine Department. She received her bachelor's degree from UNM in 2001.[2]

THE TEJAY R. COLLINS PLAQUE

Tejay R. Collins was a graduate student employed by the Physical Plant Department to work on landscaping maintenance. A yucca was planted in his memory.

MARY A. BURROWS

The memorial marker for Mary A. Burrows, who died in January 1966, sat at the bus stop on the northwest corner of Central Avenue and Yale Boulevard. Mary A. Burrows was married to Dan C. Burrows, publisher of the *Albuquerque Tribune*. The marker has since been paved over and a bus shelter and landscaping installed.

CORNELL MALL

Fig. 3. Cornell Mall – Woman with Books, circa 1960s (Center for Southwest Research, UNM Libraries).[3]

Fig. 4. Cornell Mall, 2013 (Photograph by Suzanne Mortier, UNM Landscape Architect).

Contrary to the common perception, Cornell Mall is not named for the Ivy League School, but for the Albuquerque city street that used to run through the campus. The street was named for the school, as were a whole series of streets beginning with Yale Boulevard and running eastward to Carlisle, which is presumably named for Carlisle Indian School, the alma mater of star football player Jim Thorpe.

The Warnecke Plan of 1960 depicted a proposed pedestrian mall and Garrett Eckbo, the consulting landscape architect for the University, subsequently designed the mall. Eckbo and UNM landscape architect Robert Johns designed the travertine marble fountain that formerly stood in the mall between Popejoy Hall and the New Mexico Union.

The Belén Marbles Fountain

Fig. 5. Fine Arts Center – Exterior – Fountain (The original Belén Marbles Fountain) (Center for Southwest Research, UNM Libraries).[4]

The Belén Marbles fountain, which once stood between the Fine Arts Center and the Student Union, was never officially named. The Acropolis and Stonehenge were mentioned as possible names. The name Regents' Plaza was considered for the plaza in which the fountain once stood. The site was a dirt area back in the 1970s when University Regent Ann Jordan saw Governor Bruce King getting his cowboy boots muddy walking across it and insisted that the area be developed.

Garrett Eckbo and the author went to a quarry west of Belén with Vince Lardner, the quarry owner, to look for some stones to use around the campus. On the ground they found large square stones with fluted sides that reminded Hooker of the fragments of columns lying on the Acropolis in Athens. The fluting was a result of early quarrying methods that involved drilling holes in the marble bed, driving wood pegs into the holes, and soaking them with water. The resulting swelling of the wood would break the blocks away from the bed. It has been said that the beautiful polished slabs of this travertine marble are used in the Rotunda of the State Capitol and the old Bank of New Mexico building in Albuquerque.

In a column in the *Wall Street Journal* called "Form + Function" by John Pierson, Pierson stated that more landscape architects were using the beauty of rough-hewn stones in their work. He noted, "Garrett Eckbo used giant limestone chunks to make a fountain at the University of New Mexico." Concrete pavement with brick dividers surrounded the fountain. A few years ago the fountain was demolished and the stones, sans water, were moved to a traffic circle north of the Duck Pond.

In a letter to the author, Sylvia Cooke, a student, wrote:

> For several years there has been more and more excitement in the entire campus, the new buildings, the fantastic variety of trees and shrubs, the warm, friendly areas for sitting and strolling. For me the most exciting impact was the Popejoy Plaza fountain. As an adult student taking evening classes, I would walk past the fountain at night—yes, sometimes under a full moon. I was taking an Honors class in Roots of Western Civilization last Spring and I could visualize the fountain as a perfect setting for a Greek drama.
>
> To make a long story short, our class did "The Eumenides" at the fountain last

Mothers Day, at dusk. I don't know if you were in the audience, but if you were, I want you to know that it was my admiration for your magnificent structure that inspired the theatrical production. I feel it lends itself to all forms of theatre, dance, music, drama. I believe that my group was the first to use it, but certainly not the last. I don't know if I can get enough people interested, but I envision an annual Mother's Day Myth Festival.

THE DUCK POND

Fig. 6. The Duck Pond - After Completion of Construction, 1975 (Center for Southwest Research, UNM Libraries).[5]

Fig. 7. The Duck Pond - Looking North from South of Bridge, 1995 (Center for Southwest Research, UNM Libraries).

The Warnecke Plan envisioned a large, formal, round pool where the Duck Pond is now, but Garrett Eckbo, the consulting landscape architect, who received an honorary Doctorate of Fine Arts from UNM in 1992,[6] designed the pond in a more natural setting. The pond's unofficial name came into popular use almost immediately because of the many ducks that were abandoned there by people.[7]

The Duck Pond is a public park within the campus. Students lounge, study and sleep on the grassy slopes surrounding the Pond. Parents and children feed the ducks and picnic on weekends. Many couples have fond memories of the Duck Pond, captured in photographs taken on the wooden bridge following wedding ceremonies in the Alumni Chapel.

When it became known where the Pond would be, protests erupted, particularly among staff in the administration building, as the Pond would replace the unsightly parking lot close to the building. Campus legend is that the pond was ridiculed during the annual faculty follies as the University Architect's folly. However, if anyone today suggested removing this beloved Duck Pond, the protests would be loud, and students, faculty and staff would actively work to save the Pond and its namesake, the ducks.

THE ENARSON BENCH

Fig. 8. The Enarson Bench (Source unknown).

Fig. 9. Marker – Audrey Pitt and Harold Enarson (Photograph by Ann Clarke).

Erected by the daughters of Audrey and Harold Enarson, the Enarson Bench sits beside the walk to the southeast and facing the Duck Pond. The bench and its marker celebrate their parents' fiftieth wedding anniversary. The metal plaque on the back of the bench reads:

> This Bench is Given in Honor of the Fiftieth Wedding Anniversary
> of Audrey Pitt and Harold Enarson, Who Fell in Love on this Campus.
> From Their Admiring and Loving Daughters, Merlyn, Elaine and Lisa, June 7, 1992.

Harold L. Enarson, born in Villisca, Iowa, on May 24, 1919, received a B.A. from the University of New Mexico in 1940, an M.A. from Stanford University in 1946 and a Ph.D. from American University in 1951. Enarson, who grew up during the Depression of the 1930s, served in the United States Army Infantry from 1943 to 1946. During President Truman's term, he served as a special assistant in the White House. In 1954, he became the Executive Secretary of the Western Intercollegiate Commission of Higher Education (WICHE) and served in that capacity until coming to UNM in 1960. He became Administrative Vice President for one year and then Academic Vice President. While at UNM, he was instrumental in establishing the Medical School and one of the largest Peace Corps training programs for Latin America.

In 1964, he left UNM to become President of Cleveland State University. In 1972, he was appointed President of Ohio State University (OSU) in 1972. During protests associated with the Kent State killings and Vietnam War, Enarson received nationwide acclaim for his handling of student unrest by moving into the student union and listening and talking with students for days. Enarson was also known for firing OSU Coach Woody Hayes for punching a player from the opposing team during the last few minutes of a 1978 bowl game.[8]

UNM recognized Enarson with the Zimmerman Award in 1976.[9] After retiring from OSU in 1981, he returned to UNM. As an emeritus professor, he was appointed the Carl Hatch Professor of Law and Public Administration at UNM.[10]

In addition to his work in higher education, Enarson served on many boards, commissions and committees. One of his final efforts for higher education was to head WICHE for several years. Enarson received at least eight honorary degrees from various universities, including an honorary Doctor of Letters in Humanities from UNM in 1981.[11] A building on the Ohio State University campus is named for Harold Enarson.[12] Harold Enarson died in July 2006.[13] His wife, Audrey Enarson, received a Distinguished Service award at OSU in 1981. She died on January 26, 2006.[14]

THE FRANK B. FEATHER TREE

On April 22, 2010, a "Valley Forge" American elm was planted on the grounds of the University House, located on the southeast corner of Yale and Las Lomas, in honor of Frank Feather, who died on June 5, 2009.

The June 2009 issue of the *Los Ranchos Village Vision* in an "In Memoriam" noted that Feather, who was a former Trustee of the Village, was a native New Mexican, born in Mesilla Park on October 28, 1927. Beginning premedical training at Tulane University at the age of sixteen, he soon discovered his true interests were in the study of plant life. Once back home, he established the Mesilla Park Plant Farm, a wholesale-retail nursery and farm. Feather sold the farm in 1959 and then worked at the New Mexico Institute of Mining and Technology in Socorro, after which he returned to New Mexico State University. At New Mexico State, he received his B.S. in botany in 1964 while working as a grounds supervisor for the campus.

Feather came to UNM in July 1964 to work with consultant Garrett Eckbo in developing the landscaping on campus. He also consulted on the landscaping at North Carolina State University and spent two years with the U.S. Agency for International Development in Lima, Peru, establishing a physical plant department at the Universidad Nacional Agraria. After two years, Feather resumed his duties at UNM until his retirement. For many years, he also taught classes in outdoor and indoor gardening at Central New Mexico Community College and played the oboe and English horn. Feather was active in Rotary International and served on the boards of several organizations including the International Society of Arborists (ISA), the ISA Rocky Mountain Chapter, the American Society of Consulting Arborists, and locally, Think Trees.[15]

THE F. CHRIS GARCIA TREE

On the east side of the yard of University House, a Deodar cedar tree was dedicated to former UNM President F. Chris Garcia. The bronze plaque on the east garden wall reads:

> The Deodara Cedar (Cedrus deodara) Tree to the East is Dedicated
> to F. Chris Garcia, The University of New Mexico's 19th President, by
> UNM's Staff Council To Honor His Dedication to The Staff of The
> University of New Mexico, June 24, 2003.

In the April 2009 issue of the *Albuquerque Journal*, Amanda Schoenberg wrote an article in the Mature Life Section noting that F. Chris Garcia had been selected to the Senior Hall of Fame at the Albuquerque Convention Center. She wrote:

> A thirteenth generation New Mexican, Garcia graduated from Valley High School. He spent most of his career at the University of New Mexico, where he earned his bachelor's and master's degrees and returned as a professor in 1970 after earning a doctorate from the University of California at Davis.

Garcia led several parallel careers. He co-founded the survey research firm Zia Research Associates and was a frequent commentator on New Mexico politics in national and local media, dean of the College of Arts and Sciences, vice president of academic affairs and president of UNM, a job he took after colleagues petitioned for his appointment. The Board of Regents appointed Garcia president of the university for a one-year term on June 20, 2002. Garcia said he had no interest in it as a long-term position.

A pioneer in Hispanic political studies, Garcia recently published his 12th book, *Hispanics and the U.S. Political System*. Of all his accomplishments, Garcia thinks he is most honored to have educated generations of UNM students. "I always wanted to be a teacher," Garcia says. "I can't imagine doing anything else." Garcia belongs to many academic organizations and served as officer and board member on several of them. Garcia retired as a distinguished professor emeritus of political science.[16]

THE LARRY GALLEGOS TREE

Larry Gallegos was a longtime employee of the Physical Plant Department who had a special interest in the maintenance of the campus landscaping. A tree was planted in his memory.

THE LINDA HUTCHINS MEMORIAL

Linda Hutchins, who worked at the Student Health Center, died suddenly on July 13, 2005, at age 58 in a car accident.[17] The memorial plaque dedicated to Linda Hutchins is mounted on a rock facing eastward beside walks on the south side of the Student Health Center. The plaque reads:

> Today as you read this inscription, Linda is remembered.
> She had a passion to inspire every student with the knowledge
> that nutrition and fitness solutions complement college success.
> 1947-2005, MS RD CNN Student Health Center Nutritionist. UNM 1969-1999.

THE CHARLOTTE AND WILLIAM KRAFT MEMORIAL ROSE GARDEN

The Charlotte and William Kraft Memorial Rose Garden was established on the south side of the Centennial Library by the children of Charlotte and William C. Kraft. In addition, the Charlotte and William Kraft Graduate Fellowship in the School of Engineering was created to assist Ph.D. students. A veteran of World War II, William Kraft moved to Albuquerque in 1947 and received a B.S. in physics from St. Joseph College. He worked at Sandia National Laboratory from 1947 to 1986. Charlotte Kraft, who was a passionate gardener, died on May 26, 1999.[18]

THE MACKEL FAMILY TREES

A disease-resistant elm tree was planted on the west side of Novitski Hall near Yale Boulevard by Donald L. Mackel, former director of the UNM Physical Plant Department, in memory of his brother Louis C. Mackel III.[19] Louis Mackel III received a Bachelor of University Studies from UNM in 1974 and a degree from New Mexico State University in accounting. Another tree was planted in memory of Donald's mother Adeline. Mackel intends to plant other trees to form a grove honoring members of the Mackel family.

THE JENNIE P. MORROS TREE

Fig. 10. Jennie P. Morros Tree (Source unknown).

Fig. 11. Jennie P. Morros Marker (Photograph by Ann Clarke).

An elm tree located on the southeast side of the Duck Pond was planted in 1993 in memory of 92-year-old Jennie Morros. The plaque reads:

> Dignity, Vitality, Love

TRIBUTE TO MOTHER EARTH

 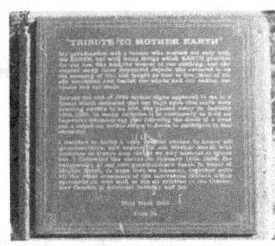

Fig. 12. Landscaping – Fountain - Tribute to Mother Earth, 1997 (Photograph by Terry Gugliotta, Center for Southwest Research, UNM Libraries).[20]

Fig. 13. Tribute to Mother Earth Plaque (Photograph by Suzanne Mortier, UNM Landscape Architect, 2013).

Tribute to Mother Earth is a beautiful fountain sculpture designed by Korean artist Youn Ja Johnson of Albuquerque and constructed in 1996. The sculpture sits at the south end of Yale Mall and northwest of the Art Building.

Youn Ja Johnson received her B.S. in elementary education from Kwang Ju College in 1961, an Interior Design Diploma from the New York School of Design in 1970, a B.F.A. in Design from the New York Institute of Technology in 1972, and a B.A. in Art from the University of Albuquerque in 1975. She received an M.A. in Art in 1982 and an M.F.A. in Art in 1985 from the University of New Mexico.

Youn Ja Johnson began her career teaching art at the Navajo Academy in Farmington in 1987. The following year she became Research Associate Professor of Philosophy in Aesthetics and Religious Studies at UNM. She has co-directed seminars at UNM and in schools in Korea and other countries.

An accomplished artist, Youn Ja Johnson's works have appeared in many exhibits around the country and South Korea. The UNM Art Gallery has a collection of her prints and she has completed a sculpture titled "Healing Herbs" at the Veterans Administration Hospital in Albuquerque. Youn Ja Johnson has written many articles in both English and Korean about a variety of subjects.[21]

DEBORAH K. LAPOINTE MEMORIAL TREE

Deborah LaPointe was born November 2, 1952, in Monmouth, Illinois, and died in Las Cruces on May 19, 2009. She studied at Northern Illinois University and Illinois State University before obtaining her Ph.D. from UNM with distinction in 2003 in Organizational Learning and Instructional Technologies (OLIT) (now known as Organization, Information and Learning Sciences or OILS). LaPointe taught at Albuquerque Technical Vocational Institute and UNM, and in 2004 at Edith Cowan University in Perth, Australia.[22] The obituary in the *Las Cruces Sun-News* stated:

> Deb's passion included learning with new technologies in the traditional and virtual classrooms and for collaboration across distances with colleagues on research projects. Envisioning learning in the future with technology and empowering those who did not have access to learning in other ways is what Deborah taught, believed in, and practiced.

A red oak tree and plaque were placed in her memory on the east side of the Health Sciences Learning Resource Center. The Deborah K. LaPointe OILS Endowed Scholarship Fund was also created in her memory.[23]

DAVID KENT MARQUESS MEMORIAL

The David Kent Marquess Memorial, which consists of a bench and three plaques, was erected by his family and is located on the northwest side of the North Campus Golf Course between the greens and the AMAFCA Flood Control Ditch. It is a good shady resting spot for a tired golfer. David Kent Marquess was a student at UNM when he died in Nevada on April 7, 2004.

David Kent Marquess was born in Rogers, Arkansas, in 1981 and spent his early life in Bentonville. He was an Eagle Scout. He attended the University of New Mexico on a U.S. Marine Corps scholarship and held the rank of midshipman first class with the Naval ROTC unit. He had completed Mountain Warfare Training in 2002 and Marine Corps Officer Training School in the summer of 2003. His obituary in the *Albuquerque Journal* stated that his interests included reading, aviation, camping, hiking, canoeing, and rock climbing.[24]

100 TREES FOR 100 YEARS

"100 Trees for 100 Years" was an effort by the Physical Plant Department to raise $25,000 to purchase 100 trees at $250 per tree. The trees could be named by the donors in honor of themselves or someone else. The drive was a success and a plaque with the names of the donors and honorees is on display in the Alumni Chapel.

JOHN K. PRENTICE TREE

Fig. 14. John K. Prentice Tree (Photograph by Suzanne Mortier, UNM Landscape Architect, 2013).

Fig. 15. John K. Prentice Plaque (Photograph by Suzanne Mortier, UNM Landscape Architect, 2013).

The incense cedar tree named for John K. Prentice is located near the Physics and Astronomy Building on Lomas Boulevard N.E. Prentice was born in Albuquerque on October 4, 1954. As a teenager, Prentice tracked satellites for the Smithsonian and received several awards at the 1972 International Science Fair. He received his Ph.D. from UNM in quantum scattering theory in physics in 1992 and began his professional career in providing scientific computational services to the national laboratories and commercial companies. He married Mary Zayin Fuka, also a physicist, in 1981. They founded Quetzel Computational Associates (later known as Quetzel Biomedical, Inc.), which developed devices for treating congestive heart failure. He lectured in the University of Colorado's Department of Applied Mathematics and created several new start-ups, such as Triple Point LLC, which focused on developing new technologies for geothermal exploration and development. According to the Jan. 24, 2010 *Boulder Daily Camera*, Prentice was "a physicist of infinitely supple and curious mind".

Prentice was a member of the American Alpine Club and climbed many peaks in Colorado and elsewhere. He died on January 5, 2010, at age 55, as the result of a fall near Boulder, Colorado.[25]

THE CYNTHIA AND DAVID EDWARD STUART MARKER

One of the more recent memorial markers on the campus is set on a stone on the west side of the Dominguez Patio. David Stuart is a man of many jobs at UNM. In the 1993-94 University phone directory, he was listed as being the Assistant Vice President for Academic Affairs, Interim Director of Novitski Dental Programs, Head of Evening and Weekend Degree Programs, and Professor of Anthropology. He later became a professor in the School of Architecture and Planning as well. *Who's Who in America* notes that David Edward Stuart was born in Calhoun County, Alabama, on January 1, 1945. After receiving his B.A. from Wesleyan (West Virginia) College in 1967, he received his M.A. in anthropology in 1970 and his Ph.D. in 1972, both from UNM. His postdoctoral work was completed at the Andean Center in Quito, Ecuador.

Stuart is well known for his many books, one of the best known being *The Guaymas Chronicles*. A reviewer in the *Journal of Latin American Anthropology* wrote of the book, "... [it is] a rich autobiographical narrative with the power of a novel peopled by a cast of resilient characters...." Other books by Stuart include *Anasazi America, True Tales of Another Mexico, Prehistoric New Mexico* (now it its third edition) and *Glimpses of the Ancient Southwest*. Stuart has also written many articles for anthropological journals.

Stuart is a member of the American Anthropological Association, the Royal Anthropological Institute (England), the New Mexico Archaeological Council, the New Mexico Humanities Council and many other organizations. He has served on many boards of directors of historical and environmental organizations, and is a member of the board of the Hibben Trust.[26]

Cynthia Stuart was Director of Admissions and Outreach Services at UNM from 1983 to 2005. Born in Pennsylvania, she attended Elizabethtown College before transferring to UNM in her sophomore year to study anthropology. In 1971, she received her B.A. from UNM, followed by an M.A. in 1983 and D.Ed. in 2008. As Director of Admissions, she was very active in the organization that provides the ACT admission tests, serving on their board of directors and as secretary for the New Mexico branch. At the time of this writing, Cynthia and David Stuart were retired and living in Albuquerque.

THE JACKIE LAWTON WELLS TREE

A desert willow tree, with no marker, was planted in memory of Jackie Lawton Wells and is located northeast of the Hibben Center for Archaeological Research on the Main campus. Jackie Lawton was a nurse at the University Hospital who married Dan Wells in 2002. Jackie Lawton Wells died in 2007.

THE FRANK RUMINSKI TREE

Fig. 16. Frank Ruminski Tree (Photograph by Suzanne Mortier, UNM Landscape Architect, 2013).

On the north side of the west wing of the Hibben Center a tree was planted in memory of Frank Z. Ruminski. The marker reads:

> Frank Z. Ruminski, 5/3/14-4/4/98,
> Beloved Husband, Father and Grandfather,
> Donated by friends at the
> UNM Physical Plant Department

Frank Ruminski was the father of Richard Robert Ruminski, a graduate in architecture at UNM who worked in the Office of the University Architect and later was the long-time manager of remodeling and the planning officer in the Physical Plant Department. Frank Ruminski, first generation son of Polish immigrants, was born in New York City and died in Albuquerque on April 14, 1998, at age 84. During World War II, Ruminski served as a combat infantryman in the North Africa campaign. In 1956, for health reasons, he moved his family to New Mexico and worked at Kirtland Air Force Base until he retired in 1973. Ruminski and his wife Barbara founded a Polish-American Club and a Polish dance club that performed native Polish dances in authentic costumes.[27]

THE HECTOR A. TORRES TREE

A Deodar cedar (*Cedrus deodara*), was planted in memory of Hector A. Torres, Professor of English, and is located on the northeast side of the Duck Pond.[28] An article in *UNM Today* of March 9, 2010, stated:

> Professor Torres and graduate student Stefamoa Gray were victims of a double homicide as described by the Albuquerque Police Department.
>
> Professor Torres was on the faculty in the UNM Department of English since 1986. He was born in Tijuana, Mexico, raised in El Paso, Texas, and with the benefit of the GI Bill, earned all his degrees, including a doctorate of English language and literature from the University of Texas at Austin. Currently, he was teaching a course on Chicano Culture, a theory course and was directing an independent study.
>
> He regularly taught courses in literary and critical theory, postmodernism, and contemporary Chicano literary discourse and film. English syntax and discourse analysis, as well as courses on writing about film.
>
> In a 2007 interview he said, "I think being a Spanish speaker who learned English in school drove my interest in linguistics, language and literature…"

STREET NAMES

As the University's main campus grew, Albuquerque city streets were run on a grid through it and carried the names the City chose for them. These streets included Plum, Terrace, Cornell, Stanford, Yale, Ash, Roma and Las Lomas. Later, New York Avenue became Lomas Boulevard N.E., Plum Street became University Boulevard, and Ash and Terrace streets were removed. In 1938, the University decided to rename the streets through the University, and architect John Gaw Meem was asked to make suggestions at a meeting with President Zimmerman. He wrote, "[it] was my thought in submitting this list that it should consist of names associated with the early Spanish colonization period of New Mexico…." The University Board of Regents approved his proposed list, which changed Terrace to Quivira, the name given by explorer Francisco Vásquez de Coronado for the mythical "Seven Cities of Gold" in the 1500's; Yale to Villagrá, named for Gaspar de Pérez Villagrá, who was a captain in Juan Onate's expedition that first colonized Santa Fe de Nuevo México, and who later wrote a history of New Mexico published in 1610; Cornell to Cibola, the Spanish translation for a pueblo conquered by Coronado; and, Ash to Coronado. Although the City had approved the changes, after a few years campus maps were carrying the old names. When the loop road around the campus was completed as recommended by the Warnecke Plan, it was named Redondo Drive, meaning "round" in Spanish.

Tucker Road

Tucker Road is a street on the North Campus that runs from Stanford Boulevard N.E. to University Boulevard N.E. and is just south of the North Campus Golf Course. The street is named for William "Willie" Henry Tucker, Sr., who was an early pioneer in golf course design. He designed the University of New Mexico courses that once stretched from the northwest corner of Girard and Central into the North Campus. Tucker was also known as a professional golfer who finished seventh in the second U.S. Open, held in 1896, and as a manufacturer with his brother of hand-made golf clubs.

Tucker, born in Red Hill, Surrey, England, in 1871, came to the United States in 1895 after learning golf course design in England, France, and Switzerland. He designed the relocated St. Andrews Club course in New York. Tucker and his son, William, Jr., established a golf course architectural firm with offices across the country. Hired by UNM in 1942 to design the University course and supervise its construction, Tucker retired to Albuquerque and served as greenskeeper for the University until his death in 1954. Since then, the William H. Tucker Intercollegiate Tournament, the second longest running college tournament in the United States, has been held at the University.[29]

THE STOUT MEDAL MEMORIAL GARDEN

The Stout Medal is given in honor of Dr. Arlow B. Stout, considered the father of daylily hybridizing.[30] Former UNM President Richard Peck and his wife Donna Peck established daylily gardens on the grounds of the UNM President's house and elsewhere at the University. Donna Peck, 1996 President of the Albuquerque Daylily Society and until 2014 the Ombudsman for the American Hemerocallis Society,[31] wrote:

> Each year since 1950 the highest honor in the daylily world goes to a daylily that grows best all around the country and gets the Stout Award, named after one of the first great hybridizers. We have a plant for each year that the award was given in that bed. It is a very valuable and educational bed.

MELISSA ANN STERLING TREE

The Melissa Ann Sterling Hawthorne tree and plaque are located on the north end of the Health Sciences Learning Center. Ms. Sterling was enrolled in the Physical Therapy Program when she died on January 22, 2010, at age 32.

THE USS NEW MEXICO QUEEN OF THE PACIFIC FLEET BELL TOWER

Fig. 17. Student Publications – Navy ROTC – Bell Tower, 1967 (Center for Southwest Research, UNM Libraries).[32]

Fig. 18. Bell Tower, 2013 (Photograph by Suzanne Mortier, UNM Landscape Architect).

The steel frame tower, designed as a courtesy by Albuquerque architect Max Flatow, holds a bell from the battleship USS New Mexico. The tower stands between the Student Union and Zimmerman Library at the top of the flight of steps leading down to Smith Plaza. The dedication plaque is mounted on the base of the bell tower and reads:

> In this tower is hung the ships' bell of the USS New Mexico as a memorial to those men and women who served their country in World War II. Dedicated April 1948. Obtained thru services of Alpha Phi Omega. The crew of the USS New Mexico.

Like an old friend, Myron Fifield, an old Navy man, wrote in *El Servicio Real*:

> Her keel was laid in the Brooklyn Navy Yard on December 14, 1915. She was christened on April 23, 1917, and commissioned there on May 20, 1918, too late to participate in World War I.
>
> It was in the Pacific in the years before World War II that she was given the name "Queen of the Pacific Fleet" because of her flagship status – a name she carried throughout her career. It was in World War II that she got her six battle stars for operations in the Gilbert Islands, the Aleutians, the Marshall Islands, Luzon, Okinawa and the Marianas. Although heavily wounded, she attended the surrender procession in Tokyo Bay at the end of the war.
>
> After a lifetime of serving her country, the "Queen's" name was struck from the Navy List on February 25, 1947. Her proud 624 feet of length, 97'5" beam and 32,000 ton displacement were sold for scrap in the city in which she was born.

YALE PARK

Fig. 19. Yale Park (Photograph by Suzanne Mortier, UNM Landscape Architect, 2013).

Yale Park, originally called Reservoir Park for the city water reservoir and pumping station at the west end, is not named for Yale University, but for the street it abuts. On April 13, 1928, the University Board of Regents approved a plan by the City of Albuquerque to beautify the park and use it as a city park until such time as the University might need it. Hodgin Grove, described in the Central Campus section, is located within it.

During the Vietnam War, Yale Park was the scene of student demonstrations, and some suggested the park be removed. When Redondo Drive went through the north side in 1975, it reduced the size of the park quite a bit. The City had to replace the steel roof on the reservoir and hired the architectural firm of Stevens, Mallory, Pearl and Campbell to design a new exterior. George Pearl designed what some people think is a building.

In the 1990s, the University proposed placing a new campus bookstore in Yale Park. An uproar ensued among people wanting to save the green belt Yale Park provided. The people prevailed and the Book Store was moved to the far east end of the Park. Today, Yale Park contains several outdoor sculptures including "Spirit Mother" by Michael Naranjo and "Cultural Crossroads of the Americas" by Bob Haozous, both installed in the mid-1990s.

Fig. 20. Yale Park Sculpture - "Spirit Mother" During Snowfall, 1997 (Photograph by Terry Gugliotta, Center for Southwest Research, UNM Libraries).[33]

Fig. 21. Yale Park Sculpture – "Cultural Crossroads" Snow-covered Ground, 1997 (Photograph by Terry Gugliotta, Center for Southwest Research, UNM Libraries).[34]

THE LONG'S 100 POPLAR TREES

Mr. and Mrs. Henry Long donated 100 poplar trees to line the streets around Zimmerman Field to commemorate their four children, who had graduated from UNM, and the 1927 UNM football team. Some of the trees lasted until the early 1950s.

MICHAEL LEYBA MEMORIAL

On July 28, 1998, Michael Leyba, a parts expediter and rental agent with the UNM Automotive Department for twelve years, passed away while at work. Daniel Apodaca, then supervisor of the UNM Automotive Department, planted a bed of climbing roses in Leyba's memory outside of the building, located on the Health Sciences Campus. Former supervisor, Lee Espinosa made a steel framework sign in memory of Leyba. A local vendor, Maco Auto Painting, painted the sign.

THE HODGIN HALL ILLUMINATED "U" SIGN

Fig. 22. Hodgin Hall – Exterior – with "U" Sign, circa 1926 (Center for Southwest Research, UNM Libraries).[35]

Fig. 23. Hodgin Hall "U" today (Photograph by Suzanne Mortier, UNM Landscape Architect, 2013).

In 1922, the University, which was known early on as "the U," placed an "electric U" on top of Hodgin Hall. The illuminated "U," which was made of tin and contained some 50 electric lights, was constructed by Albuquerque Gas and Electric Company. Sometime after 1932, the electric "U" was removed. The UNM Alumni Association commissioned a new illuminated "U," which was installed on a pedestal in the plaza in front of Hodgin

Hall as a gift to the University and dedicated on November 18, 2012. The new 12-foot by 8-foot-wide cast bronze "U" features LED lights with the potential for more than 16 million colors.

Like the original sign, the new U will be a beacon to the UNM community. It marks Hodgin Hall as The Alumni Center — a place where old traditions are preserved and new ones are created.[36]

ZIMMERMAN CHAPEL

Fig. 24. Plaque dedicated to Edward A. Zimmerman, MD (Photograph by Dr. Michelle Tatlock, BBC, Department of Spiritual Care and Education, UNM Hospital)

Fig. 25. Interior of Zimmerman Chapel (Photograph by Dr. Michelle Tatlock, BBC, Department of Spiritual Care and Education, UNM Hospital)

The Zimmerman Chapel located on the first floor of the main section of UNMH is named for Edward August Zimmerman, MD. Zimmerman received his B.S. from the University of Dayton and his M.D. from St. Louis School of Medicine. The UNM School of Medicine, established in 1964, assumed operation of the Bernalillo County Indian Hospital from the Indian Health Service in 1968. In 1969, Zimmerman left his position at Walter Reed Army Medical Hospital to join the faculty at UNM and became a professor of obstetrics and gynecology. According to a 2006 article in *Pediatrics* on the *Forty Years in Partnership: The American Academy of Pediatrics and the Indian Health Service* by Brenneman, Rhoades and Chilton, the American Academy of Pediatrics in 1965 had formed a Committee on Indian Health to address high rates of childhood disease and mortality within American Indian and Alaska Native communities. In 1970, the American College of Obstetricians and Gynecologists (ACOG) formed a Committee on American Indian Affairs and appointed Zimmerman as chairman. Under Zimmerman's chairmanship, the committees took a cooperative approach, producing a report on American Indian and Alaska Native maternal and infant health care to Congress in 1974. Zimmerman testified during hearings on the proposed Indian Health Care Improvement Act of 1976. Among his other accomplishments, Zimmerman was instrumental in fostering the use of certified nurse midwives by the Indian Health Service. The dedication plaque read:

Zimmerman Chapel
donated by the UNMH Service League
in memory of Edward A. Zimmerman, M.D.

Endnotes: Section Four—Other Spaces

1. "Alvarez," *Albuquerque Journal* (April 29, 2009), http://obits.abqjournal.com/obits/show/195381 (last accessed April 20, 2018).

2. "Coker," *Albuquerque Journal* (Mar. 13, 2004), http://obits.abqjournal.com/obits/show/142582 (last accessed April 20, 2018).

3. http://econtent.unm.edu/cdm/ref/collection/ULPhotoImag/id/3501 (last accessed April 9, 2018).

4. http://econtent.unm.edu/cdm/ref/collection/ULPhotoImag/id/3237 (last accessed April 9, 2018).

5. http://econtent.unm.edu/cdm/ref/collection/ULPhotoImag/id/2697 (last accessed April 9, 2018).

6. UNM Office of the University Secretary, "Honorary Degrees," https://secretary.unm.edu/recognition-and-awards/honorary-degrees.html (last accessed April 20, 2018).

7. See Lindsey Trout, "Duck Pond, Case Study," American Modernism Project, UNM School of Architecture & Planning, http://albuquerquemodernism.unm.edu/wp/duck-pond-unm/ (last accessed April 20, 2018).

8. Associated Press, "Harold Enarson, 87, Who Fired Woody Hayes at Ohio State, Dies," *New York Times* (Aug. 1, 2006), http://www.nytimes.com/2006/08/01/sports/01enarson.html (last accessed April 20, 2018).

9. UNM Office of the University Secretary, "Zimmerman Award," https://www.unmalumni.com/zimmerman-past.html (last accessed April 20, 2018).

10. UNM School of Public Administration, "Carl Hatch Endowment Professorship in Law and Public Administration," https://spa.unm.edu/endowments/hatch-endowment.html (last accessed April 20, 2018).

11. UNM Office of the University Secretary, "Honorary Degrees," https://secretary.unm.edu/recognition-and-awards/honorary-degrees.html (last accessed April 20, 2018).

12. See Ohio State University, Office of the President, "Harold Leroy Enarson," https://president.osu.edu/presidents/enarson.html (last accessed April 20, 2018).

13. Associated Press, "Harold Enarson, 87, Who Fired Woody Hayes at Ohio State, Dies," *New York Times* (Aug. 1, 2006), http://www.nytimes.com/2006/08/01/sports/01enarson.html, and Lloyd Jojola, "Educator Helped Start 4-year Medical School," *Albuquerque Journal* (Aug. 4, 2006), https://www.abqjournal.com/obits/profiles/481258profiles08-04-06.htm (last accessed April 20, 2018).

14. "Audrey P. Enarson," *The Washington Post* (Jan. 31, 2008), http://www.legacy.com/obituaries/washingtonpost/obituary.aspx-?n=Audrey-P-Enarson&pid=102349165, and Ohio State University, "University Awards and Recognition," https://www.osu.edu/universityawards/ (last accessed April 20, 2018).

15. See "In Memoriam: Frank Feathers," *Village Vision, Los Ranchos de Albuquerque*, p. 12 (Summer 2009), https://static1.square-space.com/static/508fe597e4b047ba54ddc41e/t/551073c0e4b0561371d5918d/1427141568287/Summer%25202009.com-pressed.pdf (last accessed April 20, 2018).

16. See "F. Chris Garcia, 17th UNM President," https://fchrisgarciaus.wordpress.com/ (last accessed April 20, 2018).

17. "Hutchins," *Albuquerque Journal* (July 17, 2005), http://obits.abqjournal.com/obits/2005/07/17 (last accessed April 20, 2018).

18. "Kraft," *Albuquerque Journal* (May 29, 1999), http://obits.abqjournal.com/obits/show/125933 (last accessed April 20, 2018).

19. See "Louis C. Mackel III – Albuquerque, New Mexico," Dedicated Trees on Waymarking (including photographs of the tree and marker) (2010), http://www.waymarking.com/waymarks/WM9ZBH_Louis_C_Mackel_III_Albuquerque_New_Mexico (last accessed April 20, 2018).

20 http://econtent.unm.edu/cdm/ref/collection/ULPhotoImag/id/3182 (last accessed April 9, 2018), and UNM Libraries, Public Art at UNM: Writing and Research, Examples of Public Art at UNM, "Youn Ja Johnson, 'Tribute to Mother Earth,'" https://libguides.unm.edu/publicart/unm_examples (last accessed April 21, 2018).

21 See Arts Albuquerque, ByArts, "Youn Ja Johnson – Biography," http://www.byarts.com/aboutus/yj_bio.php (last accessed April 21, 2018).

22 See "Deborah K. (Cooper) LaPointe," *Northwest Herald Obituaries*, http://www.legacy.com/obituaries/nwherald/obituary.aspx-?n=deborah-k-lapointe-cooper&pid=127610639 (last accessed April 21, 2018).

23 UNM Foundation, "Deborah K. LaPointe OILS Endowed Scholarship Fund," https://www.unmfund.org/fund/deborah-k-lapointe-oils/, and Mara Kerkez, "Endowments Celebrate UNM Staff and Faculty Members," http://news.unm.edu/news/endowments-celebrate-unm-staff-and-faculty-members (last accessed April 21, 2018).

24 "Marquess," *Albuquerque Journal*, http://obits.abqjournal.com/obits/show/143446 (last accessed April 21, 2018).

25 See "John K. Prentice," *The Durango Herald*, http://obituaries.durangoherald.com/obituaries/durangoherald/obituary.aspx-?pid=172661731 (last accessed April 21, 2018), and "Dr. John K. Prentice," *Boulder Daily Camera* (Jan. 24, 2010), http://www.dailycamera.com/obits/ci_14248567.

26 See, e.g., "David Stuart," New Mexico Library Association, Authors, https://nmla.org/authors/david-stuart, and V.B. Price, "Five Questions with New Mexico Authors: David E. Stuart," *New Mexico Mercury* (July 25, 2014), http://newmexicomercury.com/blog/comments/five_questions_with_new_mexico_authors_david_e._stuart (last accessed April 21, 2018).

27 See "Frank Z. Ruminski," Find A Grave, https://www.findagrave.com/memorial/82023520/frank-z-ruminski and "Ruminski," *Albuquerque Journal* (Oct. 30, 2007), http://obits.abqjournal.com/obits/2007/10/page/83 (last accessed April 21, 2018).

28 See "Slain UNM Professor Remembered," KOAT (Mar. 14, 2010), http://www.koat.com/article/slain-unm-professor-remembered/5032608 (last accessed April 21, 2018).

29 See, e.g., "William H. Tucker," *Golf Advisor*, http://www.worldgolf.com/golf-architects/william-h-tucker.html; Steve Carr, "A Golfing Oasis in the Desert," *UNM Newsroom* (July 20, 2016); and, "Wm. H. Tucker, Dean of Course Builders, Dies at 83," *Golfdom*, p. 70 (Oct. 1954), http://archive.lib.msu.edu/tic/golfd/article/1954oct70.pdf (last accessed April 21, 2018).

30 See Daylily and Hosta Gardens, American Hemerocallis Society Daylily Awards, "Stout Silver Medal Daylily Award," http://www.daylilyandhostagardens.com/DayliliesAwardsStout.html (last accessed Oct. 30, 2017).

31 Albuquerque Daylily Society, "Club Presidents," http://www.ahsregion6.org/albuquerque.htm, and Ray Houston, "Donna Joy Peck," http://www.ahsregion6.org/peck_donna.htm (last accessed Oct. 30, 2017).

32 http://econtent.unm.edu/cdm/ref/collection/ULPhotoImag/id/679 (last accessed April 9, 2018).

33 http://econtent.unm.edu/cdm/ref/collection/ULPhotoImag/id/3251 (last accessed April 9, 2018). See also UNM Libraries, Public Art at UNM: Writing and Research, Examples of Public Art at UNM, "Michael Naranjo, 'Spirit Mother,'" https://libguides.unm.edu/publicart/unm_examples (last accessed April 21, 2018).

34 http://econtent.unm.edu/cdm/ref/collection/ULPhotoImag/id/3178 (last accessed April 9, 2018). See also UNM Libraries, Public Art at UNM: Writing and Research, Examples of Public Art at UNM, "Bob Haozous, 'Cultural Crossroads of the Americas,'" https://libguides.unm.edu/publicart/unm_examples (last accessed April 21, 2018).

35 http://econtent.unm.edu/cdm/ref/collection/ULPhotoImag/id/1730 (last accessed April 9, 2018).

36 See UNM Alumni Association, "The New U: A Beacon to the UNM Community," including historical and current photographs of "the U," https://www.unmalumni.com/the-u.html, and "Relighting a Historic Tradition," https://www.unmalumni.com/uploads/images/giving/pdf/U-Brochure.pdf (last accessed April 21, 2018).

AUTHOR REFERENCES

BOOKS

Only in New Mexico, Van Dorn Hooker, UNM Press, 2000

Miracle on the Mesa, William E. Davis, UNM Press, 2006

Pueblo on the Mesa, Dorothy Hughes, UNM Press, 1939

Centennial History of the College of Arts and Sciences, multiple authors, no date

NEWSPAPERS AND MAGAZINES

Albuquerque Tribune

Albuquerque Journal

Architecture—New Mexico Society of Architects Magazine

Century Magazine

Daily Lobo, University of New Mexico

El Servico Real, M.F. Fifield Editor, PPD Department

Los Alamos Monitor

Santa Fe New Mexican

UNM Campus News

UNM Mirage (Yearbook and Magazine)

UNM Today

UNM Weekly

ARCHIVES

UNM Archives

John Gaw Meem Archive of Southwestern Architecture

COMMITTEE MINUTES

UNM Board of Regents Minutes

UNM Naming Committee Minutes

OTHER SOURCES

"60 For 60," UNM School of Law Publication

UNM Alumni

UNM Faculty-Staff Directories

ABOUT THE AUTHORS

VAN DORN HOOKER

On June 14, 2015, Van Dorn Hooker, 93, joined his wife Marjorie "Peggy" in the great architectural drafting room in the sky. Van Dorn was born in Carthage, Texas, to Anne Purcell Wylie and Van Dorn Hooker, Sr. He attended Marshall College (now East Texas Baptist U.), then volunteered in the U.S. Army Corps of Engineers from 1943-45. He served as staff sergeant, 20th Air Force, with the 58th Bomb Squadron, where he was a ground radio operator in China-Burma-India and Asia Pacific Theaters during WWII. In his spare time he painted nose art on bombers and drew cartoons for the *Army News*.

After the war ended, he met Peggy, a native of Marfa, while both were studying architecture at the University of Texas, Austin. After graduate work at the University of California, Berkeley, where he studied with Eric Mendelsohn, he established the firm of McHugh, Hooker, and Bradley P. Kidder and Associates in Santa Fe. While in private practice Van Dorn became a noted expert in the restoration of adobe churches for the Archdiocese of Santa Fe. In working with John McHugh in designing the first Santa Fe Opera, he also developed an interest in theater design.

From 1963-1987, Van Dorn served as University Architect at the University of New Mexico. He brought together the talents of many local and internationally recognized designers, while reflecting the pueblo style of John Gaw Meem, an early mentor and architect of several early UNM buildings, and honoring the 1959 Warnecke campus plan.

Van Dorn's interest in history, people and their stories led him to advocate for a University archive. His many articles and books include *Only in New Mexico*, about the University's architectural history, *The University of New Mexico*, a picture book, and *Centuries of Hands*, about the restoration of St. Francis of Assisi Church at Ranchos de Taos. His watercolors and drawings feature New Mexico landscapes and churches. After retiring, Van Dorn was the architectural design consultant for the renovation of the New Mexico State Capitol, known as the "Rotunda," which as a result displays one of the largest collections of works by New Mexico artists and craftsmen.

Van Dorn was elected a Fellow of the American Institute of Architects, 1982, and a Fellow of the Association of University Architects, 1984. He received a Silver Medal for Lifetime Achievement from the New Mexico AIA, Western Mountain Region AIA Silver Medal (highest award in the six-state region), and an honorary Doctorate in Fine Arts from UNM in 2010. A favorite accolade was his induction into the Carthage Independent School District Hall of Fame along with late country western singer Jim Reeves in 2007.

A memorial service was held Saturday, November 14, in the UNM Alumni Memorial Chapel. In honor of Van Dorn's Scottish heritage, a bagpiper piped guests into the chapel. In honor of Van Dorn's early accomplishments in the Boy Scouts, Boy Scout Troop 714 supported by Terry Brown, FAIA, presented colors to open the service.

Red roses and a U.S. flag, folded, which had been flown over the U.S. Capitol, were on the altar. A reception followed in the Willard Room within the historic West Wing of Zimmerman Library. On Sunday afternoon, November 15, at St. Michael's and All Angels Episcopal Church where Van Dorn had served on the Vestry in the 1960s, the family presented a concert by Entourage Jazz, which played pieces from the 1940s in honor of Van Dorn and Peggy and in tribute to veterans. On Monday, November 16, following a military service, Van Dorn's ashes were interred at the National Cemetery in Santa Fe as snow began to fall. His uniform, patches, sketches and memoir, *The War in Which I Did Not Fight,* were donated to the 58th Bomb Squadron Memorial at the New England Air Museum, and his papers, drafting table, drawings and equipment were placed in the UNM Archives. The family also established the Marjorie Hooker Memorial Visiting Professorship at the UNM School of Architecture and Planning.

ANN HOOKER CLARKE

A native of New Mexico, Ann Clarke attended the University of New Mexico as a freshman when Zimmerman Field was still the center of campus and the Duck Pond did not exist. She later received her J.D. from the Law School, where she was lead articles editor for the *Natural Resources Journal*. She completed her undergraduate degree in geology at Colorado College, a master's degree in geography from the University of Oregon, and her doctorate from the Yale School of Forestry and Environmental Studies. Her research and writing have focused on the relationship of the individual to society and nature. After retiring from NASA, she moved to California's Central Coast where she teaches food, agriculture and environmental law.

Naming Names

Long-time University Architect matches people to buildings in new book

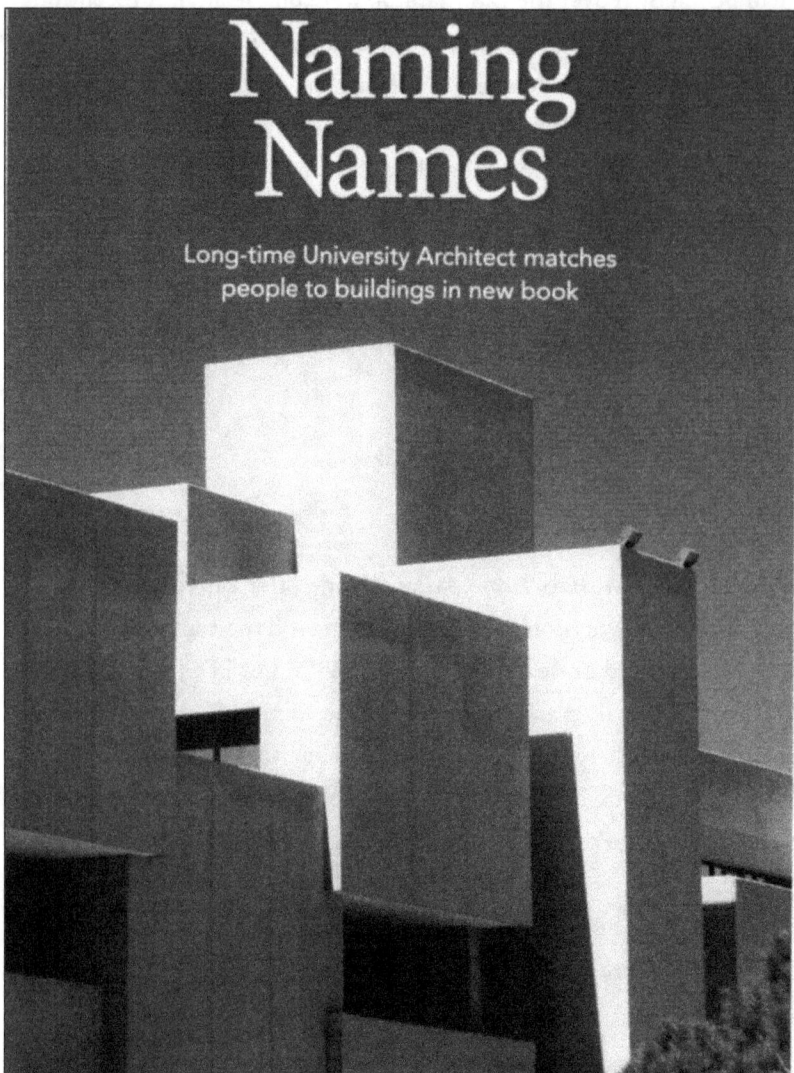

Hooker's favorite building was the Humanities Building, completed in 1974. Photo by Gene Peach.

Boal Mitchell, an advocate for expansion, was the long-serving professor, dean and academic vice president who joined the University in 1912 as associate professor of Latin and Greek. In 1951, the new classroom building was named for him.

Hooker, former University Architect, cares about buildings and their histories. In 1989, he published *Only in New Mexico: An Architectural History of the University of New Mexico*. During his 24 years at the University, 87 buildings were built.

Today Hooker is part of the history he helped create and preserve.

Van Dorn Hooker, shown here in the 1980s, continues to keep an eye on campus development at age 93.

Did you ever wonder about the people whose names identify UNM buildings?

Who, for example, is the Ortega of Ortega Hall? Or the Mitchell of Mitchell Hall?

Van Dorn Hooker wondered. "It occurred to me that most people don't know why Scholes Hall is called Scholes Hall," he said. That led him to write *Memories, Memorials and Monuments*, a book of "biographical sketches of people who have something named for them" on any of UNM's campuses. (At this writing, it's still in manuscript form.)

France V. Scholes was a history professor, beginning in 1925, who was later an academic vice president and grad school dean. Ortega Hall was named for Joaquin Ortega, professor of Spanish, director of the School of Inter-American Affairs, and editor of the *New Mexico Quarterly*. Lynn

UNM Mirage (Spring 2014) https://issuu.com/unm-alumni-association/docs/mirage_s14. Reprinted by permission from the UNM Mirage.

www.ingramcontent.com/pod-product-compliance
Lightning Source LLC
Chambersburg PA
CBHW081719100526
44591CB00016B/2434